School District No. 3
Flint
No 7

DAVIES' LOGIC OF MATHEMATICS.

The Logic and Utility of Mathematics, with the best methods of Instruction, explained and illustrated. By CHARLES DAVIES, L. L. D.

"One of the most remarkable books of the month, is 'The Logic and Utility of Mathematics, by Charles Davies, L. L. D.,' published by Barnes & Co. It is not intended as a treatise on any special branch of mathematical science, and demands for its full appreciation a general acquaintance with the leading methods and routine of mathematical investigation. To tho e who have a natural fondness for this pursuit and enjoy the leisure for a retrospect of their favorite studies, the present volume will possess a charm, not surpassed by the fascinations of a romance. It is an elaborate and lucid exposition of the principles which lie at the foundation of pure mathematics, with a highly ingenious application of their results to the development of the essential idea of Arithmetic, Geometry, Algebra, Analytic Geometry, and the Differential and Integral Calculus. The work is preceded by a general view of the subject of Logic, mainly drawn from the writings of Archbishop Whately and Mr. Mill, and closes with an essay on the utility of mathematics. Some occasional exaggerations, in presenting the claims of the science to which his life has been devoted, must here be pardoned to the professional enthusiasm of the author. In general, the work is written with singular circumspection; the views of the best thinkers on the subject have been thoroughly digested, and are presented in an original form; every thing bears the impress of the intellect of the writer; his style is for the most part chaste, simple, transparent, and in admirable harmony with the dignity of the subject, and his condensed generalizations are often profound and always suggestive."—*Harper's New Monthly Magazine.*

"This work is not merely a mathematical treatise to be used as a text book, but a complete and philosophical unfolding of the principles and truths of mathematical science.

"It is not only designed for professional teachers, professional men, and students of mathematics and philosophy, but for the general reader who desires mental improvement, and would learn to search out the import of language, and acquire a habit of noting of connexion between ideas and their signs; also, of the relation of ideas to each other.—*The Student.*

"Students of the Science will find this volume full of useful and deeply interesting matter."—*Albany Evening Journal.*

"Seldom have we opened a book so attractive as this in its typography and style of execution; and there is besides, on the margin opposite each section, an index of the subject of which it treats—a great convenience to the student. But the *matter* is no less to be commended than the *manner*. And we are very much mistaken if this work shall not prove more popular and more useful than any which the distinguished author has given to the public."—*Lutheran Observer.*

"We have been much interested both in the plan and in the execution of the work, and would recommend the study of it to the theologian as a discipline in close and accurate thinking, and in logical method and reasoning. It will be useful, also, to the general scholar and to the practical mechanic. We would specially recommend it to those who would have nothing taught in our Free Academy and other higher institutions but what is directly 'practical'; nowhere have we seen a finer illustration of the connection between the abstractly scientific and the practical.

"The work is divided into three books; the first of which treats of Logic, mainly upon the basis of Whately; the second, of Mathemetical Science, and the third, of the Utility of Mathematics."—*Independent.*

"The a ithor's style is perspicuous and concise, and he exhibits a mastery of the abstruse topics which he attempts to simplify. For the mathematical student, who desires an analytical knowledge of the science, and who would begin at the beginning, we should suppose the work would have a special utility. Prof. Davies's mathematical works, we believe, have become quite popular with educators, and this discloses quite as much research and practical scholarship as any we have seen from his pen." --*New-York Evangelist.*

Page's Theory and Practice of Teaching.

THEORY AND PRACTICE OF TEACHING;

OR THE

MOTIVES OF GOOD SCHOOL-KEEPING.

BY DAVID PAGE, A.M.,

LATE PRINCIPAL OF THE STATE NORMAL SCHOOL, NEW YORK.

"I received a few days since your 'Theory and Practice, &c.,' and a capital *theory* and capital *practice* it is. I have read it with unmingled delight. Even if I should look through a critic's microscope, I should hardly find a single sentiment to dissent from, and certainly not one to condemn. The chapters on *Prizes* and on *Corporal Punishment* are truly admirable. They will exert a most salutary influence. So of the views *sparsim* on moral and religious instruction, which you so earnestly and feelingly insist upon, and yet within true Protestant limits. IT IS A GRAND BOOK, AND I THANK HEAVEN THAT YOU HAVE WRITTEN IT."—*Hon. Horace Mann, Secretary of the Board of Education in Massachusetts.*

"Were it our business to examine teachers, we would never dismiss a candidate without naming this book. Other things being equal, we would greatly prefer a teacher who has read it and speaks of it with enthusiasm. In one indifferent to such a work, we should certainly have little confidence, however he might appear in other respects. Would that every teacher employed in Vermont this winter had the spirit of this book in his bosom, its lessons impressed upon his heart!"—*Vermont Chronicle.*

"I am pleased with and commend this work to the attention of school teachers, and those who intend to embrace that most estimable profession, for light and instruction to guide and govern them in the discharge of their delicate and important duties."—*N. S. Benton, Superintendent of Common Schools, State of New York.*

Hon. S. Young says, "It is altogether the best book on this subject I have ever seen."

President North, of Hamilton College, says, "I have read it with all that absorbing self-denying interest, which in my younger days was reserved for fiction and poetry. I am delighted with the book."

Hon. Marcus S. Reynolds says, "It will do great good by showing the Teacher what should be his qualifications, and what may justly be required and expected of him."

"I wish you would send an agent through the several towns of this State with Page's 'Theory and Practice of Teaching,' or take some other way of bringing this valuable book to the notice of every family and of every teacher. I should be rejoiced to see the principles which it presents as to the motives and methods of good school-keeping carried out in every school-room; and as nearly as possible, in the style in which Mr. Page illustrates them in his own practice, as the devoted and accomplished Principal of your State Normal School."—*Henry Barnard, Superintendent of Common Schools for the State of Rhode Island.*

"The 'Theory and Practice of Teaching,' by D. P. Page, is one of the best books of the kind I have ever met with. In it the theory and practice of the teacher's duties are clearly explained and happily combined. The style is easy and familiar, and the suggestions it contains are plain, practical, and to the point. To teachers especially it will furnish very important aid in discharging the duties of their high and responsible profession."—*Roger S. Howard, Superintendent of Common Schools, Orange Co., Vt.*

AMERICAN EDUCATION.

AMERICAN EDUCATION,

ITS

PRINCIPLES AND ELEMENTS.

DEDICATED TO

THE TEACHERS OF THE UNITED STATES.

BY

EDWARD D. MANSFIELD,

AUTHOR OF THE POLITICAL GRAMMAR, ETC., ETC.

NEW YORK:
PUBLISHED BY A. S. BARNES & CO.
NO. 51 JOHN-STREET.
CINCINNATI:—H. W. DERBY & CO.
1851.

Stereotyped by
RICHARD C. VALENTINE,
45 Gold-street, New York.

F. C. GUTIERREZ, Printer,
No. 51 John-street, corner of Dutch.

PREFACE.

I HAVE only one thing to say, by way of preface. This little work is *suggestive* of principles, and not intended to point out a course of studies. Its aim is to excite attention to what should be the elements of an American education; or, in other words, what are the ideas connected with a republican and Christian education in this period of rapid development. I wished to turn the thoughts of those engaged in the direction of youth to the fact, that it was the *entire soul*, in all its faculties, which needed education, and not any one of its talents; and that this was a need especially of our country and times. To do this, requires a complete discipline of mind and an analysis of society.

If any one should say that this is a philosophical discussion of general subjects, and not a directory treatise on practical topics, I admit the justice of the remark, and reply, that such only it was intended to be. On the philosophy of American education, I thought I might offer my reflections without presumption, while on the particular mode of actual instruction I was not qualified to advise.

Brief and imperfect as my reflections on this momentous subject are, I send them out as a well-meant, if not a valuable, offering to the teachers of the United States. They may, perhaps, aid some persons in contemplating those higher and nobler principles which lie beyond the details of books and the modes of instruction;—in fine, those principles which concern universal nature, and direct the destiny of the soul.

August 29th, 1850.

CONTENTS.

CHAPTER I.

CHAPTER II.

CHAPTER III.

CHAPTER IV.

CHAPTER V.

CHAPTER VI.

CHAPTER VII.

CHAPTER VIII.

CHAPTER IX.

CHAPTER X.

CHAPTER XI.

CHAPTER XII.

CHAPTER XIII.

CHAPTER XIV.

AMERICAN EDUCATION.

CHAPTER I.

THE IDEA OF A REPUBLIC.

A REPUBLIC is a civil community in which the PEOPLE govern. It is a community in which a large number of persons have common interests. It is a community governed by civil laws; that is, laws made by civil society, as an organized body, and not merely the laws of nature or religion. These laws are made by the people. But these laws may be made either by the *whole* people or by *part* of the people. When made by the *whole* people, then it is a DEMOCRATIC REPUBLIC. Such is the United States Republic. Here the whole people govern themselves by laws made by themselves. Hence the people here are called *sovereign;* for each individual in the United States, as one in the government, exercises, according to the principle of the government, a part of the sovereign power, which in monarchies is exercised by the monarch.

The IDEA of republican government in the United States is the idea of A PEOPLE GOVERNING THEMSELVES.

Now every reasonable person will readily grant that whatever may be the primary idea or principle in the government which a nation has adopted, all the laws and civil institutions which are also adopted in that nation should conform to that idea. For if they do not, there must be a direct inconsistency between the primary and the secondary institutions of the nation. There will arise an internal conflict, first, between the laws themselves; next, between the practical consequences which flow from those laws; and, lastly, between different portions of the nation; who will think that either the one or the other class of laws are better adapted to their wants. The house will be divided against itself; and, sooner or later, will fall. History furnishes us with many examples of this inconsistency and of its fatal effects. The growth of modern legislative assemblies in Europe, for example (just so far as they gain power), diminishes the power of the monarchy. In England we see the monarchy has become merely nominal. In France it has been twice destroyed. This is in consequence of the inconsistency of an absolute monarchy on the one hand, and of a representing assembly making laws on the other. So also we see the people in the Commonwealth of England, and in France after the first Revolution, losing their power, and the Republic destroyed, in consequence of placing monarchical powers in the hands of the first magistrate. The existence of monarchical powers in the hands of a magistrate are inconsistent with the existence of legislative power in the hands of the people. Either this despotic magistrate must be reduced to an officer of the law only, or the people will become the mere subjects of a monarch.

In the idea of a republic, then, is included the idea of a conformity or consistency between the sovereignty which the people hold in the government and their capacity to exercise that sovereignty. If the people have not both the intelligence and the virtue which is necessary to self-government, how can a republic be maintained?

It is in consequence of this obvious necessity in republics of a higher degree of intelligence and public virtue than is necessary in monarchies, that Montesquieu makes the following remarks,* which are even more strikingly true now than a century since, when they were published.

"It is in republican government that the whole power of education is required. The *fear* of despotic governments naturally arises of itself amidst threats and punishments; the *honor* of monarchies is favored by the passions, and favors them in its turn; but *virtue* is a self-renunciation, which is ever arduous and painful.

"Now, government is like every thing else; to preserve it we must love it. Has it ever been heard, that kings were not fond of monarchy, or that despotic princes hated arbitrary power? Every thing, there-

* Spirit of Laws, book iv., chap. 5.

fore, depends on establishing this love in a republic; and to inspire it ought to be the principal business of education; but, the surest way of instilling it into children, is for parents to set them an example. People have it generally in their power to communicate their ideas to their children; but they are still better able to transfuse their passions."

The idea of a republic includes in it, therefore, the capacity of the people—by means of religious and intellectual education—to exercise justly the sovereignty with which they are invested. In vain will either an ignorant or corrupted people seek to acquire or maintain republican institutions. There is a positive antagonism between the possession of civil power requiring the highest exercise of reason, and the want of that intelligence and integrity which are essential to the right use of reason itself. This antagonism renders the destruction of a republic inevitable, unless the people happily rise to a voluntary correction of the evil, and fortunately attain a successful reformation.

The idea of a defined republic, also includes in it a reference to the specific objects held in view, and the degree of civilization prevalent in the age. In the Republic of the United States the specific object is declared to be to form a UNION, establish JUSTICE, insure TRANQUILLITY, provide a DEFENCE, promote the general WELFARE, and secure the blessings of LIBERTY. All of these may be included under the general phrase,—CIVIL AND RELIGIOUS LIBERTY. For without both of these neither union, justice, tranquillity, the general welfare, or freedom can exist;—for without these there must exist a government more or less despotic, which again implies ignorance;—which again implies a want of those profound religious principles and high intellectual powers, without which a nation can neither maintain harmony, nor understand justice, nor tolerate freedom.

The Republic of the United States also exists in an age of the highest Christian light and civilization. The intelligence and virtue, therefore, which it must possess in order to maintain republican institutions, must be of no common measure or low degree. It must attain the highest measure of that natural light which science has revealed in developing the works of creation, and of that spiritual light which God has revealed in the scriptures of truth. At least such must be the ultimate measure of an education suited to this republic, in this age. We have now come to these conclusions:—The idea of a republic, is the idea of *a people governing themselves.* This includes, also, the idea of a people possessed of that *intelligence and virtue* which is essential to self-government. The Republic of the United States is founded on the principle of *civil and religious liberty.* Education in the United States must, therefore, conform to the highest standard of modern science and of Christian civilization. An AMERICAN REPUBLIC must, then, be founded on an AMERICAN EDUCATION;—an education arising out of the nature of its institutions; imbued

2

with the knowledge of its era; and filled with all that is free, true, hopeful, and glorious in the New Testament, revealed through Christ.

CHAPTER II.

THE MEANS OF PERPETUATING CIVIL AND RELIGIOUS LIBERTY.

"Add to your faith, virtue; and to virtue, knowledge."
2 *Peter*, ch. 1, v. 5.

THE idea of a republic, I have said, is substantially that of a people governing themselves, and therefore implying the capacity for self-government. This again implies the necessity of an education for the whole people; an education adapted to develop the entire faculties of man,—whether intellectual or spiritual: for we must ever recollect, that the American republic has asserted *new principles* of government, and therefore demands an AMERICAN EDUCATION. What are these new principles? They are, that the *rights* of all constitute the *basis*,—and the *happiness* of all, the *object* of government. These principles are the joint fruits of the progress made in civilization and Christianity. The first springs from science; the second is the child of the Reformation. These are the principles we have derived from the founders of the American nation;—and which, we trust, will long survive the crumbling institutions of other lands.

I propose here to discuss the MEANS OF PERPETUATING CIVIL AND RELIGIOUS LIBERTY.* I say *perpetuating*, because it cannot be doubted that the citizens of the United States do actually *possess* civil and religious liberty in the highest *degree.*

Conceding that the machinery of our government may hereafter be amended, yet it is certain that the great principles of liberty are already established here. The only practical inquiry is, therefore, *how* are they to be perpetuated?

1. *The first means* of perpetuating civil and religious liberty, is to *understand what it is*;† for when

---

* It is one thing to *acquire*, and another to *preserve liberty.* All the renowned nations of the world have, in the process of revolutions, passed from *anarchy* to *despotism;* and in that progress have, at some time or other, been at what may be called the stage of *national freedom.* At that point they have remained a greater or less period of time, just in proportion as they possessed the fundamental principles I have endeavored here to delineate. No *theory*, or *machinery of government* has, *per se*, any *magic* to preserve its salutary functions, in spite of a diseased and corrupted people. They are the *life*, while the government is the form through which they act. To trace this necessary relation between the character of the people and that of the government in a condensed form is the object of this chapter; and it seems obvious, from the signs of the times, that that relation is very little understood, and still less practised upon.

† One who does not *understand* a thing cannot *practise* upon it. Now, up to the year 1828, and in a great measure up to the present period, *well-educated* Americans studied more of the Grecian Mythology, and far more of European wars, than they did of the structure and functions of their own government. Very recently most of the colleges have ventured to place beside Hebrew and metaphysics, the study of the Constitution; and it is hoped they will not be censured

understood, strange indeed would be that being, who could prefer any form of tyranny, whether it be of the many or the few, to the beautiful system of *constitutional freedom.* The *new principle* of civil liberty, then, is that the whole people shall govern, not by instant and impulsive action, but, as gravitation holds the planets, by uniform and regulated *law.* It is new, because the records of all antiquity, and the constitutions of all other governments, will be searched in vain for any theory which acknowledges that government is the right of the *whole people,* and must be administered for their happiness. If history confirms any proposition, it is that in all the republics of the past, whether ancient or modern, the great *mass of the people* were disregarded by the institutions and separated from the interests of their country. Does

---

for so *daring* an undertaking! The great body of high schools and academies, however, are still, in relation to this subject, dumb. The people are, indeed, obliged to know something of popular government, for they are compelled to participate in the conflict of parties, and the discussions of the press; but what kind of knowledge is it? One which is made up of *inaccuracies* and *exaggerations.* Thousands think that liberty consists in doing just *what one pleases;* and recent events would lead us to conclude that this was the prevalent notion. A still larger portion think that it consists simply in the right of *representation,* no matter what the representative may do, or what may be his character for integrity and intelligence. But very few think that freedom is a creature of checks and restraints, rather than of license and impulse. The American government is composed wholly of the former, and is strong just in proportion to its *complication:* for this very reason its study should be made as general as possible among the people.

any one doubt this? Let him go to that land, whose laws more than those of any other have been the study of the statesman, whose people were the most ingenious and inquiring, as they were the most refined of the ancient nations, whose glory lives, even here, in whatever of art or genius can survive decay. Go to the fierce democracy of Athens, and who were its citizens and governors? Were they the *mass* of the people? Were they the cultivators of the soil? Were they the few or the many? The least numerous part of the people were those who held the rights of citizenship. A large class were *metics*, residents for the purpose of trade and manufactures; and the largest portion slaves. Such also was the condition of Lacedæmon, of Rome, and of all the ancient republics. In all the spirit of *domination* prevailed; and whilst, aided by the then existing science, by the hardihood of the rugged virtues, and by all the spirit of eloquence, they subdued from the weakness and ignorance of barbarism province after province, and nation after nation, they added nothing to the family of Grecian or of Roman citizens. The conquered were left on the vast, dead level of slavery, or in the condition of tributaries to the wealth and strength of others. Such is the picture of ancient liberty. And did Venice, or Genoa, or Florence improve upon the example?—See the terrible aristocracy of Venice, and the alternate prevalence of faction and families in Florence, the once happy seat of letters and the arts.

There is, then, a radical difference between the *origin* and *object* of government in our republic and those of other countries. But there is another difference equally distinct, and equally necessary to the happiness of the people. This is, that now liberty can act only through defined and limited organs, created by the people. These are responsible to the power which created them, and are yet unchangeable, except by its *deliberate* action. In other free countries, it acted by *the instantaneous, unrestrained impulse of the popular will.** Here, however omnipotent this popular will may be in the creation of laws and constitutions, it can only act *through* them, while they exist. The difference between these systems is as wide as that between a meteor and a planet. Both obey a common force; but one, unre-

---

* The Athenian democracy, for example, was, with little exception, one of *impulse*, without regulation. A pure democracy must always be so. In such a case the people govern by their direct action, without representation—a form of government which is only possible in small communities. In the United States it is otherwise. Here is the government of a great nation, with its powers divided among *states, representatives, departments*, and a great variety of checks and balances, by which the popular will is restrained till time is given for deliberation.

Among the Grecian people the majority were *slaves*, and the tendency of all their institutions was to increase the *servile class*, and diminish the citizens. When Xenophon drew up a plan of government for Athens, his sole desire was to subsist the citizens *wholly* by the labor of slaves, and, for this purpose, to diminish the number of the former. Hence, Mr. Mitford remarks, that to the slave *war* was a blessing; for it compelled the master, by the *fear* of desertion, to treat him with kindness.—*Mitford's Greece*, vol. iv. chap. 21.

strained by law, shoots its glory forth, quickly to perish; while the other, governed by the regular action of constant and balanced principles, returns from time to time to yield its steady light to the mariner, and fix the eye of a glorious faith.

To illustrate this difference by obvious examples, take the *separation of departments*. The power to *judge* was never, it is believed, wholly separated from the power to *legislate*, or to *execute*, till our republic was instituted.* How disastrous their union has been in other governments, is fearfully exhibited in the long and melancholy record of popular as well as despotic tyranny. For the union of these distinct powers of government in one department, makes, in itself, a despotism.

The definition of *treason*, say the most enlightened statesmen of modern times, is inseparable from *liberty*. This *definition*, without the admission of any construction, was first made, with precision, in the Constitution of the United States.† Without it, treason becomes just what the momentary passions of the people, or the monarch, make it. The *patriot* of to-day, becomes the *traitor* of to-morrow.‡ To

---

* See Adams's "Defence of the American Republic," vol. i. p. 362.

† United States' Constitution, art. iii. sec. 3.

‡ By the ancient common law of England, *treason* was undefined and *constructive*. This gave rise to a statute defining treason, entitled of the 25th of Edward III. From that statute, as far as it was applicable, the *very words* of the American Constitution was taken, in order that they might receive the same interpretation which had long

be called *the just*, is enough to make an exile. Such was Aristides, Cicero, and Sydney. The same passions are everywhere common to humanity. They have swayed, and will again sway our country. But sad will be the day when the wishes of the populace shall become the definition of treason, or the tumults of passion mistaken for the duties of patriotism.

2. Next to *understanding* what liberty is, the great means of perpetuating it will be found in the *adaptation of popular action to the new constitution of things*. Nations, like individuals, are *organized* bodies. The state of anarchy is only a state of *transition;* never of permanent rest. And whether we regard a nation as subsisting under the lifeless civilization of China—the military domination of Russia—or the patriarchal government of an Arab tribe—we shall find them acting upon principles adapted to *their mode* of organization; without which, indeed, they might have continued their national existence, but must have *changed its form*, and its principles. If, for example, the Arab tribe, living under a patriarchal government, would give up the principle of social equality, or create an individual *tenure in the soil*, they would cease to be what they are—the un-

been attached to them in the administration of the English courts. *But* it must be observed that only a small part of it was applicable; for, under the English statute, there were no less than *seven* kinds of treason, and some of them very indefinite; so that any one who consults iv. Blackstone, 76–90, will discover that, at last, it is only in America that treason is certainly and accurately defined.

subdued children of the desert—a living testimony to the truth of prophecy. If the Hindoo had abandoned the *caste*—the peculiar principle of his *aristocracy*—he would long since have melted into Mohammedanism, or now have opposed a less icy barrier to the progress of Christianity. Popular action, then, must conform to the organization of a nation, or that nation must *change* its organization.* What, then, *is* the

* There are but *three* ways in which aristocracy can be maintained:—1st. By a distinction, which is made part of the *religious code*, and perpetuated by the superstitions of the people; 2d. By *military gradation*, and which can only subsist where the bulk of able-bodied men are employed in military service; and 3d, Where the *law*, and not talents or industry, creates an *unequal distribution of property*. The first is exemplified in the *castes* of Hindostan; the second was exhibited in the *feudal system;* and the third may be seen in the restriction on inheritances and sales which have prevailed heretofore in a large part of Europe. In America none of these exist, or can exist, till every thing which is peculiar in American political institutions have been destroyed. The destruction of *primogeniture, fee-tail*, and other feudal contrivances, has taken away the *possibility* of a continued ascendancy of particular families by means of continued wealth, unless there be with it the union of talents, industry, and integrity. The constant succession we see around us in particular families of poverty, or wealth, or competence only, is like the ebb and flow of the tides. Nor can this elevation and depression be prevented, except by the universal diffusion of that which every family and every nation ought to seek—*sound principles* with *sound knowledge*. These bring with them the economical virtues of frugality, temperance, and industry. It is true, these cannot prevent the inequalities of natural capacity; yet they modify them so far as to prevent total poverty or imbecility. Fools and geniuses are seldom such by *nature;* there is little of folly, which was not originally

popular action required by our organization? What should be the elements of social character in that nation, who are both governors and governed? that people, who have written upon their standard in golden characters, and unfurled it from the *mountain top* to the gaze of nations—that government is the *right*, and is instituted for the happiness of *all?*

There are two principles which are fundamental in all governments wholly free; and to which popular action must be adapted, or they must change their form. They who govern must know *how* to govern; and they who govern *rightly*, must themselves be *right*. Intelligence and virtue, therefore, are presupposed, by the very organization of our government.

They are the necessary elements of its existence. And this is *peculiar* to governments wholly popular. For whether we take a military domination, or an hereditary despotism, or a limited monarchy, or an aristocracy, or any other form which excludes the majority, the character of the mass, however much it may con-

---

occasioned by neglect or idleness; and little of the admirable in talent, which had not its origin in industry and *will.*

The *equality of distribution* created by the *law* in respect to property and political privileges, is elemental in republics. But that species of equality, or rather *levelling*, which destroys the distinction between industry and vice, by destroying the property which one has acquired and the other lost, and the social distinctions arising from virtue and talents on the one hand, and vice and folly on the other, belongs only to the worst species of *anarchy*, in the worst period of human degradation.

cern themselves, has nothing to do with institutions *directed by others.* It is then the necessity, as it certainly should be the glory of our country, to cherish whatsoever is wise, or excellent, or elevating in the human character.

3. The most important object of popular action, then, under a free government, is *to make the principle of intelligence general in the mass, and to elevate it as knowledge increases.* What is intelligence? It is *cultivated mind, the developed faculties of the human understanding.* To be capable of that development is, next to immortality, the most glorious gift of God to man: to be permitted to seek it, a right guarantied by all institutions which do not seek to fetter *soul* as well as body. To seek it free as the mountain air—the very element of republics. . To seek it under forms which allure to heaven as well as adorn the earth—the privilege of the Christian system. *This* development of the faculties, which is a combination of *knowledge* and of *thought,* is the object of all systems and schools of instructions. But to attain that object there is, and there always has been, *two* very *different* methods of *teaching.* The one teaches to *think,* the other to *repeat.* The one teaches *principles,* the other *rules:* the one *systems,* the other *particulars.* About these different plans there are different opinions. The great majority of mankind, however, from the Egyptian to the Hindoo, from the Chinese to the Roman priesthood, have followed *repetition;* and even at this hour, the mass of

enlightened modern Europe prefer *rule* to *principle*, whether it be applied to the teaching of childhood or the greater affairs of government. On the other hand, a few in ancient and many in modern times, believed it better to exercise their own faculties than to have them moved by others. The philosophers of Greece, and the Apostle of the Gentiles reasoning with them, the men of science and the disciples of the Reformation, are of this school. What has been the result, as exhibited by history and observation, of these different modes of teaching upon the earth and its inhabitants?

A few men, while the mind was yet unfettered, in the early ages of Egypt, or India, or China, discovered the mere elements of mechanics, of astronomy, of written language; but, about the same time, the people discovered they could be relieved from the troubles of conscience, by just imposing them upon the priesthood; and from the cares of government, by just confiding them to some particular class, or family, who by some freak of nature had acquired the sole capacity to govern, and, by some still odder freak, had the power of perpetuating it. Science had done enough to enable monarchs to build cities, erect monuments, and sleep in the dust with their faces to the east; and then, deprived of its power to inquire, slept the dreamless slumber of indolence. And what became of the nations—the people? *They* learned to *repeat*. The million did as they *had* done. They continued to build sepulchres, write hieroglyphics, gaze at the moon, obey castes, follow Brahma, and despise the barbarians. They continued from age to age to look back with increasing astonishment, as increasing mists magnified the lights of antiquity, at the wonderful intelligence of their ancestors, who had brought such a wonderful system as theirs into being!* Through three thousand years, they still look back with unmingled surprise at the miraculous powers of that mechanic who first learned how to raise one

---

* The Chinese have long believed that they really were the sources of all *civilization;* and that to prevent degeneracy, it was absolutely necessary to erect an *iron barrier* between them and all other nations. What the effect of this is, is easily seen in the state of their institutions, arts, and manners. It is not discoverable that they have at all changed in their habits, or made any advances in knowledge, for many generations. Yet it is very evident that they learned all that they do know, in early ages. When the embassy of Lord Macartney visited them, the Europeans, who for the first time were permitted to visit the interior of China, were surprised to find the Chinese artists capable of repairing some of the most refined parts of their astronomical instruments; yet it did not appear they knew any thing of the *uses* of these instruments: it was the *mechanical* part they could understand, and that was not of modern acquisition. More recent travellers have shown the hollow, yet antiquated frame of things in that ancient empire. Indeed, as the author of "Saturday Evening" has well remarked, every thing in the civilization and superstitions of those eastern nations, is in a state of *decrepitude.* They are like an old tower still standing in Italy, so far decayed and bent over from its base, that every passer-by expects to see it fall. The eastern nations are incapable of doing what Europe can—accommodating themselves to the new constitution of the moral world. They have not done so, in the least. The consequence is, that they are ready to fall, comparatively, at *a touch.*

stone upon another*—the great *genius* of him who first discovered that the sun rose in the east and set in the west! Such are the *results* in the school of *repetition*. It found the world with the beginnings of civilization, and it took care to perpetuate them, by erecting a system of civil *machinery*, by which the last mind should be *ground out* precisely on the *model* of the first. How extensive, and how terrific this system has been, is exhibited in the history of the oldest and most populous portion of the globe. Nor in that alone, but in every land—as in Spain or Turkey—where infallible systems, whether of religion or

* The great pyramid which stood near Memphis was larger than the Temple of Diana, and, as well as that, was called one of the *wonders of the world*. The Temple of Diana was 426 feet at its base, and contained columns of white marble, of which the shafts were 60 feet in length. The great pyramid was 660 feet at its base, and 466 in height. So massy and extensive were these structures, that many even now inquire how they *could* have been erected. They who make this inquiry know very little of mechanics, and still less of science, when they adduce these monuments as evidences of ancient superiority in that branch of knowledge. If the assertion of an ancient philosopher, that he could move the earth if he had a place for his lever, be true, there could be little difficulty in devising a mode of erecting the pyramids, provided only that *men* and *money* could be obtained for such a purpose. The latter difficulty did not stand in the way of the Egyptian king; for we are informed that it took *one hundred thousand men ten* years to hew the stones, and *twenty years* to build the edifice! And at last—sad lesson to the vanity of human greatness!—he was not permitted to rest in the mausoleum his ambition had built; but, pursued by the vengeance of an injured people, the burial place of the oppressor was hid from the face of the oppressed.

government, have sent their opiate influences, there are monuments, which, like those of Egypt, stand out from the sands of the desert, to point, not so much to the skill and power which erected them, as to the utter obliteration of heart and mind which follows him who manacles the human intellect.

But what have been the results in the school of *thinking?* It transferred the power of *originating* and *improving* from those who had discovered the best *pattern* of mind, to a nation of barbarians, yet a people of *inquirers.* It polished their language till it became a model for all who would study the relation between words and things. It cultivated the arts, till the forms of physical beauty were exhausted. It taught mathematics with ceaseless ardor, and inscribed upon the doors of the greatest philosopher, "Let none enter here who have not studied geometry." It imbibed the spirit of poetry, and swept the lyre of Mœonides till its notes, rising clear and high above every sound, still echo from the hills, still linger around these abodes of learning. It courted the mountain nymph, sweet Liberty; nursed the republics of old; and when the outward form in which it was encased perished under the weight of pagan institutions, it remodelled other nations and other times, perpetuating its living and ever-growing power from age to age. The royal Alfred and the monk Bacon, the wild Arabian and the gay Florentine, in turn received its mantle; till at last concentrated in the spirit of the Reformation, it is hurrying forward the chariot wheels of knowledge till they are *heated with motion.*

Such and so wide is the history of nations between those who learn to *repeat* and those who learn to *think.* And is not the principle the same when applied to individuals? is it not exhibited as plainly in the humble school by the roadside as when expanded through the aggregate mind of millions? Are not those who are taught without *thought* still the majority? If there are troublesome spirits in the world who *will* think for themselves, and a few who arrive at great truths without the aid of "royal roads," are there not a great number who will not travel any path of knowledge till it is strewn with down, nor then till they are drawn by the intellect of others? Sustained by natural indolence, and yet more by the belief that nothing but to make a part in the *machinery* of life belongs to the mass, the system of *teaching without thought* silently, but surely, creeps over nations like the livid green upon the stagnant pool.

To comply then with the fundamental law of all republics—to create that *development* of the general mind which constitutes *intelligence,* we must teach men, not merely the thoughts of others, but *how to think themselves;* and by what means shall thinking be taught? Whatever may be the case with the acquisition of mere facts, or the cultivation of taste, the arts, and the imagination, *thinking* can be taught only by something which excites *inquiry,* and still leaves something to be *discovered.* Nothing has done this more successfully, either in nations or individuals, than the study of the great body of natural principles which constitutes *science;* and by that term, I mean no particular subject or department; but include as well the analysis of language as the demonstrations of mathematics—the philosophy of history, as the investigation into the powers and structure of the human mind. It teaches men to think, by compelling them to reason; and allures them to learn, by leading them from discovery to discovery; as the wayfaring man is tempted to follow a path which opens upon new fruits, and soothes his spirits with the strains of a music before unheard by mortal ears. Science, considered merely as a teacher of the intellect, in this general philosophic sense, has some advantages which, whatever may be thought by the learned, are appreciated by the mass neither in theory nor in practice; and for the want of which, none suffer so much as the multitude. There is a simplicity and a durability in exhibiting great elementary truths which pervade the whole system of nature, and are equally applicable to all conditions of things, not possessed by the particular rules formed from them; for a thousand rules may flow from one principle, and he who learns one of them has only learned one application of the general truth, while he who has learned the principle may apply it when and how he pleases. It is this mistaking the *end* for the *beginning,* which has converted the minds of thousands into confused storehouses of miscellaneous goods, where the master knows neither name nor place, and throws a dense obscurity over the great subjects of *morals* and *politics.** Thus, he who has acquired a discriminating idea of falsehood, will need no metaphysics to distinguish it in all the variety of phases it assumes among men. Thus, too, he who has learned that the principle of *appropriation* is universal, has learned something which lies at the foundation of *property*, and consequently of society and government. Thus, also, he who has learned the idea of the *refrangibility* of light, will understand it wherever he sees it, whether exhibited in the colors of the prism or the beautiful phenomena of the rainbow, the uses of the telescope or the tranquil image in the water. And whenever he sees these exhibitions of original truth, he will see greater cause to rejoice in the existence of that wise Providence which has made the elements of nature as

---

* Some say this generalizing, *philosophizing* is of no use; we want to learn *practical* every-day things. Now it is precisely because general elementary *principles* are of the *greatest use*, the most practical of all things, that they should be learned. All the great rules of political economy are general, elementary, of every-day use. So, many of the rules of human life, as those in the Book of Proverbs, are general principles, which, if adhered to, will make men wise and great. In fact, *generalization* is the only means by which we can acquire or retain the constant accumulations of knowledge from age to age. We now learn and demonstrate, in a few hours, general truths of Chemistry and Natural Philosophy which ages of experiment scarcely served to discover and establish.

simple as they are *harmonious*—ministering spirits to the wants and the pleasures of life.*

---

* The *religious uses* of natural science seem not to have been fully appreciated at all times. If science, in all its complicated departments, is that *language* by which " day unto day uttereth speech, and night unto night showeth knowledge," and like the firmament has displayed, step by step, the glory, wisdom, and mercy of our Almighty Father; if it be (as it is) in perfect harmony with the scriptural history of the world; and if it be found to corroborate, by the testimony of nature herself, the minutest statements made therein, then is it the most powerful of all testimony to the truth of the *Old* Testament, which is the ground of belief in the *New*. Of the *humility* with which this subject should be approached, and the little ground it affords for the presumptuous boastings of human knowledge, none but the blind to all spiritual influences can be ignorant. On this subject I have met with the following extract from a Discourse by the Rev. Bartholomew Lloyd, D. D., Provost of Trinity College, Dublin:

" What I insist on, then, is—that when we seek God through the indications of his power or his will, contained in his word or his works, we should apply ourselves to the task with patient self-distrust and humble reverence, amounting to religious awe. This is the frame of mind which becomes us when we would approach the Father of Lights; and I would add, that this is the frame of mind which every advance in the study of his works no less than of his word is fitted to produce. In fact, it is only the grossly ignorant who is insensible to his own ignorance; the more extensive our knowledge, the greater the number and the variety of the subjects which present themselves for further inquiry. The wider the sphere of illumination, the more expanded is the surface which separates it from the region of darkness; and the greater the extent of our intellectual domain, the more numerous the points in that boundary by which we are sensibly confined. This growing sense of our insufficiency adequately to comprehend the workings of Divine power, serves but to increase the wonder excited by what is already brought within the compass of our discernment; and whilst man is humbled, God is exalted. Can we

No better example of the effect produced by such a mode of instruction can be found, than in the Fathers of the American republic. They were men who, for the most part, studied *science* as I understand the term—a system of principles, developing the laws of moral and political, as well as physical existence. They were generally educated, sometimes learned, but always *thinkers*. Consult their history, follow them to the councils of the Revolution, and go to that convention whose work is now our noble Constitution, our study and our glory, and you will find them taking lessons from the learning of the past; comparing results, adhering to recognized principles, and combining them in forms applicable to their state of society. See Richard Henry Lee scanning the volumes of history, and gathering the principles of government from universal experience ;* the Adamses, Samuel and John, comparing the republics of

---

then fail to acknowledge with the illustrious Bacon, the religious uses of natural science, when in that glowing language so peculiar to himself he thus expresses his convictions: *Philosophia naturalis, post verbum Dei, certissima superstitionis medicina est ; eademque probatissimum Fidei alimentum. Itaque merito religioni donatur tanquam fidissima ancilla, cum alteram voluntatem Dei, altera potestatem manifestat.*"

* Biography of the Signers of the Declaration of Independence, vol. ix. His biographer says: "The histories of the ancient republics inspired him with a love of liberty, taught him the fate of tyrants, and elated him with hope, not, however, unmingled with apprehension; for he saw them at times tossed by the storms of faction, and again awed to the stillness of despotism."

old,* and learning to perfect the new government by avoiding the defects of the old; and Hamilton, availing himself of the practical discussions of Europe to establish the political economy of the young republic of America.† Was not Chancellor Wythe a student of the classics and the mathematics?‡ Was not Washington himself, practical as his life was, always a student, always thoughtful, reflective, judicious?§

Science, as a teacher of the intellect, has this invincible argument—that it is, and ever has been, *inseparable from human improvement.* It is *progressive,* and *never retrogrades.* Aside from the light of Christianity, in what *but* this can we boast of superiority over the nations of antiquity? If a defender of ancient systems were to be attacked, simply on the ground of the *arts,* his position would be impregnable. He would point, in the cities of Europe and the plains of America, to architects building upon the models of the temple of Minerva, and the columns of Corinth and Ionia. He would point to sculptors spending their nights and days over the Apollo Belvidere, satisfied that beyond it their genius could not go. He would show you a poet, taking rank with the first of

---

* John Adams's "Defence of the American Republic" is one of the most learned and instructive works on the subject of government.

† Hamilton's "Report" is recognized as one of the ablest works extant on the subject of finance.

‡ Wythe was an accomplished scholar. See Biography of the Signers.

§ See Sparks's "Correspondence of Washington."

his race as the *translator* of Homer; and he would make you feel at every step, by the testimony of the senses, that you were following a long-discovered and long-beaten path. How different is the aspect and the progress of science! Has modern Europe added nothing to the knowledge of Greece; or did Greece add nothing to the models of Egypt? Did Newton make no discoveries, or add no principles to former systems? Did Bacon learn his philosophy from Aristotle? Did Davy and Cuvier study chemistry and geology in ancient books? Did Fulton build no other boat than those which navigated the Nile or the Indus? The value of science is embodied in the *history* of the *human mind.*

And why should not science be associated with human happiness? Is it not eternal truth? the *lens* through which the light of nature is converged upon the *intellect?* But, it will be said, this is *well;* yet it is not for the mass of the people; they can never learn science—that belongs to *philosophers;* and government—that belongs to *politicians;* and religion—why, that belongs to the *clergy!* The million have the catechism, and the newspaper: one teaches what to *believe,* and the other how to *vote;* and what business have they with more knowledge?

The answer is written in the fundamental law of your country, as it was before in that of heaven; both suppose man to be an intelligent being, capable of administering government—the subject of noble aspirations and of infinite improvement. And with this constitution of temporal and eternal freedom about him, shall the laborer plod on unmindful of the world of beauty and glory spread before him? Shall the ploughman turn up, day after day, the flowers of the field, listen to the song of birds, gaze upon the stars set in the firmament, and yet be unconscious that all are moving forward in ceaseless progression round the throne of Him who formed them? Shall he hear, as confused sounds in his ears, of heroes and patriots, the wise and good, who once lived in this land of liberty, and yet know not *who* they were or *what* their doings? Never think that they left an example for imitation, as well as principles to be perpetuated? Shall he hear of that revolution which established the republic, which has shaken the nations, and is felt by thrones, dominions, principalities, and powers; and yet know nothing of the means by which it was accomplished? Let him remain then unconscious of the world of light and life around him; let him believe, that to supply the *necessities* of life is his only business, while to *thirst* and *know*, belongs to philosophers, statesmen, theologians: let him believe and act thus; and can this government be maintained as a government of the people? How long will this morning star of nations continue to attract and fix the eye of faith?

4. Another principle presupposed in the establishment, and necessary to the existence of our republic, is public virtue. One of the means necessary to perpetuate American liberty, is the *adaptation of popular*

institutions to sustain the sentiment of public virtue. But what *is* public virtue? This word is of uncertain signification, according to some authors, but is employed by Montesquieu as having a precise bearing. It has a meaning easily understood in popular language. A man of public virtue is one who loves the republic, and its institutions; who obeys its laws from a high sense of duty; who does nothing to impair its interests; but, who acts for the public interests as if they were his own. In his case, the *feeling* of patriotism becomes a sense of duty; and duty implies honorable and trustworthy conduct, founded on moral obligation. Virtue then is a *sentiment,* in contrast with *intelligence,* as a result of intellectual investigation. To be intelligent, is not always to be *virtuous;* and to think, is not always to think *rightly. Intellect, thought,* are the foundations of *power.* Man holds dominion over the creatures of the earth, as he holds dominion over his fellow-men, by *superior strength of mind.* But to acquire and enjoy happiness, the intellect must be used in conformity with another principle, which in popular language is called *virtue.* Men must be virtuous, as well as intellectual. And the experience of the whole human race stands ready to prove that this principle is as applicable to nations as to individuals. Though you should look with dull eyes upon the volume of nature—though you should reject any demonstration which philosophy could make—though you should have the hardihood to deny the *Scriptures of truth*—yet will you read it in the record of those events which, from age to age, have brought nation after nation—from hoary Egypt, in the depths of antiquity, to the fair republics of modern Italy—to the untimely grave which their corruptions had prepared. Does any one ask, *why* Athens, or Sparta, or Corinth could not preserve a liberty which genius, art, song, and science had conspired to acquire? Let him read the laws of Lycurgus and of Solon. Let him dwell, if it pleases him, upon the noble, self-sacrificing spirit of an Athenian, offering himself up for his country; let him speak of the hardy virtues of frugality, prudence, and fortitude: then let him turn to those other scenes, where an American seeks his highest happiness—the altar and the fireside. Where was the worship of the heart in a land over which Mars and Apollo held divided sway? Where was domestic happiness in the circle in which woman was reduced to the level of the savage; where conjugal rights were almost unknown, and licentiousness scarcely left a seat at the table for the wives and mothers of freemen? Where was security for property among a people who converted power into right? Where was the safety of *person*, when the definition of treason depended upon the fancy of the populace; and where every man was a licensed assassin of those who opposed the popular government? And will the inquirer ask again why liberty fell in Greece? or will he *hope* to sustain the freedom of his own country, without the virtues which alone have power to withstand the mutations of time? Nor, even under Christian institutions, is there any example to show that liberty can be sustained without that practical spirit of virtue which gives them life. Take the commonwealth of England as an example. The nation had brought the chief of the house of Stuart to the scaffold, exiled his family, and levelled the nobles with the people. They had become, in principle, republican. The experiment could be fairly made—and why was it not? Because the people had lost the virtue which commenced the revolution; had fallen into indolence and licentiousness; and from a military dictatorship, easily returned to the ancient monarchy, the reign of unabashed vice, and unawed tyranny. From England turn to Italy—to republics rising and falling with every popular excitement; yet unstable as the winds, because unsustained by nutriment from the soul. Behold freedom courted to dwell in the beautiful land of the vine and the olive; yet compelled at last to take refuge among the simple virtues which abide with the spirit of Tell on the mountains of Switzerland. In all the past, whether we view it in the shades of ancient time, or in the light of modern ages; whether seen from the hills of Attica, or those of the Tiber; whether where Venice looks out upon the Adriatic, or Andes frown upon the changing governments of South America—liberty, when lost, is entombed in the grave of virtue.

5. But public virtue, I have said, is founded on the

sense of *moral obligation.* In every country the sense of moral obligation is founded in the character of its *religion.* The religion of Hindostan gives rise to one form of morals; that of Persia to another; and that of Europe to another. In every country the morals of a people, whatever they may be, take their form and spirit from their religion. For example, the marriage of brothers and sisters was permitted among the Egyptians, because such had been the precedent set by their gods, Iris and Osiris. So, too, the classic nations celebrated the drunken rites of Bacchus. Thus, too, the Turk has become lazy and inert, because dependent upon Fate, as taught by the Koran. And when in recent times there arose a nation, whose philosophers discovered there was no God and no religion, the nation was thrown into that dismal case, in which there was no law and no morals. The *fool* only hath said in his heart, There is no God.

In the United States, Christianity is the original, spontaneous, and national religion. It is revealed from heaven, and therefore perfect. Its morals are the morals of a perfect society, untouched and unspoiled by the selfishness and tainting expediencies of worldly policy. If the virtue of the nation conform, in any degree, then, to this acknowledged standard, it so far approaches that elemental right, which is the single principle lying at the foundation of republics. The fathers of the republic, our glorious ancestry of Pilgrim memory and revolutionary fame, acknowledged and worshipped the God of the Bible, who had borne them safely over the waves of the ocean and through the fires of battle. In the forest sanctuary, on the blood-red fields, in the halls of solemn council, they worshipped and they prayed; and their prayers were heard in the fruits of success, in the glory of victory, in the strength of growth, and in the full vision of that Future which is now rising full orbed on the horizon of Time. If such were their virtues, and such their conduct, what was the example left to us? It is as unphilosophical as it is impossible, to found morals in Christian countries upon any other basis than the Christian faith. There is no such phenomenon as a nation teaching one code of religion, and another code of virtues. What is the fundamental principle of Christian ethics? Love, in all its relative forms, is the active principle of Christian morals, as it is the foundation of all true civilization. And it is such a principle which forms the basis of the highest patriotism, as it does of the private affections. It is such a principle only, when dwelling with a mind acquainted with its own immortal powers, which can at once refine manners, purify the heart, and energize the understanding. The institutions of the republic must, therefore, conform to the religion of the people. In a Christian republic they must be Christian. If they be not, there must arise that *antagonism* of which I have already spoken. And if there be, which is likely to fall, the religion or the state? Let history answer. No power of the state has yet been able to martyrize religion, whether true or false, from the minds of a people.

6. Another thing to be noticed as necessary to the perpetuity of republics is not so much a principle, as a *tendency*, a constitutional tendency, to be cherished and encouraged. This is *activity of mind.* Accurate logicians may say this is not an element of itself, but a mere result of free society and free government. Be it so. It is yet something to be increased or diminished. We can easily understand what it is when we reflect on the intellectual condition of Greece or of Persia. It is not easy to *define* what the American people mean by " enterprise." But the meaning is understood by every one. It is activity in action. I mean by activity of mind the same thing when applied to intellectual processes and productions. It is that activity of intellect and feeling which is ever undertaking new enterprises into the world of creation around it, whether it be in matter or in mind—whether it be the discovery of new powers in mind itself, or new conditions of the social structure. *Action* is the life of nations as of persons. Neither ever stand still. The course of a republic should be the eagle's flight—upward, sunward, still seeking purer light.

It is *activity* of mind which creates *improvement;* and it is *that* we wish to perpetuate—and not merely columns of art, or volumes of learning, or passive sentiment. *Original, vigorous thought* is the sturdy oak; while art and literature are the flowers and tendrils under its shade. The oak must shoot forth new limbs, grow green in the free air, and imbibe the vigor of the earth, before it can protect the frail plants beneath. Neither art, nor taste, nor erudition, nor books have been able to preserve any people. It is recorded of Greece,* that learning was never greater, scholiasts more numerous, or books more abundant, than when in her declining years she presented the melancholy spectacle of *art surviving freedom*—the perished tree made green by the vine which still lingered about its branches. Indeed, it is impossible that either mere art or mere erudition, however necessary to the ornaments of life or the acquisition of facts, can ever do much towards creating new or improving old systems of thought or of happiness. The one derives its power from the forms of beauty in the

---

* In the last chapter of Sismondi's Fall of the Roman Empire, pages 470, 471, the reader will find authority for what is said in the text. "The degeneracy of the Greeks took place when they were in the midst of the accumulated treasures of knowledge and the enlightenment of the world." Knowledge without *thinking* is useless, and *thinking* without knowledge is like a mechanic without tools. It remains yet to be tested in the experiment made in America, whether nations have not, as well as individuals, the *lassitude* and *decay* of declining age; and whether the energy of nations is not peculiar to their youth. The glory of Greece was but about 300 years in duration; that of Rome somewhat longer; that of Egypt much longer than either; while that of England—counting from Alfred—promises to be of yet greater continuance. There seems, then, to be no particular limit to the *life* and *prime* of nations; and we may fairly conclude there is none, but that created by their *vices*.

natural world, and the other from existing knowledge. Both are limited. They may form the intellect of a Canova, or Parr, or Porson; but never the minds of Newton, of Locke, of Milton, or of Washington. *These* were made by THINKING; not, indeed, without the *materials* of knowledge, but without the *vassalage* of opinion, which binds men to rules and forms. And in exact conformity to this, we find that when a people like the Greek, the Arabian, the Italian become commentators, and cease to cultivate the great principles of science, or to bring the great truths of virtue round the fireside, indolence soon subverts the energies of the soul; rule is substituted for principle, the ordinance for the spirit, and art and learning weave their beautiful woof round the dying body of Liberty.

But activity of mind, like strength to youth, is the gift of young republics; and must be, as it ever has been, kept up by excitement of some kind. On the early ages of mankind, as, indeed, those of the highest refinement in modern days, war and its conquests have been the effects of national ambition.

The glory of battle, like the blaze to the insect, seems to have been the brilliant point around which the warrior energies of men have gathered for destruction. Yet conquests are not consistent with republics. It is contrary to their system. Macedonia could conquer, but Athens fight only in self-defence. Rome lost her liberties when she made extensive conquests; and, till the late war with Mexico, it was the doctrine of both statesmen and people in the United States, that we should make no conquests. Nor is it easy to see how we can make war an object of ambition, when, except a few weak neighbors, there are no nations on this continent whose conquest would add new lustre to the national glory. We are already an ocean-bound republic, whose frontier invites no hostile attack; and whose career must consist in the peaceful pursuits of commerce, in building and adorning a home for the uncounted millions of posterity, and in sending round the earth the principles of liberty, the charms of civilization, and the reviving and invigorating truths of Christianity.

What then, some may ask, shall employ that activity of mind, whose outbreaking spirit we see in the excitements of society? These excitements are but the foam on the tide. If men are alarmed by the white caps raised on the waves by some stormy wind, would they not have much greater *cause* of alarm if that stream sunk into a still lifeless pool, mantled by the green and putrid form of disease? What is wanting is to convert this activity into a blessing and not a curse. The energies of freedom *cannot* be suppressed. They ought not to be, because there would no longer be freedom. The tree might retain its *foliage*, but would be stripped of its *fruit*.

What then are the proper channels for that intellectual activity which cannot be left to itself without danger? America, more than any other country existing, contains new avenues for that ceaseless exercise of mind and heart, without which there is neither energy nor progress. Its very social condition, the first object of inquiry with a foreigner, and which should be the first to engage the care of its citizens, is a problem, as new as it is curious. The traveller from other countries in vain endeavors to understand or describe an equality, whose compatibility with the existence of government he cannot comprehend. Our own statesmen sometimes mistake its nature, and are lost in the results of a principle whose operations elude speculation. The formation and modification of public opinion—whether by education, by interest, by the press, or by social assimilation, in a land where public opinion governs, should be thoroughly watched and investigated. Subtle as the water, the public sentiment of a free people is yet subject to the laws of motion and attraction; and these must be well understood before it can be made steadily to bear on great plans of improvement. The general mind is yet uninformed on the true relation existent between law-maker and law-subject, in a nation where every citizen is both; and upon the correlative necessity of *obeying* as well as enacting wise laws.*

* The laws are made both practically and theoretically by the *whole* people, in a collective sense. But they are to be obeyed *individually*. While it is true that an individual has his share in the making of laws, it is also true that he must individually yield obedience to that *law* which is made by the whole, and which, as an individual, he has no right to repeal. To be a *law-subject* as well as a law-

If we pass from this subject to that of *moral truth,* what country upon earth ever presented a wider range for inquiry! What government ever before admitted the principle of universal toleration? In what other land could it be said that error of opinion might be safely tolerated, while reason was left free to combat it? What people are more susceptible of *moral* impressions? Upon whom could you have greater hopes of fixing the abiding truths of time and eternity? That the spirit of Christian civilization has, in fact, a deeper root in this than in any other country, may safely be inferred from the more elevated *condition of women.* The treatment of women is rightly said to be the *standard* of civilization. Among barbarians they are slaves; in France the idols of pleasure; in Germany drudges; in England the respected companions of masters; in America the cherished wives of freemen. Such is the testimony of foreigners.* Nor does America ask from

---

maker, *obedient* as well as sovereign, is the highest virtue of a republican citizen.

* All foreigners agree in the superior purity of American women, and the high degree of respect paid them by their countrymen. The following is the remark of M. de Beaumont, an intelligent French traveller. "You may estimate the morality of any population, when you have ascertained that of the women; and one cannot contemplate American society without admiration for the respect which there encircles the ties of marriage. The same sentiment existed in a like degree among no nation of antiquity; and the existing societies of Europe, in their corruption, have not even a conception of such a purity of morals."

their jealousy a higher or a nobler tribute to her institutions. The same *principles* which have produced such a result are ready to be trained into other channels of moral sentiment; and if we do look back with something of shame at the superior frugality and temperance of ancient Sparta, it is not that we value those hardy virtues *less*, but that wealth and pleasure have tempted us *more*.

New materials for thought and activity in the paths of science—those regions of invention and discovery where human power has exercised its highest functions, and poured back upon society its uncounted blessings—where will it find a fresher or a wider field than in this new-risen continent? Indeed, it is obvious that no country can furnish higher inducements in the development of its multiplied resources for the improvement of practical science; and it is equally obvious that here the great improvement must be made for generations to come. The philosophers of England have distinctly declared that there the cultivation of science is on *the decline;** the German mind is occu-

---

The same thing is admitted by the London Quarterly, in the number for April, 1835.

* "Four English philosophers, Sir Humphry Davy, Sir John Herschel, Mr. Babbage, and Sir David Brewster, under a deep concern for the honor of England, boldly pointed out the fact of the decline of science and the scientific arts."—*Edinburgh Review, January,* 1835.

This declaration produced the formation of the British Scientific Association, which has held four meetings, and made many reports on the state of science.

pied with metaphysical subtleties; the French have lost the genius of the Institute; and are, as, with few exceptions, they have ever been, occupied upon the *details* rather than the *foundations of knowledge.* It is in America that the great additions to science and social improvement must be made. Nor are they, like the *fine arts, limited* by the forms of beauty. They are not required to imitate the models of the past. That knowledge which is based upon the *structure* and *uses* of the world which infinite *wisdom* created, and infinite *love* sustains, cannot be exhausted. It is as perennial as nature herself; as fresh upon those hills and vales, as when blooming Eden first opened upon the father of men, or the shepherd first gazed upon the firmament from the star-lit plains of Chaldea. So *wise* is the constitution of things, that curiosity must ever find something ungratified; some secret unrevealed in the bosom of nature; some land undiscovered to the vision of genius. And yet the conquests of mind still go on; science multiplies herself at each added step; allures forward by all the mystery of the promised future, and all the sublime of glory possessed. Her weapons are from the armory of heaven; her dominion wide as the universe of mind.

Lastly, there is full employment for activity of mind, in the culture and practice of *social science.* I mean the discovery of the laws, and carrying into effect the principles, which produce the happiness and improvement of human society.

The time is past, in which intellectual power can

seclude itself in monasteries, or spend its life in solitary studies. The light of a thousand eyes is poured upon it by the press, the extension of social intercourse, and the rapidly increasing freedom of opinion. Man can no longer live for himself, but is compelled to make other men his companions, and the world his theatre. The very principle announced by America, that government was constituted for the happiness of *all*, was one which pledged the energies of its citizens to the improvement of the human family. *That improvement*—moral, intellectual, physical—is an object of effort and desire, which cannot cease to exist, while there remains oppression to destroy, knowledge to diffuse, or regions of possible attainment yet unsubdued to the dominion of mind. This is an object, also, which is constantly accumulating power over the feelings and judgments of enlightened nations. Already we find it recognized in Europe, that a war of subjugation will no longer be tolerated. The piratic trade in slaves is outlawed by the most powerful nations.* The ablest statesmen frown upon the

* After the abolition of the *slave trade* by Great Britain, she made many treaties with other nations, stipulating for its abandonment. Among others was Brazil, where slavery was carried to an extreme of cruelty and debasement, known to but few countries. There it ceased to be legal in 1830. Notwithstanding which, immense importations of slaves are clandestinely made. Treaties containing the same stipulations have been made with Sweden, Denmark, and various other nations.

It is to be regretted that these measures have not proved as effectual as was hoped.

system of privateering. The hereditary peerage is crushed in France, and crumbling in England. England herself is carrying our common language to the dwellers on the Ganges, the Indus, and the Niger. Colleges and schools in distant India teach the learning and the science of our common race. The castes of Brahma tremble at their touch; and the lofty Mandarin of the Celestial empire wonders and fears, as truth approaches his shore. Our own republic is founding in Africa new republics from that exiled race, who have returned to renew in glory the country which they left in gloom.

In all civilized countries a practical freedom, in accordance with the ameliorating spirit of Christianity, is abroad upon the earth. It must be instructed and enlightened, but cannot be successfully opposed. By mother, by school, and by college, in the popular assembly, in the press, and in the pulpit, the active energies of mind and heart must be trained in every sound principle and perfect law. Whatever may be thought by timid, or even philosophical persons, of the present tendencies of the human mind, it must be admitted, as a *fact*, that the masses of mankind have, in Christian countries, been awakened to the past degradation of their condition, and are looking restlessly and anxiously for a new order of things. Nor can any candid person read the ancient prophets of Judea, announcing a future of life, light, and knowledge, in the glowing poetry of Oriental language, without admitting that this condition of things is, *in part* at least, a realization of that magnificent vision!

The people have harnessed themselves to the chariot of knowledge; and though the weight of long ages of darkness rest upon it; though clouds and shadows still throng its path; though error and fanaticism cling to its wheels; it rolls on, and must forever roll, till the last system of oppression, of ignorance, and of false belief, shall have crumbled into the dust and ashes of the tomb.

CHAPTER III.

THE IDEA OF AN AMERICAN EDUCATION.

"To develop in each individual all the perfection of which he is susceptible, is the object of education."—*Kant.*

It cannot fairly be denied that the greater number of those who have written and spoken upon education have taken far too limited and narrow views of that most important subject. They have often spoken well and forcibly in regard to the particular branches of the general topic which they have considered; but how few have written in regard to the ultimate object, and the whole measure of means by which it can be attained! What is the *ultimate* object? No less than to develop all the faculties of the human soul to the utmost extent of which they are susceptible in this temporal life and condition. This is a sublime object; but not more sublime than practical, if the human will interpose no obstacles to the completion of the enterprise. I readily grant that it is neither possible nor desirable to raise the intellectual standard of every man to the same elevation with that of some one individual who may be a model of eminent genius and high attainments; but we should never forget that the greatest and brightest of the human race are but examples of what the human faculties are capable of attaining. And who can truly say that he knows the human spirit can never soar higher than even the greatest and brightest have done? Who can say that he knows philosophy will never be adorned by a brighter than Bacon; or astronomy advanced by a nobler than Newton? Has he ever heard of a divine decree, that he who was made in the likeness of God is limited by the earthen barriers which confine the body? Has any one taken measure of the elasticity and velocity of the soul? does he know where it must cease to inquire, and when it must cease to soar? If we know not these limits, then neither do we know that the highest attainments of human knowledge, and the sublimest pursuits of science, may not become the common possessions of the common people. We know that one star differeth from another star in magnitude; but we also know that every star shineth with a continual efflux of light—flowing perpetually through the visible creation.

The idea of education then, in its absolute, ultimate, and universal sense, is that of a perpetually growing and never-exhausted growth of the human soul. In the language I have quoted, it is "to develop in each individual all the perfection of which he is susceptible." This, too, corresponds with the original meaning of the word, as derived from *educere*, to lead, or draw forth the mind, passions, and affections. In this sense, not merely the school, but all that meets the soul of man in its passage through time, become its educators. Every sense draws in knowledge, and every faculty goes forth to meet the elements of nature: history repeats the lessons of experience; the world fascinates with the delusions of pleasure; the church calls to the performance of duty; and the state invites to share in the glories of ambition. Whatever there is in life to draw forth its emotions, to dazzle its imagination, to excite its inquiry, to induce reflection, to impel it forward, or to delay its career—all these things enter into that aggregate of results which is called education; all have been ministering spirits—whether of good or evil—to this wondering soul, striving continually to gather up something of its original inheritance.

In a practical view of education, however, we must confine ourselves to narrower limits; we must take for education what is commonly meant by instruction—the work of teachers. In this sense, however, there are general and universal principles to be applied in the adaptation of this instruction to the ends in view. If we were, for example, to adapt a system of instruction (and had the power to do it) to the people of the United States which was adopted and has for ages been employed to teach the religious ideas of Brahminism, and the despotic power of princes in India, it would be impossible to preserve the republic. There is an absolute, positive antagonism between such a course of instruction as that and the existence of free institutions. So, also, if we could teach the great body of the children of India the doctrines of Christianity and the operation and effect of republican laws, it would be utterly impossible for India to remain in its present condition. Hence we must adapt instruction to the means we have and the object in view. We wish to perpetuate the institutions of the republic, because we believe them wise, beneficial, and well calculated to produce public prosperity: hence we must adapt instruction to that object. In the preceding chapter I have discussed the general principles of perpetuating civil and religious liberty. It now remains to apply those principles.

1. The education of a free people must correspond to the necessities of freedom, in regard to intelligence, public virtue, activity of mind, general growth, and Christian progress.

2. In order to attain these results, those studies should be principally regarded which tend to instruct the mind in the structure and operation of republican government; in the principles and value of science;

in history and social science; in eloquence, or the art of talking; in the moral capacity and spiritual destiny of man; in the coequal value, responsibilities, and destiny of woman; in the education of mothers; in the Bible, as the charter derived from Heaven; and, finally, in whatever shall make man a thinking, spiritual, active, responsible agent. Such he must be before this world can realize, even in a small measure, those beautiful and exquisite pictures of a renovated earth, so forcibly depicted by the holy prophets.

3. American education, in order to attain the perfection of society and perpetuate the institutions of freedom, must adopt these general principles in practice; and also adapt itself to whatever is *peculiar* in America, peculiar in Christian civilization, and peculiar in the laws of social progress, as developed in history.

The idea of American education, then, is of an education, in fact and theory, in conformity with the idea of a complete republic; in conformity with the idea of a Christian republic; and in conformity with the idea of both a physical and spiritual development of all the faculties in each individual. It is not necessary, in order to attempt this, that we should assume the perfection of any such system, or of society itself, at present. It is only necessary to place before us such an IDEAL of what education ought to be, in order to stimulate zeal, excite ambition, and energize effort. It is impossible for an individual or society ever to improve, without placing before it the ideal beauty of something better than exists, or has existed, in our experience. It is thus that scripture continually places before us, for imitation, the character of God, the beauty of excellence, and the loveliness of a holy society; and is it not certain that he who strives to form himself upon such models will attain a purer and a higher character, than he who shall confine himself to any standard of character yet attained among even the brightest of men? American education must ever keep in sight the fact that it is not the most glorious nation of antiquity, nor the greatest of modern days, that we are to imitate; but that, on the contrary, there is no model for us. We are to be ourselves a model: we are a model. If America has presented any thing new to the world, it is a new form of society; if she has any thing worthy to preserve, it is the principles upon which that society is instituted: hence it is not a Grecian or a Roman education we need—it is not one conceived in China, Persia, or France. On the contrary, it must have all the characteristics of the American mind, fresh, original, vigorous, enterprising; embarrassed by no artificial barriers, and looking to a final conquest over the last obstacles to the progress of human improvement.

The organization of the business of education concerns chiefly three things: 1st, The teacher, and his qualifications; 2d, The process of instruction; and 3d, Knowledge and its classification.

The first two, the teacher and his method of teaching, are intimately connected ; for whatever the mind of the teacher is, that he will, as far as depends on human power, impress upon what he does and upon those he instructs. The power of mind upon mind, in this respect, is most wonderful. Could the whole truth on this subject be known, we should be more careful in selecting teachers than in making laws. So far as biography and history give us an insight into the effects of education upon mind, there is scarcely a single example of a really great mind whose early bent or impressions have not been derived from a mother or teacher remarkable for the strength or brilliance of their own minds. If, then, we could secure the thorough education of mothers and teachers, we should secure the best education of society. In the following chapters I have considered first the teacher and his qualifications, for in them are laid the foundations of all education.

Knowledge and its classification constitute the *subject* of teaching; and its special topics must be chosen and *emphasized* (more or less) according to the principles I have already indicated. They must conform to the organization, the civilization, and the religion of the nation, if, as I suppose, the object is to perpetuate the institutions already existing, or to improve them, if the primary ideas of those institutions are correct.

At the foundations of this knowledge, in regard to the republic of the United States, lie these ideas :

1. The idea of its government, contained in the Constitution.

2. The idea of modern science, as developed in modern civilization.

3. The idea of Christianity, contained in the Bible.

These are the elements *peculiar* to our nation and times; and while they are by no means all the topics which enter into a complete system of instruction, they are those which require an *emphasis* in America. One who reads and reflects will see that they hardly touch upon what were the great *staples* of ancient instruction. Metaphysical philosophy, which was then discussed among all classes of people, scarcely enters into the above account except as a systematized branch of modern science; but does it follow that we shall be deficient in that branch of philosophy? Not at all; for a free country is the very cradle of metaphysical discussion. At this moment there is hardly a political question in the nation which does not involve metaphysical arguments; but yet more has Christianity rendered that instruction unnecessary, by defining all that it was necessary to define, and leaving to human reason all that can fairly be deduced from revealed facts.

In this volume I have confined myself chiefly to those subjects which belong to the idea of an American education, as it has been here described.

CHAPTER IV.

THE TEACHER—HIS QUALIFICATIONS, HIS TEACHING, AND HIS CHARACTER.

"It requires great wisdom and industry to advance a considerable estate, much art and contrivance and pains to raise a great and regular building; but the greatest and noblest work in the world, and an effect of the greatest prudence and care, is to rear and build up a man, and to form and fashion him to piety, and justice, and temperance, and all kind of honest and worthy actions."—*Tillotson.*

Who is the teacher said to be *abroad* upon the earth,—once the subject of inspiration—now of legislation,—seeking to mingle with statesmen in the government of men? What are his limits? In vain I seek to confine him. It seems to me that earth has no prison-house for him. His limits are the boundarics of mind itself. For into what circle of the arts does he not enter? Over what secret emotions of the soul has he not control? What field in the wide domain of knowledge does he not penetrate? Into what lonely nook of society does he send no influence?

Though the business of teaching (considered in its absolute sense) may be as wide and as durable as the universe of intelligent beings, yet we may study and deduce the laws of right instruction, from our knowledge of the laws of mind, and its operation in society. The philosopher in vain attempts to trace the rays of light through the pathless heavens as they fall in succession on each object of creation ; but he can analyze and comprehend its principles. It is the light of knowledge upon which we speak, and the laws of instruction we would investigate.

The term *teacher* is generic, signifying one who conveys knowledge, informs, instructs. There are certain general characteristics which belong to all *good* teachers, and these are the characteristics upon which I now propose to dwell.

The qualifications of teachers relate *chiefly*, I think, to three different topics; and may be stated thus:—

1. Their qualifications, in reference to the *subject-matter* taught.

2. In reference to the *mode of teaching*.

3. In reference to *personal character*.

Under these three heads I shall endeavor to bring most of those qualities, natural and acquired, which are peculiar to the *profession* of *teaching*.

THE TEACHER AND SUBJECT-MATTER.

The qualifications of a teacher, in reference to the *subject-matter* of his teaching.

To be a teacher at all, supposes a knowledge of the subject taught; and to be a *good* teacher, that knowledge *perfect*, — limited only by the existing boundaries of human science, in that department. This then is *fundamental* in the qualifications of a teacher. But what sort of knowledge upon any given subject, should the teacher possess? For it is obvious, there are various kinds of knowledge of the same thing. Nothing is more common than to find an artist who does not understand the principles of his art; or a man of science who knows little of its applications; or a man of education who can enunciate a proposition, and point out its uses, but who knows nothing of either the principle or the art. Yet it will be conceded that neither of these constitutes the proper *kind* of knowledge for a teacher. In what then does it consist? Is it an acquaintance with the best text-book of the best author? Is it a familiarity with the various rules constructed to facilitate the applications of science? Is it any form of words? or is it, rather, a *conscious understanding*, not only of all the *facts* of the subject, but of all the *relations*, whether of *cause* or *effect*, which they bear to each other? The *latter* is the proposition I maintain. For what is the *business* of a teacher? He is neither a *manipulator* in the laboratory of arts, nor yet an eccentric *philosopher*, seeking new discoveries in the region of speculation. His position is strictly that of a conveyer of knowledge—moral and intellectual—to a yet unoccupied and growing mind. To do this successfully, requires that his instruction should carry to that waiting mind a conviction of its *truth*, and that he should also *connect* that truth with the *duties* of life.

Now to convince of truth, in matters of human

learning, requires reasoning; and to *reason* upon a subject, requires that the instructor should understand what is called in science its *rationale,* as well as its *facts.* And this is not only an *à priori* deduction of theory, but a manifest indication of nature; for what is the first question of every inquisitive pupil, young or old, in school or out of school, to the enunciation of a new fact, but—why? as if men were taught by instinct itself that the pathway of mind is to ascend, by the golden chain of cause and effect, to the source of immortal light. If this question, thus naturally put, be not properly answered, it implies the ignorance of the teacher, and leaves the truth doubtful. We are told to give a "reason for the faith that is in us;" and he must be a poor teacher of human knowledge who cannot. Again, this *rationale* of which we speak is nothing more nor less than a thorough *analysis* of the subject taught. Whoever teaches, *must analyze.* He must not merely say that he has a machine, which will perform this and that thing, and that his pupil, by turning certain screws, will inevitably obtain certain results; but he must take that machine to pieces—must count every cog, and calculate the movement of every wheel; for the works of nature are but a series of *contrivances,* and science is but a *development* of those contrivances; and mind is so constructed as never to be satisfied with the announcement of a problem, without seeking its solution. Nor is this true of science, so called, only, but of every thing which embodies thought or speech. This living language with which I now write; those anciënt classics, dead types of the glorious past; that brilliant literature, now coming with softened tones through the depths of time, now shooting up fresh verdure under our feet;—all are but the interpreters of thoughts and emotions; and thoughts and emotions have their being in things, and it is by reasoning upon things only they can be explained.

Thus, he who would teach grammar understandingly, would not surely content himself with announcing the parts of speech; that every verb must have a nominative, and that an adjective must agree with its substantive, and thus on. In this disconnected state it would be as arbitrary and as uninstructive as the decrees of an autocrat: taught, however, as what it is, the strict translation of acts and things into words, it becomes a complete system of philosophy, whose progress in any given language is the very history of its literature.*

And this is the *distinction* between the *kind* of knowledge on the same subject which a teacher must possess, and that which is necessary to the common

---

* The "Hermes," or Universal Grammar, by Mr. Harris, and the "Diversions of Purley," by Horne Tooke, are beautiful treatises on the philosophy of grammar: it would be well if they were more read. In reference to the necessity of reasoning from effects to cause, Mr. Harris makes this observation: "Those things which are *first to nature*, are not *first to man. Nature* begins from *causes*, and thence descends to *effects; human perceptions* first open upon *effects*, and thence by slow degrees ascend to *causes*."

business of the world. He must be master of its *analysis*, that he may *explain* the reason, the use, and the connection of every part; while the mass of men are but operatives, who are to perform but one function in a complicated system: it is the difference between the soldier and the general. And while I admit the painful fact that the larger portion of his pupils may never seek or need the knowledge he possesses, I still would not abate one whit of his responsibility. The million may, if they please, remain the victims of pretenders in science, of sciolists in literature, and of demagogues in politics; but the teacher must understand for himself. I will not require every passenger in a steamboat to understand the machinery; but the *engineer* I will, for the safety of the whole depends upon it. And though the teacher may find the mass of his pupils slow to apprehend and of humble destiny, yet every school contains some inquiring minds of more spiritual mould, whom it will require all his powers of thought and instruction to accompany in their ascending flight. It is not the village church-yard, but the village *school-house*, which contains

> "Hearts pregnant with celestial fire;
> Hands that the rod of empire might have sway'd,
> Or waked to ecstasy the living lyre.
> But knowledge to their eyes her ample page,
> Rich with the spoils of time, did ne'er unroll."

I have given this view of the kind of knowledge which the teacher should possess in relation to the subject-matter of his teaching, because it seems to me the prevailing error of teachers is *not* to have that *kind* of knowledge. Many respectable, and in most respects well-educated teachers, will perform any problem, and enunciate any rule upon the subject under examination, and yet be completely *nonplused* in any attempt to explain what they have done, or analyze the principles upon which it is performed. Nor is this, in my opinion, confined to any class of teachers; but is a defect in some measure common to the majority, from the village school to the lofty university. The American mind, like that of its English ancestors, is more *deductive* than *analytical.* Nor would I have it otherwise; for it is the most useful, and, provided always there are philosophers enough in the world to do the reasoning and to make the rules, the most productive. It is a working and a thinking mind, too; but it works and thinks towards *results,* rather than *causes.*

The proposition I maintain is, that the position of a teacher is one which requires the constant analysis of the subject of his teaching; and that to do this, he must understand not merely its results, but all the connections, dependencies, and relations by which those results are obtained.

Besides this particular knowledge of the subject taught, there are two species of general knowledge, derived from reading and observation, which I believe to be of *peculiar use* to the teacher. I mean the *philosophy of history*, on the one hand, and the *phenomena of the human mind*, on the other.*

In relation to the former it may be said, in general terms, there can be no mode of ascertaining the principles and course of human conduct, under any given circumstances, so certain as by referring to the open volume of recorded experience; for it contains the long series of experiments upon which the science of human nature is based—a science, like that of chemistry, wholly experimental. When the wisest of teachers said, "there is nothing new under the sun," he referred, as the context shows, to the inevitable results of those few original principles which, like gravitation or evaporation, are immutable in their tendencies; but not to the ever-increasing and multiplied combinations of those principles, as various as

* In reference to the study of the political sciences, the social sciences, and history, Sismondi, in his Fall of the Roman Empire, remarks: "But even were the study of the moral and political sciences utterly prohibited, their practice could not be suspended for a single moment. There are nations in which the theory of government has never formed a subject of reflection or of discussion; but have they therefore found it possible to dispense with all government? No; they have adopted at random some one of the systems which they ought to have chosen after mature deliberation. Whether in Morocco or in Athens, in Venice or in Uri, at Constantinople or at London, men have doubtless always desired that their governments should facilitate their way to virtue and happiness. All have the same end in view: must they act without regard to this end? must they walk without endeavoring to ascertain whether they advance or recede?"—*Sismondi's Fall*, chap. i.

those of motion and of light, which make up the forms and movements of civilized society. These are the study of the historian, and should ever be consulted, as we refer to the history of our own lives, to gather wisdom from the experience of the past. But there *is* a reason why this is peculiarly fit for the instruction of the teacher: he, of all men living, needs the means of constant illustration; he wants some common ground for himself, his pupils, and the subject he teaches; and, like a lexicographer in search of a definition, is compelled to seek words and figures which the most ignorant may comprehend, and he will be most apt to find them in the common treasury of human action. A child cannot read the simplest lesson without reference to men and things which have figured in the past; and to his question of who is this, and what is that, the teacher should return an answer at once full and correct.

Again: I ask any practical teacher or observer of life, if there be any truth in the art of teaching plainer, than that the elementary process of reading is never taught well by one who does not himself thoroughly understand the subject read about?

But if this faculty of illustration given by history be true of men and events, much more so is it of science. Such is the unity of nature and the kindred blood of all her children, that the arts and sciences are never found far apart. They are, like the virtues, social. If you are acquainted with one, you have a better chance of being introduced to the rest;

and if you would illustrate the character of one, you will most readily do it by the biography of another. Hence the history of arts, science, and philosophy, —itself a history of the progress of civilization,— throws a steady light on the social relations of every branch of human knowledge.

It is often the subject of vulgar astonishment, that one could in a single life, like Sir William Jones,* acquire a facility in writing and speaking twenty-eight living languages; or, like Peter of Russia, acquire in a few years, some familiarity with numerous arts: yet, when we consider that all languages have a common root, and are grouped in classes, whose members are strongly analogous, and that all sciences are kindred, we come to admire, not a mysterious phenomenon of intellect, but a patient investigation worthy of all renown.

If you would study astronomy, study geometry; if you would study anatomy, study mechanics; and if you would study the effect of any or all education upon human conduct, study history. From that vantage ground you will see, as the optician discovers that all colors are necessary to make up the pure white light of day—that all principles of knowledge are but parts of one great and glorious whole.†

---

* The character of Sir William Jones was quite a model in goodness as well as learning.

† This idea was thrown out by Cicero in one of his most beautiful orations; but the truth of it is far better illustrated now than in

In respect to the second general subject, the phenomena of mind in action, I do not of course mean that knowledge of mind which is acquired from particular books or partial systems. They are but aids to reflection. The teacher is, however, in the very nature of things, compelled to analyze the operations of mind. He has it constantly under his care, and sees its growth, from the blossom to the fruit. The analysis of the subject taught, which we have seen he must possess, compels him also to trace the investigations of other minds on the subject; and if it be one involving moral affections, he must first place it in the crucible of his own heart and consciousness. Now it is this analysis of consciousness, and especially of the grounds of moral action, which the teacher needs. To look abroad upon others we are compelled to do, for indolence does not take away sight or hearing; but to *reflect* upon what we observe requires some *activity* of intellect; and to compare the reflections and emotions of others with our own, is a yet more abstract and difficult undertaking. Such, however, is the task of the moral teacher, and especially at those periods of his teaching when, in seeking to correct some vicious bent of character, he is compelled to look into motives of action. It is then that he will find a knowledge of the constitution

---

his time. The sciences seem now mutually contributing to each other's glory, and all illustrating the harmony and order which prevail in the work of creation.

of mind available to the practical purposes of education; a knowledge which, as it relates to the most subtle and least tangible of all agents, is to be gained only by the most careful observation. The qualifications of a teacher in this respect should be simply that of a mind patiently and quietly inquiring after truth. To depart from this and amuse himself with dividing mind into little compartments, like the squares of a chess-board, would be as wise as he who should attempt to mark out upon the clouds the course of the lightnings.

THE MODE OF TEACHING.

The qualifications of teachers are next to be considered, in reference to the *mode* of teaching. This has strict relation to the end to be obtained. Among the ancient heathen nations, the Persians, in the time of Cyrus, considered the *virtues*, especially justice and gratitude, as the main object of education; among the Athenians, *accomplishments* in *arts, sciences,* and *letters,* were the end; and among the Spartans, *obedience* was the sole principle of instruction,* because that would preserve the ascendency of the

* In Rollin's History of the Greeks and Persians will be found an account of many particulars in the education and manners of the ancient nations. Each of the ancient nations seems to have laid great stress on some particular quality which they thought adapted to their character and circumstances.

laws. Yet neither of these answered their designs Persia acquired some of the milder virtues, but failed in strength and hardihood; Athens found that neither art nor science would avail against depravity of morals; and Sparta found that it was not enough to secure obedience to laws without considering their nature and effect; Persia fell a victim to luxury, Athens to licentiousness, and Sparta to tyranny. Such are the lessons of antiquity; and its splendid wreck remains an example to warn us against the dangers of *partial* systems.

But under the new light which the Christian system has thrown over the power and destiny of the soul, a different view has been taken of the end and means of education. We consider the object of education now as twofold:—one to improve and strengthen the mind itself; the other to endow it with whatever is valuable or auxiliary in the duties of life. The second relates chiefly to topics of education, and may in this place be passed by. The first, however, requires an adaptation of means to the peculiar condition of a thinking and spiritual being.

1. For this purpose the teacher must first place himself upon terms of *good-will* with his pupil. One comes to receive, the other to give instruction. There is, therefore, a community of pursuit and of interests. Their minds should therefore come together, without which, I apprehend, little instruction is ever conveyed: it will be but the rolling stone of Sisyphus. Now to effect this mutuality of mind, the

teacher must from the first show himself capable of instructing, and that it is his happiness and his pupil's gain. Then he will have the powerful aid of that sympathy which is the strongest bond of union in the human heart: then he can effect that with kindness which no force can do; then he will sharpen the dull and strengthen the weak; then will the rugged steeps of science be clothed with verdure, and the school-house ever after looked back upon as a sunny spot in the pathway of life. The quality we speak of is a tact in the teacher; but one which he must come by from nature or from art. Every good and successful teacher has it. Some acquire the confidence of their pupils, in spite of austere qualities, by their open, hearty, up-and-down *enthusiasm* for the subject of their teaching; others, by the milder virtues of the heart, attracting by the cords of love; others again, by an art which readily adapts itself to the well-understood movements of mind. But all who would succeed must have it. As well might we expect to warm ourselves by light reflected from the impassive ice, as to gather knowledge from that cold indifference, from which the eager inquiries and aspiring zeal of youth pass unregarded. It may exhibit in its own medium the prismatic colors, but sends forth no genial beam of heat.

2. The next step in the process of teaching, is to inquire how a subject is to be taught. What functions of mind are we to call into activity? What principles are we to use? We cannot so well an-

swer this question as by referring to some notable errors in education; errors which have prevailed in times past, and still prevail; which have governed whole nations; which have influenced the affairs of all mankind, and whose contrasted results are valuable to us.

THE FIRST ERROR OF TEACHING.

The first of these errors is teaching men to *imitate*, or *repeat*, rather than to *think*. We need to take but a very cursory glance at the great theatre of human life, to know how deep a root this radical error has struck into the foundations of education. Look abroad among men, and ask yourselves how many of the moving multitude inquire into the springs of action? How many seek to know the causes and consequences of those scenes in which they themselves are actors? Or to descend to details, how many attempt to understand the true principles of the business in which they are engaged? How many can correct a blunder arising merely from the application of a principle? Analyze this boasted liberty of ours; look again upon republican society in this freest land upon earth; separate the living agents from the mere automata in this game of life, and tell me how many of the latter—how many of the former! And if you are not pleased with the result, tell me whether this is a decree of nature, or a fault of education; whether you believe if men were taught to be independent thinkers, and that while they revered all that was good, or glorious, or valuable in the works of their ancestors, that they too had an indwelling spirit whose high prerogative it was to extend the conquests of mind, they would cease to inquire, and remain dull floats upon this ocean of being!

But if you would know what the effects of thinking are, compare Athens with China. Here are three hundred millions of people—more than one-third the human race—whose history goes far back into remote antiquity, and who commenced with no small share of the arts and sciences, but who have added not a single particle to knowledge nor taken one step in improvement; whose only policy is to prevent innovation, and whose only power is to perpetuate succession.* Here is another people, whose population does not exceed one-tenth that of Ohio, whose place can scarcely be found on the map, who commenced barbarians, yet who have given to the world new sciences and new arts, and whose mighty men infused into language

"Thoughts that breathe and words that burn;"

who reconquered their conquerors by the spirit of eloquence, and whose renown has filled the earth.

What makes this mighty difference? The one learned to *repeat*, the other to *think*.

---

* The Chinese are esteemed, by philosophical historians, one of the four primitive nations. What may be the effect of European commerce upon them we cannot tell; but it is certain they have produced no intellectual impression upon the world in a long time.

THE SECOND ERROR OF TEACHING.

Another error which has prevailed in some places and times is, that the pupil can acquire nothing except by observation or experiment. It assumes that the mind can deduce nothing from given premises, but is a manipulator in the great school of art, where every thing must be reduced to the senses; and because illustration is a very good thing, therefore you cannot have too much of it; and because experiment is a good way for philosophers to make discoveries, therefore it is the best way for children to learn them. Something like this was the theory of J. J. Rousseau, who proposed that a boy should be taken at one season of the year on a hill-top and shown the sun in a certain position, and at another in another—and thus of other things; but how long it will take a boy to go through all the experiments of all the philosophers he has not informed us. Others, however, have improved upon this example, and introduced the world in miniature into the school-room. Cubes, cones, and pyramids, sun, moon, stars, and comets, dance attendance upon their levee; and when these fail, the art of engraving is exhausted to exhibit upon the pages of the school-book things human and inhuman, from the wonders of the deep to "gorgons and chimeras dire." Now, doubtless, good maps, globes, or even a well-executed picture of some great event, and still more a social walk with some instructive friend, who could say, with David, that "day unto day uttereth speech, and night unto night showeth knowledge," may be made useful aids of a good teacher; for such a one cannot be supposed not to know and adapt to his purpose the strong attractions of sense for the young; but, on the other hand, neither will he be expected to teach abstract truth by models or experiments.

The fallacy of this error consists in overlooking the real advantage which science confers upon the teacher—that of generalization. It is the *condensation* of knowledge which is the great facility in the art of teaching, afforded by constant improvements. How else could education keep up at all with the accumulation of knowledge? It takes a generation for philosophy to discover and demonstrate a principle which, in after times, the pupil learns in a single hour.

THE THIRD ERROR OF TEACHING.

The third error, and in a great measure that of our times, is to interpose a patent machinery between the teacher and his pupil; a labor-saving machine by which we shall print off minds just as we print off calicoes: flimsy, parti-colored, cheap enough they are. We get up a long array of text-books, which are so good we hardly know how to choose among them; and which facilitate the art of teaching so much, there is nothing left for the teacher to do except, as the ancients did with the oracle of Delphos, to ask questions and receive answers. And then we have discovered another great facility in teaching: it is rather laborious to lead the pupil *up* the hill of knowledge, and as the teacher and he have to meet somewhere, why the teacher must walk *down;* and as the child cannot talk *learnedly*, why the teacher must talk *simply*. In this manner the grand desideratum in teaching, as in many other arts, that of getting along *by doing nothing*, is at last discovered. The pupil and the teacher are *both* contented. The one has found an *easy chair*, and the other has *no hill to climb.*

The recapitulation of these errors, if indeed you are prepared to admit them such, shows them to have one common origin—*indolence of thought*, on the part of both pupils and teachers. It is not the body merely that has its *vis inertiæ;* the soul partakes of that common tendency which has made man, in every age and clime, seek some escape from that law of his nature—the necessity for labor. And while we admit, what is certainly true, that mind has an upward principle, seeking new and better things, we must also admit that in the mass of mankind its *sensualism* has ever overcome its *spirituality*. Few and far between, angel visits, are those inspirations of intellect which lead the patient scholar in the face of poverty, humiliation, disease, and death to seek the *viginti annorum lucoubrationes;* to spend the midnight vigil and the morning watch in ascending through the works of God for that wisdom which he sought in vain among men.

It is no libel then upon teachers, to suppose them possessed of this common infirmity of human nature What Gibbon said of his professors, that they remembered they had a salary to receive, but forgot they had duties to perform, would have been true of thousands of others had they been placed in similar circumstances.

In combating this difficulty, we have here in America, a great encouragement and consolation. There is a vast difference among nations as well as individuals, in the natural activity of mind, and a still greater in institutions, climate, and resources. The American mind comes of a good stock. It has never yielded to any thing on earth in vigor of intellect or purity of purpose. Nor has corruption of manners taken that hold upon it which history tells us was the case with the ancient nations, and of which modern France displays so vivid a picture. Our ancestors, too, have placed it in the midst of institutions, allowing the utmost freedom of inquiry, and tending to the utmost cultivation of heart. If then we have high responsibilities, we have also a full treasury to draw upon.

THE TRUE MODE OF TEACHING.

Let us now recur to the true mode of teaching, as I conceive it, in opposition to the errors we have alluded to; which is nothing more than what the ablest teachers of the world have always followed to teach the use of their reason. There is one fact in the human constitution so obvious that every body notices it, and every body does or may draw instruction from it. When a man is an infant, no animal is a greater imitator than he; it is then he learns his mother tongue; and thus he does whatever he sees done. But just in proportion as his understanding strengthens, he ceases to imitate, till bye and bye, he reasons upon every thing, glories in his freedom, and seeks new varieties of being and action throughout the universe.

Now this seems an intimation from nature of the only mode by which the human understanding can be successfully improved; and this is by constant inquiry and constant investigation. We cannot go on like the animals, governed by instinct, repeating and imitating the same thing. The models made for them are perfect; but the models of human workmanship are altogether imperfect. The bee may build forever, and if it were gifted with reason, could never build better than it does; but man may build and forever improve.

We have already said the teacher should arm himself with an analytical knowledge of his subject, and that he should then acquaint himself with some of the observed laws of the subtle body upon which he is about to act; and having now determined to use reason as his chief means of instruction, he will have need of all the powers he has acquired. He will find the awakened mind of his pupil ever inquisitive and ever seeking novelty. He must carry it, as in geometry, by clear, strong, dovetailed deduction, from step to step, to the result; now, as in chemistry, bring the aid of analysis to disintegrate every part, and show its rationale from the element to the product; now, as in philosophical grammar, examine all its relations, and bring the illustrating light of history to bear upon it: he must now excite the imagination with a view of distant triumphs, and now check its aspiring flight through unconquered realms; now excite it with the glories of science, and now humble it with a sense of immeasurable infirmity to the Almighty Architect.

To do this, there is but one plain rule. Bring mind to mind, and heart to heart. The Scripture saith. "As iron sharpeneth iron, so does the countenance of a friend his friend:"—and in all intercourse of thought and emotion, the most direct is the best. The less interposition of artificial machinery, the stronger will be the impressions of the teacher. Not by any means do I mean to say, that good text-books and practical illustrations are not needed; on the contrary, there is not a school-room in the country where they may not, within certain limits, be profitably used: but I do say, they may be and they frequently are relied upon as the chief means, instead of the adjuncts of teaching. They are but the skeleton which the teacher is to animate with life. How can the teacher transfer to the dull instruments of his trade, his directing soul? How can we substitute the hot-bed appliances of the nursery for the living beam of the mother's eye?

THE PERSONAL CHARACTER OF THE TEACHER.

We shall now consider the qualifications of a teacher, in reference to his *personal character*. Among these are included all the qualities which relate to government and example. The first of these qualities is *good breeding*. The teacher should be a gentleman; and by that name I mean nothing artificial, beyond the universal customs of society; nothing which fashion can guide; nothing to which the gaudy glare of wealth is necessary; nothing which rank or power can give or take away. It is simply that character which Christianity carried into action must inevitably produce—a man of gentleness and good-will: qualities which were esteemed as necessary to the character of a true knight in the days of chivalry, as was that of his renown in arms.*

Some men, and good men too, have thought, if they only walked through the world uprightly, certainly the grand desideratum, it was little matter

* "For what, I pray, is a *gentleman?* What properties hath he; what qualities are characteristical or peculiar to him, whereby he is distinguished from others and raised above the vulgar? Are they not especially two—courage and courtesie?—which he that wanteth is not otherwise than equivocally a *gentleman*, as an image or a caskare is a man; without which *gentility* in a conspicuous degree is no more than a vain or an empty name."—*Barrow, vol.* 3, *ser.* 21.

what else they did; if they could only act *fortiter in re,* the *suaviter in modo* was of little consequence. Now this is a mistake of which bad men in every age, from Pericles to Louis XIV., from Chesterfield to the butterfly of fashion, have taken advantage by presenting the contrast. They have covered up their own ruined systems with the beautiful garments of grace and courtesy: literally, as was said by Professor Frisbie of a renowned poet, alluring "the tender and the young till they breathed the damps of disease with the dews of heaven;" while the man of virtue stood afar off, presenting rough repellancies, rich as the jewel in the rock, but as difficult to get at.*

Nor let the teacher suppose, in this or any other matter of morals, of conduct, or of opinion, that it is no matter, provided he does his duty in the schoolroom, what examples he leaves behind him. The very evil we have spoken of, the tendency to constant repetition and imitation, makes example of most powerful effect. Let him not think, then, that if he does not teach *well,* he therefore does not teach *at all;* that if he does no good, he does no evil. He will teach, in spite of himself; his examples will be like the positive and negative poles of electricity: if they do not *attract,* they are sure to *repel.* And he will find his pupil taught; not, indeed, by the central

* On this subject I can add nothing to the remark of Mr. Locke, who certainly valued intellect as high as other men. Vide Locke on Education, 120.

influences of attractive love, to revolve harmoniously round a centre of warmth, but to shoot off, like some lone star, carried away by its centrifugal force, seeking the void immense, "in wandering mazes lost."

Next to good breeding we may place that power of command which is necessary to preserve order. In ancient times, we are told, there dwelt a sage called *discipline;* but, if we are to believe Cowper, he long since fled from our mother land, and I think none of us can say he has yet taken up his permanent residence here. Yet, that his influence was salutary, the ancient nations never doubted; and all Scripture testifies, in the strongest language of precept and example. Obedience was alike the doctrine of Persian and of Spartan philosophy—of the Hebrew dispensation and of the more glorious system of Christian liberty; and who is wild or mad enough to suppose that we can do without it? If such there be, over him we can never hope that reason or philosophy, or even revelation itself, could hold an influence. We might indeed enforce its necessity, by an inductive process, drawn from every analogy of nature, and every law of mind. We might point to the volume of enlightening experience, to the pages of the written law, or at last address him, with England's purest, noblest poet, in strains of mingled grief and satire; yet, when all was done, we should be compelled to adopt the ancient, well-known maxim—

"Quem Deus vult perdere, prius dementat."

Assuming, then, that among common-sense men obedience is to be the first rule of the school, what is to be the deportment of the teacher? Whatever he may be to other men, however mild to the pupil himself, he cannot forget, without ruin inevitable, that the school-room is his domain, and in that he must rule alone. His government may be a monarchy, a republic, or he may be a patriarch at the head of a family; but in all its forms he is the supreme executive. Rebellion may produce revolution, but government cannot exist without a head.*

Nor should he be unmindful of the impression of awe, and dignity, and learning produced by his character upon the mind of his pupil, for that alone is often a sufficient means of government, while the reverse is sure to destroy all control over the lawless young. Is it not a case of every-day occurrence, that knowledge alone does not carry with it powers

---

* "There, in his noisy mansion skilled to rule,
The village master taught his little school;
A man severe he was, and stern to view;
I knew him well, and every truant knew.
Well had the boding tremblers learn'd to trace
The day's disasters in his morning face;
Full well they laugh'd with counterfeited glee
At all his jokes—for many a joke had he;
Full well the busy whisper circling round
Convey'd the dismal tidings when he frown'd:
Yet he was kind; or, if severe in aught,
The love he bore to learning was in fault."

Deserted Village.

of government? I remember to have examined a young man, whose classical and scientific acquirements would have fitted him for a professorship, and to have heard, a few days afterwards, that his boys had turned him out of his own school-room. The severe disciplinarian of former days has almost passed away; yet there is a simplicity mixed with dignity of character which commands respect, and which is a gift rather than an acquisition. That gift must be the teacher's.

CLEAR THOUGHTS AND CLEAR LANGUAGE.

The next qualification is the facility of communicating clear thoughts in clear language. This is a grand *sine qua non* of a good teacher. I cannot think any one ever made a good instructor without it; and no one who has it not, at least in a tolerable degree, need expect to be any thing more than a ploughboy in breaking up the fallow-ground of human ignorance. I do not mean merely fluency or elegance of language, for I have heard gentlemen discourse most rapidly and elegantly, for hours together, when it would have defied the wisdom of Solomon to have told what they said; and I know a distinguished clergyman of whom it was said in college, that he could not state a proposition in distinct terms. And yet this capacity to state clear thoughts in clear language, without one word more or less than is necessary, is an element of the highest eloquence, and the greatest power in the range of human acquisition. It has distinguished some of the most remarkable men of modern times: it was the peculiar talent of Swift and Cobbett, and marked the genius of Chatham and of Webster; and this power should always be, in some degree, the attribute of a teacher. I care not whether he is to officiate in a country school-house or in the halls of science, or address an Athenian audience in the groves of the academy, he must in any event be able to convey thought clearly and forcibly, or be forever shut out from the high rewards of a successful teacher; for when we come to consider, it is only the conveyance of something from the mind of the teacher to that of the pupil, in the way of thought, explanation, or strong illustration, that constitutes the peculiar functions of a teacher. If it be merely to set lessons, or hear them repeated, a monitor, an assistant, or any one who can read, can perform that office, and we need not resort to cultivated intellect and peculiar qualifications for that purpose: but our common sense teaches us that more than that is necessary; and all who are educated or are familiar with public teaching, *know* that the greatest possible difference exists among teachers in their power to impress and interest their pupils, by the clearness and force of their expression. Life is too short for either young or old to spend much time in hunting up an idea which an instructor thinks he has put away in some corner of his head, but cannot exactly find; nor does it make the matter much better if he throw out fifty at once, so confused that, like the goods and chattels of an auctioneer's room, it will take half our life to separate and classify them. No; we want him to hand them out distinctly, one by one, and just in the order they should be stored away. He that can do this has a clear head, and clear language, too; he is not a rhetorician, but he is one who is remembered when rhetoricians are forgotten.

THE TEACHER A LOVER OF HIS COUNTRY.

Again, the teacher should be a lover of his country—not from any mean spirit of selfishness, but because there is in it something worthy to love, and worthy to preserve; because it is the result, not merely of a people struggling against the oppressions of government, but of mind against the servitude of its own corrupt tendencies—the last rich fruits of ages upon ages of trial, experience, and long-suffering among nations past; and because to him (the instructor of youth) is intrusted, upon all the principles of our ancestors, in the very nature of our institutions, and in the very words of our fundamental law, the solemn guardianship of its life and its destiny. None of the founders of our government ever contemplated the possibility of its existence without religion and education, and they have written it over and over again in all their constitutions. To what high duty, then, is the teacher called!

Nor should he regard it as a light thing that he is

in America, in these green and fresh lands; not some unhappy Hindoo worshipping crocodiles on the banks of the Ganges—or some serf making a unit in the masses of the Russian autocrat—or in some more doubtful land waiting the fearful issue of revolution; but that he is here, to partake with the republic in its matchless freedom, in the mighty velocity with which it ascends the most daring heights of human hope, and in those high responsibilities, too, which God has, in every age, attached to his peculiar blessings.

THE TEACHER A LOVER OF HIS PROFESSION.

We come now to a qualification for teachers without which I cannot conceive of success in any thing: it is a zeal and a love for his profession. And who has a better right to that zeal and that love than he? whose labors are to be more durable in time, or wide in extent? who, much more than liberty, gives to fleeting life its color and its perfume? whose influence shall survive the monuments of mental glory?

Would he compare himself with artists—with Phidias or with Angelo? He is not forming a work like theirs, from the cold marble, lifeless and perishable; but is vested with power to mould a heart warm with the beatings of youth, and direct a mind perennial in freshness and immortal in youth. Does he compare himself with musicians—with Handel and Mozart? He is a performer upon a more complex instrument than theirs, strung with a thousand chords, and each chord susceptible of a thousand tones. Is it the hero with whom he would compare himself? *That* destroys—*this* creates; *that* conquers a kingdom of earth—this the dominion of mind. Is it the fame of the statesman that he would reach? The statesman governs empires—he teaches statesmen how to govern; that gives laws to property—this to soul.

If it be fame he seeks, let him look at the roll of practical teachers only; what a record of renown! it is a sheet of fire! With whom is he enrolled? With Plato, with Euclid, with Cicero, with Descartes, with Boerhaave, and Newton; with Rush, and Adams, and Dwight; with Socrates, teacher of men, and Paul the apostle of God.

THE GLORY OF TEACHING.

Let the teacher then remember the glory of his profession: nor let him suppose that men are unwilling to learn; the history of the world is against such a supposition. Wherever there have been found men willing to teach, there have been pupils willing to learn. How else did the ancient philosophers draw multitudes to their audience? How else did Abelard, in the midst of the dark ages, draw listening thousands? Did they draw them to the mere sound of the voice? How did they teach geometry and arithmetic? Let me take one example from the close of the middle ages: the Abbot of Croyland, when he was appointed, sent for four Norman monks to teach;

they went on to the farm of the monastery with all the zeal of itinerant preachers; they hired a barn to teach what they knew of science and philosophy. In a short time a concourse of pupils gathered about them; in the second year the accumulation from all the country round was so great that neither house, barn, nor church could contain them. They separated their labors, and one taught grammar, another logic, another rhetoric, and a fourth preached. "In this unadorned account," says the historian, "we have a striking proof of the attachment of mankind to intellectual improvement, and their eagerness to embrace every opportunity of acquiring it. The soil is ever ready; the laborers only are wanting where it continues unproductive."* Yes, never did the teacher step into the arena of life without followers; never did he tread the path of instruction that light did not fall upon it; never did he go armed with fit instruction, but he went "conquering and to conquer." Yet I cannot flatter him with the hopes of ease and idleness; there is no royal road to geometry—and there can be no downy couch for the teacher.

And now let me refer the reader for one moment to a well-known structure of science and of art. On the coast of England stands the Eddystone lighthouse, many miles from the land, on a sunken rock of the

* Sharon Turner's History of the Middle Ages, vol. iv. book vi. chap. 2: "One monk taught the Latin grammar, another taught the logic of Aristotle, a third lectured on rhetoric, and a fourth preached to the people."

ocean. It was built and swept away; it was built again and burnt. Science comes to the aid of commerce: it gathered the materials, and the tide washed them away; it collected them again; secured, bolted and dovetailed them into the rock. It rose slowly but steadfastly above the waters; and the higher it rose, the faster it grew; and at last, after years of patient labor, the light was hung on high. The ocean breaks over its top, but the watchman is there to trim it; and still, that white light burns brightly through the mists. And never again, till some convulsion, sent through the works of nature, by nature's God, shall that light fade away.

And now, my friends, that tower is the labor of the human race; that light is science, revealed alike by the works and by the Scriptures of the Most High; that watchman is the teacher; knowledge has been slowly, patiently, laboriously accumulated; many times has its materials been swept away by floods of error and of barbarism; little by little have its foundations been bolted and riveted by experiment, by demonstration, and by revelation. And now its light is upon the mountain top; but still the waves and winds of error and of doctrine beat upon it. Who shall keep it? You are the watchmen. And long as storm and darkness shall abide upon this wide ocean of being, you will hear a cry ringing abroad, "Watchman, what of the night?"

CHAPTER V.

THE IDEA OF SCIENCE.

"I think science may be divided properly into these three sorts:

"First, The knowledge of things as they are in their own proper beings,—their constitution, properties, and operations.

"Secondly, The skill of right applying our own powers and actions for the attainment of things good and useful.

"Thirdly, The third branch may be called the doctrine of signs—the most useful whereof being words—it is aptly enough termed also logic."—*Locke on the Human Understanding*, B. iv. ch. 21.

SCIENCE may be generally defined as *systematized knowledge*. It is sometimes confounded with knowledge merely: but there is a vast amount of knowledge which is no science; nay, which never can become such. For example, a piece of intelligence is received that a battle has been fought, or an earthquake occurred. This is knowledge; but it is neither science nor part of science. In one sense, and in another and a distant period of time, it may become a fact, which, with a number of similar facts, make up a general result in the philosophy of history. At the present, however, it is not and cannot be science. Science cannot be wholly disconnected from the ideas of system and reason. It is the former condition of knowledge. It implies, in the term itself, reason, deduction, method, conclusion, system. Science, therefore, is more properly the system which reason has deduced from facts, than any arrangement of the facts themselves.

Science thus systematized naturally divides itself into three very distinct branches, having their basis, not only in what is called nature, but in that which is far higher and superior to nature in the order and method of creation.

In the Book of Genesis,* we have a record of the order of succession in the creation of the earth and its inhabitants. First, we have the creation of all things *necessary to any thing which succeeded them.* Hence we have the substance of the earth, the water, the light, the stars, the sun, the fruits, the animals—all in succession created before man, to whom they all were necessary. This was the creation of matter—the material world—constituting the visible abode of spirit. The laws of matter then make the first subject of science, and exist prior to and independent of man. Geometry is the science of form and the relations of form, derived from matter only. These laws began to exist with the creation of matter, and continue to exist independent of man. The principles of geometry existed, and the science would exist, perhaps in a dormant state, though man had never been created. This is obviously true of all the principles and laws which relate to the physical creation. *Physical science,* then, is the first and most distinct form of general science.

* Genesis, chap. 1—The order of creation.

Continuing to trace from divine history the order of creation, we find that when the physical constitution of things was completed, then man was created, and there was breathed into him the breath of life. This *life* was not the same life as that given to the animals; but it was something which being breathed into man from God, gave him dominion over the earth, and made his spirit immortal.*

This was in regard to this earth—the metaphysical creation—the creation of a spirit, whose laws of action make a new subject of science. Hence we have metaphysical science, and that which is an application of metaphysics to the relation of things, such as logic.

Pursuing still the path of divine history, we find that when organized matter had been created, and life had been given to man, with dominion over all other things, that then there was given to him a manner of *expression;* a sign of ideas; a means of communication, and of stating and making known the relations of things abstracted from the things themselves: this is language, grammar, philosophy. It is the doctrine of signs. Algebra is an example of it in the expression of physical science; and all literature is but a system of signs for the expression of thought.†

Thus we find the three great foundations of science

* Genesis, chap. 2, verse 7.—" And the Lord God formed man of the dust of the ground, and breathed into his nostrils the breath of life; *and man became a living soul.*"

† Genesis, chap. 2, verse 19.

traced out in the very order and succession of creation. Science is itself but a development of the laws of creation, so far as man has been able to discover and develop them. Creation is its cradle, and every new discovery but a new testimony to the order, beauty, and harmony which dwell forever in the works of God.

This deduction of science from the order and system of the universe, as exhibited to man, by the right use of reason, proves clearly for what end and purpose it is to be used in education. We have first the strengthening of reason by this exercise of its powers. Next we have the recognition of order and method, in the pursuit of any design, or object, as it is illustrated in all the works of creation. Next we have the knowledge of fixed, eternal truth, as the basis of all created things. Then we have demonstrated the superior power of the spirit, by its faculty of abstraction, in taking the principles or laws from the material objects and laying them before the mind in an independent condition. Finally, we find the higher power of creating a language of signs, which shall express their relations, and convey them from mind to mind, in a state of abstraction and independence. Thus we have the science of physics, the science of metaphysics, and the science of a logic in language and signs, which expresses, explains, and connects, and communicates the laws deduced from the system of creation.*

* The recent work of Professor Davies, on the "Logic of Mathematics," supplies a *desideratum*, which has long existed, in reference

The IDEA of SCIENCE, then, is, in its general and complete sense, the idea of the constitution; properties and laws of all created things, whether of matter or mind, as developed and expressed from the works of creation by the reason of man. There are three corollaries consequent upon this idea of science: 1st, That it is the best exercise to improve the reason to the highest point. 2dly, That as the works of God are found to be perfect, this development of them gives the most complete idea we can have of form, order, beauty, and harmony. 3dly, That as the works of creation are exhaustless, and the spirit of man immortal, science affords an exhaustless field for the investigations, the improvement, the strengthening, and enlargement of the human mind. For science is not, in this idea of it, limited to the science of matter, nor to the science of mind, nor to the discoveries of man, independent of Revelation. In one word, it is true science, and not science "falsely so called," that I have here defined. It is that law, of which Hooker said, "No less can be acknowledged than that her seat is the bosom of God; her voice the harmony of the world."

---

to the connection of the physical and metaphysical sciences. That work is, so far as I know, original; and it will be found as useful as it is novel. The connections of the various branches of physical science, and of the whole with metaphysics and logic, constitute now an open field of inquiry.

CHAPTER VI.

THE UTILITY OF MATHEMATICS.

"I have mentioned mathematics as a way to settle in the mind an habit of reasoning closely, and in train; not that I think it necessary that all men should be deep mathematicians, but that having got the way of reasoning, which that study necessarily brings the mind to, they might be able to transfer it to other parts of knowledge, as they have occasion."—*Locke on the Human Understanding.*

To the scholar and lover of knowledge, the sciences are a harmonious brotherhood; a golden circle, which he would fracture with scarcely less reluctance than he would pluck from the heavenly system one of its glorious planets. He may look upon another with a longer and steadier gaze, or to him another light may be purer and brighter; but he will recollect that the illumination of the mind, like that of the firmament, is made up of *many* lights, each shining in its own sphere, and each, as it rolls on, casting its rays over that intellectual pathway in which he moves to his immortal destiny.

While, however, each one of the sciences may thus claim its own excellence and its peculiar prerogatives, I shall consider only those which, in a direct way, strengthen the reasoning powers, or aid the manifestation and development of the human mind in a very remarkable manner.

Mathematics belong to this class, and have, at all

times, constituted a portion of a liberal education. Indeed, arithmetic, a very important branch of mathematics, is so necessary to the business calculations of the world, as never to be omitted in any course of instruction, however slight. This, therefore, no theorist, wild as he may be, will ever neglect. But all the elementary parts of mathematics are equally useful, as *a means of education*, though not as universally necessary to the *wants* of mankind. And I lay it down as a fundamental principle, that this science is so accessory to the received methods of human reasoning; is the foundation of so many arts and sciences, and so interwoven with the various operations of society, that its study cannot be wholly omitted in the schools, without destroying nearly all that is solid and valuable in education.

Indeed, I cannot conceive of any such thing as an *education*, in a fair sense, without mathematics. Words, literature, and a certain species of metaphysics, may be acquired without any direct study of mathematics; but how can any accurate ideas of any thing in nature be obtained without just notions of form, measure, magnitude, and quantity?

What are the objects of intellectual education? I suppose them to be twofold: First, the discipline of the mind. Second, the attainment of such knowledge as may be of practical use in after life.

I shall now proceed to ascertain the real value of mathematics as a means of education, comparing its uses and results in reference to human improvement.

THE KINDS OF MATHEMATICS.

Mathematics, in its extended sense, comprehends more than that of which we now speak. It is both *pure* and *applied:* pure, as respects its elementary branches—algebra, geometry, etc.; applied, as regards those sciences, mechanical philosophy, astronomy, and others dependent upon the former. The pure mathematics are commonly understood by that term, and in this sense I now understand it.

To improve the reason, as well as the heart, is the peculiar care of that branch of education whose object is the discipline of the mind. To do this, indeed, and to secure the ultimate object of that improvement, happiness was the end of those various systems of philosophy, which, under glorious names and beautiful forms, have from time to time fastened the attention of mankind. But those systems have successively sunk; the reason of verbal philosophy has crumbled to pieces, while that of demonstration, based upon experiment, has strengthened and increased; and with it knowledge has enlarged its bounds, as the successive circles in the water increase from the centre of motion.

To measure the influence of mathematics as an intellectual power in producing these results, would be to analyze the whole machinery of civilized society. But without doing that, we may yet go far enough into mental history to prove this science, either as a part of education or of knowledge, the most powerful instrument, after the growth of true benevolence, in the progressive improvement of the human race.

MATHEMATICAL REASONING.

Mathematical reasoning, as in fact all other, is divided into two great and opposite *methods of demonstration*—the analytical and inductive. The one would prove the principles of a machine by taking it to pieces and examining its parts ; the other by puting those parts together. At the head of one stands algebra, and of the other geometry. Algebra assumes the conditions of a proposition as it is, and, analyzing it, arrives at its elements. Geometry takes those elements, and, putting them together, step by step deduces a conclusion which cannot be resisted. And these two methods comprehend in general all the varieties of demonstration—moral or physical—which human wisdom has devised, from the philosophers of the academy to those of the institute. Any other than these appeals not to reason, but to the fallible testimony of the senses. In fact, all treatises upon logic teach nothing, except terms, which may not be found in the elementary propositions of geometry ; and when the youth, who in his collegiate course has mastered the mathematics, comes at the close of it to peruse some book of logic, he smiles with contempt at what appears to him an inferior method of reasoning. What form of syllogism—the sophism excepted—has he not found in Euclid ?

The mode of reasoning, and the things reasoned about, which give no result but the exactness of truth, claim a superiority for this system over every other. Observation deceives; consciousness itself errs; but demonstration never. This method of investigation, however, though in general applied only to physical objects, may be transferred to any upon which the mind can be employed. It was the opinion of Mr. Locke that moral as well as mathematical science may be reduced to a demonstration. The improvements in moral investigation seem fast leading to this result; and Mr. Locke, like some other great minds, has, I believe, published a truth which posterity may see accomplished though we may not.*

If it be true then that mathematics include a perfect system of *reasoning*, whose premises are self-

---

* What is a demonstration but a *series* of *connected truths* with a *conclusion* drawn from them? Now these *truths* may be derived from *any source*, and may be *exhibited in any* form, provided the connection is kept up and the conclusion clearly drawn. Mathematics assumes truths drawn from the relations of *figure and extension;* natural philosophy those drawn from *experiment.* Moral science deduces its conclusions from *testimony* and *consciousness.* The *demonstration* in either case is the same. But as the *facts* of mathematics are at once obvious to the *senses* and incapable of denial, the demonstrations are the most perfect. For this *very reason*, they furnish the best means of studying logic. If a man wished to learn the art of *engraving*, would he go to the worst engraver in the land? No—to the best. Then shall he not learn reasoning in its best form?

evident, and whose conclusions are irresistible, *can* there be any branch of science or knowledge better adapted to the discipline and improvement of the understanding? It is in this capacity, as a strong and natural adjunct and instrument of reason, that this science becomes the fit subject of education with all conditions of society—with all conditions of society, whatever may be their ultimate pursuits. Most sciences, as indeed most branches of knowledge, address themselves to some particular tastes or subsequent avocations; but this, while it is before all as a useful attainment, especially adapts itself to the cultivation and improvement of the *thinking faculty*, alike necessary to all who would be governed by reason or live for usefulness.

HE ORDER OF REASONING.

But, by teaching geometry first* and algebra subsequently, an inversion of the usual order, these sciences prevent the very method by which the human mind in its progress from childhood to age develops its faculties. What first meets the observation of a child? Upon what are his earliest investigations employed? Next to color, which exists only to the sight, *figure*, extension, dimension, are the first objects which he meets and the first which he examines.

* This idea is derived from a discourse delivered by Mr. Grund, a teacher of mathematics in Boston.

He ascertains and acknowledges their existence; then he perceives plurality, and begins to enumerate; finally, he begins to draw conclusions from the facts to the whole, and makes a law from the individuals to the species. Thus he has obtained figure, extension, dimension, enumeration, and generalization. This is the teaching of *nature;* and hence, when this process becomes embodied in a perfect system, as it is in geometry, *that system* becomes the easiest and most natural means of *strengthening* the mind in its early progress through the fields of knowledge. Long after the child has thus begun to generalize and deduce laws, he notices objects and events, whose *exterior* relations afford him no conclusion upon the subject of his contemplation. Machinery is in motion—effects are produced. He is surprised —examines and inquires. *Analysis* is begun, and he reasons backward from effect to cause. *This* is algebra, the metaphysics of mathematics, and the *second step* in the order of nature; and through all its varieties, from arithmetic to the integral calculus, it furnishes a grand armory of weapons for acute philosophical investigation. But algebra advances one step further; by its peculiar *notation* it exercises, in the highest degree, the faculty of *abstraction,* which, whether morally or intellectually considered, is always connected with the loftiest efforts of the mind. Thus this science when taught subsequently t geometry, comes in to assist the faculties in their progress to the ultimate stages of reasoning; and the more these analytical processes are cultivated, the more the mind looks in upon itself, estimates justly and directs rightly those vast powers which are to buoy it up in an eternity of future being.

The minds of *nations,* as well as of individuals, have pursued the same order; generations have their infancy and age, and the great public mind of the world has cultivated its understanding and aggregated its knowledge by the *same processes* which are natural and necessary to individuals. Thus, the philosophers of ancient Greece perfected *plain* geometry, and Euclid is still a text-book in modern schools.* But not so with analysis; the Greeks knew not the numerals,† and their whole arithmetic was exceedingly imperfect, while in algebra they were but beginners, having scarcely advanced beyond equations

* Geometry, like most other sciences, is supposed to have had its *origin* among the Chaldeans, or Egyptians. But however that may have been, their knowledge upon the subject must have been slight; for it was Pythagoras, in the year five hundred and ninety before Christ, who discovered the fundamental proposition that the square of the hypothenuse is equal to the sum of the squares of the other two sides. Euclid appeared in the year three hundred B. C. His object was to systematize the scattered discoveries in science, and clothe them in the strictest form of reasoning; and he did it with such success, that no book of science ever attained the duration and celebrity of Euclid's elements. They were for many centuries taught exclusively in many schools, and translated and commented upon in all languages.—*Vide Bossuet's History of Mathematics.*

† The Greeks, and all other ancient nations, used *letters* and other *characters* for arithmetical operations, but of arithmetic itself they knew very little.

of the first or simplest order. The invention of numerals,* the algebraic notation, the solution of equations of the higher order, the invention and use of logarithms,† and finally, the integral calculus, were reserved for that period‡ in the progress of knowledge when the human mind at once overthrew the Aristotelian philosophy and substituted that of reason and experiment. And it is not unworthy of remark, that the disappearance of the verbal school was coeval with the advance of analysis. A mathematician, Descartes, with one hand overthrew the verbiage of the ancient metaphysics, and with the other improved the analysis of algebra.§

We thus see that mathematical reasoning conforms itself, step by step, to the *order of nature*, and that the history of mathematics is, in fact, the history of human improvement.

---

* The invention of the numerals is by some attributed to the Hindoos; but this, like many other tremendous drafts upon credulity by the Brahmins and mandarins of Hindostan and China, is an *unproved assertion*. Our numerals were derived directly from the *Arabs*. They were introduced into Europe about the year 960, by *Gerbert*, who was Pope Sylvester II.

† It was in the sixteenth century that equations of the higher orders, third, fourth, and fifth degrees, were resolved by Carden, Vieta, and others. Logarithms were invented by *Napier*, of Scotland, who was born 1550, died 1617.

‡ About the years 1684–6 the method of fluxions was discovered, by Newton and Leibnitz.

§ Descartes was born 1596, died 1650. He introduced the notation by *exponents*.

BIOGRAPHICAL ILLUSTRATIONS.

The use of this science as a *discipline of the mind,* derives a strong practical argument from a fact which *biography* spreads before us; that, aside from the realms of fiction and fancy, almost all great minds which have exercised *power* over human affairs, whether for good or for evil, have been aided and strengthened by the study of mathematics. They have pursued it not merely as a task prescribed by the *routine* of education, but resorted to it at subsequent periods as a great mental arsenal, with whose keen and powerful weapons they were to subdue to their purposes the will and the resources of others. Let us take a few examples from modern history, recorded as beacon-lights in the progress of mind.

Heroes and statesmen, those brilliant points in the eye of fame, have not disdained to profit largely by mathematical studies. Peter the Great,* who, whether we contemplate his private or public character, or the results of that character in the subsequent progress of his empire, was a sublime anomaly in the race ol monarchs, owed his early education to a diplomatist, a mathematician, and his mother. His subsequent acquisitions, in naval architecture and in various branches of mechanics, were such as could only have been made by the aid of mathematics.

Napoleon, in whom intellectual power was the

---

* Encyclopedia Americana, art. "Peter the Great."

foundation of greatness, was all his life an enthusiast in this science. In the school of Brienne he pursued it with youthful ardor. It was the subject of his midnight studies, and the element of his unsurpassed success.

Jefferson, the statesman and philosopher, was so much an adept in mathematics, that he drew from private life to public station a distinguished mathematician from the perusal of his works alone; and is it a small honor to the memory of the illustrious dead to say, that he and Clinton, likewise the friend of letters and science, contributed more to their improvement and encouragement, than all the other statesmen of our country united?

If we pass to theologians, we find Barrow, whom the witty Charles the II. called an *unfair* preacher, because he so exhausted the subject as left nothing for others to say, a mathematician second only to Newton.

In our own country, Dwight, whose name and influence will be transmitted through many generations, was several years both a student and instructor of mathematics.

There are few greater names in medicine than Boerhaave,* yet so convinced was he of the necessity

* Boerhaave was a great improver of medicine, a learned scholar, and an eminent Christian. He was highly skilled in Latin, Greek, and Hebrew. He was a chemist, a professor, a lecturer in the universities, and a practitioner to whom patients resorted from all parts of Europe. He studied mathematics *con amore*, and declared in an

of mathematical learning, that in the university he pursued it with assiduity, and in his later years, with still greater industry. He went further, and recommended the application of mechanical principles to practical anatomy, of mathematical reasoning to the investigation of diseases.

One of the greatest of England's lawyers—Erskine, I believe—carried Euclid in his pocket, and gave as a reason, that it was the best book of logic, and therefore the best adapted to his profession, of any he had ever met with. And it is due to that *profession*, who move in the advance guard of nations, and are *wise*, at least in the wisdom of this world, to say that the greatest of its number, from Bacon and Hale to Brougham and Parsons, have laid the foundations of their education deep in the mathematics. The late Chancellor of England is said even now to be a stu-

---

oration, delivered before the University of Leyden, that as to philosophy, "all the knowledge we have is of such qualities alone as are discoverable by experience, or such as may be deduced from them by mathematical reasoning." And this is the simple *truth*, known and acknowledged by all improvers of science.

As a Christian, he was pure, active, and practical. Once, after fifteen hours of exquisite pain, he prayed that God would take his life. This he sincerely regretted, on account of its impatience and want of confidence in God. A friend, who was by, consoled him by attributing it to the unavoidable infirmities of human nature. But he replied, that "he that loves God, ought to think nothing desirable but what is pleasing to the Supreme goodness." Thus died Boerhaave, a man formed by nature for great designs, and guided by religion in the exertion of his abilities.—*See Johnson's Life of Herman Boerhaave.*

dent of this profound science. And in what other school could those illustrious minds have acquired that clearness of method, and strength of illustration, which make their very statements arguments, and their conclusions conviction? These were practical men, who never left the substance before them, like the dog in the fable, for the shadows of imagination.

If we take examples from the lives of those who have improved the world by mechanical ingenuity, we shall find them not less striking. Fulton received a common English education, but subsequently studied the arts and sciences in England, and, before the invention of the steamboat, acquired the higher mathematics at Paris.

Whitney, in his early youth, except his great mechanical propensity, had no predilection for any study but arithmetic; and afterwards, in college, preferred the mathematics to other pursuits. And his biographer remarks that he was a distinguished example of the beneficial effects of a liberal education upon a practical man, as well in respect to the economy of business as in the triumphs of mechanical skill.*

And these were men whose minds were strengthened by *mathematical studies.* They were mighty men—the one covered the earth with the moving monuments of science, and the other added forty millions annually to the resources of his native land;

* Life of Whitney, by Professor Olmstead. See *Silliman's Jour.*

and both did more for the physical comfort and improvement of the world than all their generations besides.*

The examples I have given are none of them drawn from the ranks of *professed* mathematicians. These men studied other sciences, and followed other pursuits; but they resorted to mathematics as an in-

---

* I said, above, "aside from the realms of fiction and fancy," but mathematics has not always been excluded from them. Where is he, whom the world equals with immortal Homer?

> "Is not each great, each amiable muse
> Of classic ages in thy Milton met?
> A genius universal as his theme;
> Astonishing, as chaos, as the bloom
> Of blooming Eden fair, as heaven sublime."—*Thomson.*

To show what were the studies of Milton, I make this quotation from Bishop Newton's Life of Milton.

"Here he resided with his parents for the space of five years, and as he himself has informed us (in his second defence, and the seventh of his familiar epistles), read over *all the Greek* and *Latin authors*, particularly the historians; but now and then made an excursion to London, sometimes to buy books, or meet his friends from Cambridge, and at other times to learn something new in the *mathematics* or *music*, with which he was extremely delighted."

Five years of *such studies voluntarily* pursued, after the usual course of education, were certainly different vocations from those which engage the mass of reformers in learning, but not more so than are their moderate attainments from the splendid results exhibited in the character and productions of John Milton. From the classic authors he may be supposed to have derived that fund of ancient learning which shines so conspicuously in all his works; from mathematics that strength of logic, which made him the best controversialist of his day, and from music, that sense of melody, which is essential to the formation of a good poet or good writer.

tellectual *instrument* as well as a useful attainment. They used it as an element of power. They acquired power; and they have poured its influence, for good or for evil, for the present and the future, through all the mass of human kind.

The biographical facts to which I have alluded arise from *fixed principles of mind.* A great mind influences others, so far as intellect is concerned, by the superior rapidity and certainty, almost amounting to prophecy, with which it arrives at results; and it obtains these results by assembling the facts, that is, the elements of the question, combining them and deducing a conclusion. Now these are the very faculties—comparison, combination, and judgment—which mathematical reasoning quickens and invigorates;* and it is the exercise of these powers by the study of mathematics which has given superior strength to so many minds over others who have cultivated other faculties.

It was thus that Peter the Great compared his bar-

---

* The faculty of *combination* is that of (what is called) *genius.* Let any one examine carefully the creations of a great poet, as Milton, Shakspeare, or Scott; and the results of a great military mind, as exhibited in the conduct of Cæsar and Bonaparte; or the inventions of great mechanical skill, as in Arkwright and Whitney; or the sublime discoveries and demonstrations of Newton, and he will find an instructive volume, illustrating this department of intellect. This volume affords no space to enlarge upon this subject; but the intelligent inquirer can easily refer to the facts. It is sufficient to say that mathematical studies are full of exercise and employment for this faculty.

ren empire with the rest of Europe; assembled the means of civilization, and brought his nation from darkness to light: it was thus that Bonaparte comprehended the principles of the revolution; combined the resources of his empire upon single points; and crushed nation after nation, till physical force accomplished in his overthrow what the genius of Europe could not perform: and it is thus that Brougham, in the simple declaration that "the schoolmaster is abroad," shows the comparison between the modern and the ancient world; while he announces to corrupted governments and decrepit superstitions, that their sceptres have departed.

Thus have history and biography* confirmed my proposition; and if on the one hand these eyes ot wisdom exhibit positive examples of those who by the aid of mathematical reasoning and method have performed their functions with the power and regularity of planets in their course, so also our own

* It is certain that too much value cannot be placed upon history and biography properly studied. *Public* history contains the embodied mass of human *experience; private*, the *means* by which the natural faculties and affections have been made to produce the practical *results* we see exhibited in the life of an individual. It is in fact, when philosophically written, a *picture of education* acting upon mind and heart. But to study it properly, books must be written differently from the mass of modern history. *Tacitus*, Robertson's *Introduction to Charles V.*, Hallam, and similar authors, must be the models, instead of the confused and uninstructive details of blood and glory which have so long dazzled the eyes of unreflecting historians.

observation furnishes negative illustrations in the lives of many, who, *without* that aid, but with no less genius, have beat the air with vain efforts, till at last, like shooting-stars, they went out forever.*

I have now endeavored to show that the mathematics contain a complete system of reasoning; that as such, they conform to the order of nature in the development of the faculties, individual and national; that their progress is consistent with the history of human improvement; and that they have successfully assisted in the cultivation of the greatest minds.

Now if these propositions be *true*, I think it irresistibly follows that they present the best known *means* of strengthening the intellect, of disciplining the faculties, of cultivating the thinking principle; and, in one word, of *improving the human understanding.*

THE ATTAINMENT OF PRACTICAL KNOWLEDGE.

The *second* great object of intellectual education *is the attainment of such practical knowledge as may be of use in after life.* Now it is clear that in a *general,* not professional education, those branches of

---

* How many men of brilliant faculties fail from instability of character! "Unstable as water, thou shalt not excel." And what is the cause of this instability, but *want* of *balance,* as well as strength in the faculties? And what can give this balance and strength so well as mathematical investigation?

science which contribute the most to others, and which are connected with the most numerous pursuits of life, are the most useful attainments. And in this point of view, is there any science comparable in utility to this? What sciences, not wholly moral, are disconnected from it? Where shall we go and not find its principles in active and profitable operation? The connection of mathematics with the arts and sciences of civilized life, are strikingly illustrated in many of the most common occupations of society. Descending from the ambitious heights of intellectual renown, let us consider the simple operation of house-building: how much is it indebted for its improvement to practical mathematics! and how clearly and how certainly would all the operatives connected with it be better qualified for profit and success in their vocation, by a knowledge of its elementary principles! They have to call into operation at every step the *practice*, if not the theory, of three branches of this science—practical geometry, the strength and stress of materials, and the principles of stone-cutting. The very works written to instruct the young carpenter in his profession, are works upon geometry; and he cannot understand them till he understands its principles. It is true that he may plane and square timber without geometry; that he may receive the dimensions of the rafters, the beams, and girders of the roof, from the master-builder, and make them all fit; the master-builder may himself have received the practical rule without a knowledge of its principles; yet can there be a doubt that they would both have worked with more economy and accuracy, if they had understood the common properties of a right-angled triangle? And when they advance to the more difficult cases of spiral stairways and vaulted roofs, it is easy to see that an ignorance of principle may lead to both error and waste.

The difficulty in positive rules prepared for uneducated men is, that they can never bend to circumstances; and the workmen go on in a fixed track, in cases where they might have changed it without a variation of principle, but with the greatest economy of time and money. The calculation of the strength and stress of timber, though very simple in itself, is, notwithstanding, an *analytical* problem, which one unacquainted with the principles of algebra could not solve; yet is it everywhere important that it should be properly determined. Very recently the roof of a large cathedral in England, which was supposed to be a model of architecture, fell by its own weight, destroying in a moment the result of a great expenditure of time and money; a fact which could never have occurred had the architect resolved a practical problem in the strength of materials. In the construction of groined arches, whether for roofs, door-ways, vaults, or bridges, the principles of descriptive geometry are equally applicable and necessary; the catenary and elliptical curves, which are their best form, cannot be understood without the higher geometry; the arch cannot be built, without the greatest extravagance in the use of materials, unless the *precise form* of every stone is known before it is cut from the rock. Such was the fact in some of the finest specimens of modern architecture; and such also was the case in the building of Solomon's temple; for it is recorded in the book of Kings* that "the house, when it was building, was built of stone *made ready before* it was brought thither, so that there was neither *hammer* nor *axe,* nor any *tool of iron,* heard in the house while it was building." And this fact also corroborates a former position, that *geometry long preceded analysis.*

If the quantity of timber, stone, and other material wasted in building, from the want of a very little knowledge of mathematics, could be calculated, I have little doubt its price would educate all the young mechanics of the land. *Science is economical;* it repays the people a hundred-fold for what is expended in its cultivation.

Let us take another example in the case of *surveying.* Everybody knows that carrying the chain and compass, and blazing trees, is no very difficult operation; yet of what USE would it be, if there was not mathematical knowledge to calculate the results? The surveyor himself must at least have some knowledge of trigonometry; and is it not obvious that every chainman in the forest would perform his duty better, if he were acquainted with the objects and

---

* 1 Kings, vi. 7.

principles of the business in which he is engaged? He would then know *where* and *how* to apply his labor to the best advantage. But in the beautiful survey of the Northwestern Territory, mathematics has exercised a still higher faculty; all the section-lines are based upon the *meridian-lines,* and these meridian-lines were fixed by the nicest astronomical calculations, while yet the Indian had not learned the mastery of the pale-face, and civilization announced itself only in the triumph of its proudest sciences!

In *hydraulics* we find the principles of mathematics equally necessary: here, all the calculations of the velocity, power, and quantity of moving fluids depend upon these principles. How can a millwright be master of his business without understanding them? The very shape of the cogs in his wheels are determined by them; their form is that of the cycloid—a curve generated by a fixed point in the circumference of a circle revolving in a right line; and he must understand that curve, or he can never judge whether his wheels are fit for use. And *how* is he to ascertain the quantity of water necessary to move them? and how is he to ascertain the quantity discharged? If he will turn to a practical treatise on mills he will readily find a *rule* for it, but one which neither improves his understanding nor his pocket. If, however, he would study a few of the laws of forces, of descending bodies, and moving fluids, he could then make a rule for himself, and could adapt it to all the changing circumstances of locality and power.

In the construction of canals, railroads, bridges, and in all the operations of civil engineering, mathematics are the essential element. In addition to algebra and geometry, trigonometry and the conic sections find him full employment. Mountains and valleys are to be reduced to a level, rivers turned from their channels, and all to be done with a certainty and economy which nothing but the calculation and reasoning of mathematics can effect. And when the beautiful and grand result *is* obtained; when the high hills are brought down and space traversed with the speed of the winds; when the people and products of the most distant nations meet together with the ease and safety of near neighbors; when knowledge is borne over the earth by the chariot-wheels of all-conquering science; when civilization and Christianity herself look to these results as their kind and beneficent aids; shall *we* not inquire by what means they were accomplished? Shall we learn *nothing* from the principles by which this vast machinery is moved? Or shall *education* neglect them, when she is gathering the elements of a great and useful mind? Of the millions who rejoice and wonder and admire over these achievements, few are either taught or seek to know the means by which they are produced. *Genius*, cries the assembled multitude, *genius* is great and glorious! Yes; genius is indeed great—the admirable work of a perfect being:

yet genius unaided has done none of these things; but with industry and vigilance she *has* gathered the aggregate wisdom of uncounted ages; she has called arithmetic from the land of Chaldea; geometry from the plains of ancient Greece; logarithms from the hills of modern Scotland; and from the darkness of deep antiquity, as well as from the brightness of the fresh and living present, she brings the treasures of science to aid her in blessing mankind.

The connection of mathematics with the arts, sciences, and employments of civilized society are far too numerous for reference here. Those I have selected are cases of ready and familiar observation: and if they enter thus into the accustomed walks of life, still more do they into those higher and nobler studies, whose object is to develop the laws and structure of the universe. Man may construct his works by irregular and uncertain rules; but God has made an unerring law for his whole creation, and made it, too, in respect to the physical system, upon principles which, so far as we now know, can never be understood without the aid of mathematics.

THE STUDENT WITHOUT MATHEMATICS.

Let us suppose a youth who despises, as many do, these *cold* and *passionless abstractions;* yet he is intellectual—he loves knowledge; he would explore nature and know the reason of things; but he would do it without aid from this *rigid, syllogistic, measur-*

ing, calculating science. He seeks indeed no "royal road to geometry;" but he seeks one not less difficult to find, in which geometry is not needed. He begins with the mechanical powers. He takes a lever, and readily understands that a weight will move it; but the principle upon which *different* weights at *different* distances move, he is forbidden to know; for this depends upon *ratios* and *proportions.* He passes to the inclined plane; but quits it in disgust when he finds its action depends upon the relations of angles and triangles. The screw is still worse; and when he comes to the wheel and axle, he gives them up forever—they are *all mathematical.* He would investigate the laws of falling bodies and moving fluids, and know why their motion is *accelerated* at different periods, and upon what their *momentum* depends; but roots, lines, squares, angles, and curves float before him in the mazy dance of a disturbed intellect. The very first proposition is a *mystery;* and he soon discovers that mechanical philosophy is little better than mathematics itself. But he still has his *senses;* he will at least not be indebted to diagrams and equations for their enjoyment. He gazes with admiration upon the phenomena of light; the many-colored rainbow upon the bosom of the clouds; the clouds themselves, reflected with all their changing shades from the surface of the quiet waters. Whence comes this beautiful imagery? He investigates, and finds that every hue in the rainbow is made by a different *angle of refraction;* and that each ray reflected from the mirror has its angle of incidence equal to its angle of reflection; and as he pursues the subject further, in the construction of lenses and telescopes, the whole family of triangles, ratios, proportions, and conclusions arise to alarm his excited vision.

He turns to the heavens and is charmed with its shining host, moving in solemn procession through the "halls of the sky," each star as it rises and sets, marking time on the records of nature. He would know the structure of this beautiful system, and search out, if possible, the laws which regulate those distant lights. But astronomy forever banishes him from her presence; she will have none near her to whom mathematics is not a *familiar friend.* What can *he* know of her parallaxes, anomalies, and processions, who has never studied the conic sections or the higher orders of analysis? She sends him to some wooden orrery, from which he may gather as much knowledge of the heavenly bodies as a child does of armies from the gilded troopers of the toy-shop.

But if he can have no companionship with optics, nor astronomy, nor mechanical philosophy, there *are* sciences, he thinks, which have better taste and less austerity of manners. He flies to chemistry, and her garments float loosely around him. For a while he goes gloriously on, illuminated by the *red lights* and *blue lights* of crucibles and retorts. But soon he comes to compound bodies—to the composition of the elements around him, and finds them all in fixed relations. He finds that gases and fluids will combine with each other, and with solids only in a certain *ratio,* and that all possible compounds are formed by nature in *immutable proportion.* Then starts up the whole doctrine of chemical equivalents, and mathematics again stares him in the face. Affrighted he flies to mineralogy; stones he may pick up, jewels he may draw from the bosom of the earth, and be no longer alarmed at the stern visage of this terrible science; but even here he is not safe. The first stone that he finds—quartz, contains a *crystal,* and that crystal assumes the dreaded form of geometry. Crystallization allures him on; but as he goes, cubes and hexagons, pyramids and dodecagons, arise before him in beautiful array. He would understand more about them, but must *wait* at the portal of the temple, till introduced within by that honored of time and science, our friendly *Euclid.*

And now where shall this student of nature without the aid of mathematics go for his knowledge or his enjoyments? Is it to natural history? The very *birds* cleave the air in the form of the cycloid, and mathematics prove it the *best.* Their feathers are formed upon calculated mechanical principles; the muscles of their frame are moved by them: the little bee has constructed his cell in the very geometrical figure and with the precise angles which mathematicians, after ages of investigation, have demonstrated to be that which contains the greatest *economy of space and strength.* Yes, he who would shun mathematics must fly the bounds of flaming space, and in the realms of chaos, that

> ——————" dark,
> Illimitable ocean,"

where Milton's Satan wandered from the wrath of heaven, he may *possibly* find some spot visited by no figure of geometry, and no harmony of proportion. But nature, this beautiful creation of God, has no resting-place for him. All its construction is *mathematical;* all its uses are *reasonable;* all its ends *harmonious.* It has no elements mixed without regulated law; no broken chord to make a false note in the music of the spheres.

THE STUDENT WITH MATHEMATICS.

Let us take another student, with whom mathematics is neither despised nor neglected. He sees in it the means of past success to others: he reads in its history the progress of universal improvement; and he believes that what has contributed so much to the civilization of the world, what is even now contributing so much to harmonize society, and what the experience of all mankind has sanctioned, *may* perchance be useful to his own intellectual development. He opens a volume of geometry, and steadily, but not coldly, pursues its abstractions from the definition of a right line, through the elegant properties of the right-angled triangle, the relations of similar figures, and the laws of curved surfaces. He finds a chain of *unbroken* and impregnable reasoning, and is at once possessed of all the knowledge of postulates, syllogisms, and conclusions, which the most accomplished school of rhetoric could have taught him. He looks upon society, and wherever he turns, arts, sciences, and their results, from carpentry to civil engineering, from architecture to hydraulics, from the ingenious lock upon a canal, to the useful mill upon its sides, disclose their operations, no longer mysterious to his enlightened understanding. Many an interesting repository of knowledge this key has opened to his vision; and as he thus walks through the *vestibule* of science, he longs to penetrate those deep aisles and ascend that magnificent stairway, which lead up to the structure of the universe.

With the properties of the ellipsis, the laws of motion demonstrated by mathematics, and two facts drawn from observation—the one, that bodies fall towards the earth, and the other, the regular motion of the planets—he demonstrates beyond the power of refutation, the laws of the celestial system. He traces star after star, however eccentric their course, through the unseen immensity of space, and calculates, with *unfailing certainty*, the hour of their return after ages have passed away. He does more, he weighs matter in the balances of creation, and finds that to complete the harmony of the system, a planet is wanting in some distant corner of its wide domain. No mortal eye has ever seen it, no tradition tells of its existence; yet, with the confidence and zeal of prophecy, he announces that it *must exist*, for *demonstration has proved it.* The prediction is recorded in the volume of science. Long after, astronomy, by the aid of mathematics, discovers the long-lost tenant of the skies; and fractured though it be, while its members perform their revolution, no living soul can be permitted to doubt the *worth of mathematics*, or the powers of his own immortal mind.

And what were the glorious contemplations of that pupil of mathematical philosophy, as he passed behind the clouds of earth to investigate the machinery of celestial spheres! Alone, yet not solitary, amidst the glowing lights of heaven, he sends his spirit forth through the works of God. He has risen by the force of cultivated intellect to heights which mortal fancy had never reached. He has taken line and figure and measure, and from proposition to proposition, and from conclusion to conclusion, *riveting* link after link, he has bound the universe to the throne of its Creator, by that

> "Golden, everlasting chain,
> Whose strong embrace holds heaven and earth and main."

And is there no *moral* instruction in this?* Does he learn no lesson of wisdom? Do no strong emo-

* It has been said "there is no Christianity in mathematics:" *intrinsically*, what is there, except the Bible and the renewed heart, which *is* Christian? The Christian does not hesitate to eat, drink, clothe, sow, and plant, like other men, without once inquiring whether his food or clothing be Christian. It is enough for him that he *uses* them with Christian motives for Christian ends. It is necessary for a

tions of love and gratitude arise towards that Being who thus delights him with the charms of intellectual enjoyment, and blesses him with the multiplied means of happiness? *Harder* than the adamant of his own reasoning, *colder* than the abstractions in which he is *falsely* supposed to move, must be he who *thus* conducted by the handmaid of the arts and sciences, through whatever humanizes man—through whatever is sublime in his progress to a higher state—through all the vast machinery which the Almighty has made tributary to his comfort and his happiness—yet feels no livlier sentiment of duty towards him, no kinder or more peaceful spirit towards his fellow-man. We

---

Christian, in the fulfilment of his duty, to cultivate the energies of both *body* and *mind.* He uses food and exercise, *temperate in all things,* for the former; and shall he not use mathematics for the latter? Is there not too frequently a mistake made in distinguishing between *means* and *ends?* And do not some persons suppose that the world is to be Christianized by some *direct* interference of providence, independent of human means? If the latter are to be used, then are the mathematical sciences among the most powerful ever brought to bear upon the human mind. They who deny this, know very little either of the science itself, or of its connection with the civilization and consequent moral refinement of the world. How much has the modern astronomy alone done to exhibit and illustrate the glorious attributes of the Creator! How much has the improvement in naval architecture done to facilitate the progress of the Gospel among pagan nations! Would the missionary cross the Pacific in a birch-bark canoe? How much have the improvements, even in the science of war, produced by mathematics done to establish the dominion and consequent influence of Christian over uncivilized nations!—See the British Empire in India; the open ports of China; the Sandwich Islands, and the Australian Colonies!

have now *traced* many of the most useful arts and sciences to the *knowledge of mathematics;* we have seen that it contributes to the most necessary and practical operations of society; and we have further seen that we cannot *understand* the *works* of nature, nor *commune with the Almighty*, in the sublimest portion of his creation, *without* the aid of this *benign* and *civilizing* science.

But if mathematics be a part of education in *general*, there are some reasons why it is peculiarly so in a well-devised system of education *in the West.* Education must adapt itself to the *wants* of the people. It must be that which draws the treasures from the earth as well as the blessing from the heaven. Now after fixing the general subjects of instruction, the first inquiry is, What will the next generation in this country need? How are they to be engaged? What are to be the effects of their business? I answer, that aside from the cultivation of Christian benevolence, their pursuits and the improvements they aim at will be in those arts and sciences which are *physical;* it will not be a matter of *choice* with them. It arises from the necessity of their condition. And if it be so, then is the science of which we are speaking, of all others the best calculated for facilitating their progress. Let us glance at the existing state of things in the region of the Ohio and the Mississippi. We are a young people—a thrifty plant, it is true, grafted by knowledge with the best fruit of the wise and ancient world; yet a *small* plant, scarcely risen above the green grass of our beautiful prairies. Our population has hardly begun: here and there you find a mart of commerce and civilization; and you read of the millions within the borders of Ohio, as of a vast multitude: yet within that very state you may travel fifty miles with but little appearance of cultivation, and when you come to take an accurate view of it, you find the forest scarcely broken by the dwellings of man. If you pass to Wisconsin, the native of the woods is there to tell you that the wilderness has not passed away. On the plains of Iowa it is the same; and if you go beyond the Mississippi, the traveller may wander five hundred miles within an organized territory without meeting a cabin. Yet this is all a region of arable land—*rich* in the resources of nature, yielding whatever adds to physical enjoyment or rational contemplation. It will therefore in time be *populous*. It will go on as it has done, to speak mathematically, in geometrical progression, doubling from period to period. I am no optimist, no gilder of futurity in the hues of imagination; and it requires no aid from fancy, or even calculation from arithmetic, to know that the shores of the Ohio and the Mississippi will be crowded a century or two hence with a mass of humanity, dense as that which looks upon the waters of the Rhine and the Ganges. The generations which pass from this to that period, like our own, are preparatory. They are to build the physical as well as moral temple for the habitation of posterity. And where are we? Standing at the corner-stone, laying the very foundation. And what shall these intermediate millions do? Shall they not appeal to the full storehouse of nature? And shall they not call science to unlock their doors? They *will* do so, because they *must.* The *resources* of the land must be developed before the *mass* of the people can cultivate the charms of taste or the refinements of speculative philosophy. They will first look to the products of the soil. They will go to your salt-springs and bore the earth for that necessary of life, and they will call upon the mechanic for forcing-pumps and lifting machinery; and *he* will call upon mathematics to aid him in economizing time and labor. They will open your coal-banks, and look to the mechanic arts to aid them in its transportation; and in the mines of iron and lead, and copper, gold, and quicksilver, they will need geometry as well as chemistry to aid them in mining and smelting. They will send engineers to construct vast bridges over those noble streams, and to lay the track of that magnificent highway which is to connect the Atlantic with the Pacific, and make a path for the nations as they still roll on to the interminable West! And in all these operations mathematics will be the active agent and kind assistant; and as it helps others, it will help itself to *increase,* still propelling the wheels of knowledge, till, with the *light,* they have *rolled round the circle of the earth.*

And in this great work who has the responsibility and the honor more than the teacher? Cicero demanded for his client, the Poet Archias, the citizenship of Rome, *not* because it was his *legally*, but because he had done that for which the republic owed him everlasting gratitude. "He has given you," said he, "those intellectual gifts which nourish youth, delight age, adorn fortune, and soften adversity;" and to do this is the office of the teacher. Let him who is worthy in that calling be honored by the praises of the good and the gratitude of the republic

CHAPTER VII.

THE UTILITY OF ASTRONOMY.

In the fourth day of the creation God made the stars; he set them in the firmament of heaven, so that from every part of the material universe light fell upon the earth. He made them shine forever, that while this globe continues to circle on its axis, each falling ray should be a recording hand to write upon its circumference the passage of time to eternity! There was then no human voice to praise the mighty work; but there *was* music in the skies; the morning stars sang together, and the sons of God shouted for joy!*

* The passage from which this idea was taken is from the 4th to the 7th verses inclusive of the 38th chapter of Job. The whole of it is this: "Where wast thou when I laid the foundations of the earth?

Man was yet in the silent dust: God breathed upon it, and man became a living soul. He was made *erect*, with his countenance upturned to heaven, that while he walked upon the earth he might behold those glorious messengers of the Creator rolling their chariots of light through the skies from morn till night, from night till morn, immutable in law, unshaken in their courses, undiminished in power. From age to age they have continued to shine; from age to age man has gazed and marvelled at the sight; and yet they beam as brightly upon the last eyes opened upon earth, as upon those which first looked out upon the bloom of creation. Forever fresh, forever shining, forever rolling—eternal power their source, eternal light their element!

On the plains of Chaldea Job saw them, and in midnight meditations marked their wandering constellations careering through the firmament; on Judah's hills David looked up, wondered at the sight,

---

declare, if thou hast understanding. Who hath laid the measures thereof, if thou knowest? or who hath stretched the line upon it? Whereupon are the foundations thereof fastened? or who laid the corner-stone thereof, when the morning stars sang together, and all the sons of God shouted for joy?"

This passage intimates two things: 1st, That there was no man in being when the foundations of the earth were laid; and, 2d, That the stars were then in being, and another race of beings called the sons of God. The harmony of the stars and their perfect system is the foundation, without doubt, of the metaphorical phrase, "sang together." The intelligent beings then existing also rejoiced in the progress of the work of creation.

struck his harp to notes of praise, and poured them into the songs of Israel. By the waters of Euphrates the Babylonian saw that host of heaven pass before him, and mistaking the creature for the Creator, worshipped it on the false altars of Baal. The Persian, too, transferring the worship from the sun to the fire, bowed down under the open skies to the coals upon the altar, as the life and image of the stars above. The Egyptian marked the seasons by the signs of the zodiac, and recorded them on the ancient monuments of Thebes. The Greek, the Roman, the Hindoo, the Christian, the men of every age and every nation, have gazed upon those wandering fires above, and, gazing, been fixed with astonishment, filled with admiration, and made silent with awe!

When the great light of day sinks beneath the horizon, the portals of heaven open wider to your vision. Ten thousand suns come out from the dark firmament behind: each seems but a little light, twinkling for a moment. You watch it, and its light never ceases; it comes, and comes continually; its rays fall, but never stop. You look upon that light as the traveller upon the rocks of Niagara looks upon that world of rolling waters; it flows, and flows, and flows on forever! The light comes, and comes, shining and gliding on, like the spirit of man towards some vast, distant, unknown, untold eternity!

This work of the fourth day of creation is not merely the admiration of prophets and philosophers; but it is one of the most instructive subjects of contemplation, and therefore one of the best topics of a broad and useful education.

ASTRONOMY is derived (as a term) from the two words, *aster* and *nomos*, the first signifying a *star*, and the second a *law*. Astronomy may therefore be defined, the law of the stars. It comprehends, however, all that relates to the different bodies in the system of the universe, and the material laws by which they are governed and sustained. I shall consider here both the *practical use* of astronomy, and the *effect of its theory*, in the improvement of the human mind.

ASTRONOMY DETERMINES TIME.

The first and the greatest use of astronomical observations is declared in the first chapter of Genesis: "And God said, Let there be lights in the firmament of heaven, to divide the day from the night; and let them be for signs, and for seasons, and for days, and for years."

Imagine, if you can, a world inhabited by finite and mortal beings, without time! Such a world would have been ours, if the rising and the setting of the stars had not cut off from infinite space, and marked on the visible horizon, those small measures which we call time. Space is the measure of time; and the idea of infinite space is the idea of eternity. Space can be made definite only by motion: he who attempts to measure space only by the eye, will mistake a foot for a furlong, and a furlong for a mile.

There is no measure of space but by motion; and there is no record of time but by space. It follows, then, that to give the idea of time at all, there must be bodies moving continually through the vacuity of space. It follows, also, that there must be more than one body so moving; for it is only by the *transition* of those bodies, passing one another at regular and continuous intervals, that we get by relative motion an accurate idea of time. The revolution of the earth on its axis determines our day; but it is only by the existence of other bodies, which appear to ascend and descend from the horizon, that we have the least idea of such a period of time. So also it is by the relative motion of still other bodies, that we get correct ideas of the year and its seasons. These stars, then, by their relative motions, divide space, and space determines time.

Had there been, then, in the councils of Infinite Wisdom, no other reason for the creation of stars than this, it would have been enough. It is enough, that in the vast vacuity of space there was created a world of innumerable beings, for whose happiness it was necessary to give, by the records of time, the idea of a finite, fleeting, and mortal life! It is in contemplations such as these we can realize the solemn declaration of holy history, that one great use of those glowing orbs was, that they might "be for signs, for seasons, for days, and for years."

Nor was man dull to perceive or slow to understand these significant records of passing time, as they were, one by one, written with a pencil of light on the face of creation. No sooner had men looked upwards than they noted these transitions of the heavenly bodies, and measured their own history by those revolutions. There is no memory of man which goes so far back, that certain fixed methods of measuring time by observations on celestial objects were not known. These bodies were no sooner placed in the firmament than they became what they were appointed for, *dividing signs* between day and day, month and month, and year and year.

In the temperate zone, where man was first placed, the most obvious of all divisions is that made by the setting and rising of the sun and stars on the horizon. The day thus became the first measure of time. The seventh day marked a fourth part of the lunar revolution. It was also the day of sacred rest, and has thus been handed down through the whole descent of the human family, by commandment, by observance, and by tradition, in perpetual memorial of the creation. The lunar revolution made the month, and the solar revolution the year. Thus there is no measure of time known to us, which is not either a unit, or an exact proportional part of the great and visible revolutions, regularly performed in our planetary system.

When these divisions were earliest made and recorded as time, no history informs us. Why may we not suppose them to have occurred to the first man, and by him have been transmitted through successive generations?

It is in these terms of time, the inspired historian of the Hebrews has recorded, in the only history of the early ages of the world, the chronology of the antediluvian patriarchs. In those times, he has recorded the very day, and month, and year, in which the deluge occurred. It was in the seventeenth day, of the second month, of the six-hundredth year of Noah. This chronology has been subjected to the severest criticism of science, of history, and of human reason. Yet, neither the traditions of the oldest nations, the monuments of the most aged ruins, the authentic records of the most remote antiquity, nor the profoundest researches of science herself, have been able to throw a reasonable doubt on the accuracy of the antediluvian dates.* It is thus that yonder orbs of light

* There have been various and very ingenious attempts to invalidate the chronology of the Bible, especially in relation to two facts: the duration of the human race on earth, and the deluge of Noah. Geology has been used as an instrument for this purpose. But, so far as relates to the race of man, it has furnished no fact contrary to the biblical chronology. Its facts, so far as they relate to time at all, bear only on the structure of the earth and the lower order of animals.

There was a time, however, when astronomy itself threatened to overturn all our received chronology. This was at the close of the eighteenth century, by the discovery of the East Indian, or Hindoo astronomical tables, professing to give the position of the heavenly bodies, at a period anterior to the deluge. These were accompanied by the histories and affirmations of the Hindoos, that their origin went back to a date far more remote than our Christian annals. The bold production of astronomical tables to establish a date in antiquity was certainly a strong attack on the authenticity of our chronology. It was hardly possible to present the attack in a more plausible shape.

have become the historians alike of nature and of man. Their record is ineffaceable from creation.

It must be admitted, that if the Hindoo system of astronomy could be established as originating at the time claimed, and demonstrated on astronomical grounds, it would be the strongest argument against biblical chronology, and in favor of Hindoo antiquity, which the annals of science or of literature could furnish. This Hindoo astronomy, found in the tables of Tirvalore, was seized upon by M. Bailly, a French mathematician, with great avidity. In his *Traite de l'Astronomie Indienne et Orientale,* he founded a theory, that there had once been an immense and learned nation which flourished some thousands of years before our most ancient accounts, and that these tables were a part of the wreck of an astronomical system! Such theories have a great effect on the human imagination, where the mind is not firmly based in a belief in the truths of the Bible *as they are written.* It is one of the most remarkable facts in literature, that the Edinburgh Encyclopedia, compiled by learned men, adopted this theory, and contains the record of its faith, in the article Astronomy, vol. 3, page 550. Professor Playfair also supported it. But it was doomed to meet with strong opposition, and final defeat when least expected. La Place declared, the Tirvalore tables were invented "for the purpose of giving a common place in the zodiac to all the motions of the heavenly bodies, and that they were constructed or invented in modern times." Even Voltaire, in whose time Bailly first announced his theory, expressed his doubts of its truth.

The mode in which the question was solved was a curious one. A volume of Hindoo astronomical tables was subsequently discovered, which the Hindoos believed to be inspired. From these tables Mr. Bentley drew a deduction, which completely disproved their supposed great antiquity. As these tables gave the astronomical calculations for a great length of time, there seemed an easy way of ascertaining their date. From these Hindoo tables the calculation was made of the position of the heavenly bodies *for the present time.* Then their true position was ascertained by the European tables. From these

Their circuits through their orbits are no more certain than the certainty they have given to every measure

---

two results it was calculated, at what time the position of the sun, moon, and planets, *was the same according to both sets of tables.* It is plain there must be such a time; and that time was, when the Hindoo astronomer made his observations and calculations; for it is manifest, that he or any other observer, whether he proceeded on true or false systems, would give the true position of the heavenly bodies at the time he observed them. The true tables would of course give it. The time *at which both coincided* would be the demonstrated time at which the Hindoo calculation was made. This was ascertained to be about *seven hundred years* before Mr. Bentley's calculation, or about the beginning of the twelfth century of the Christian era.

Another mode of calculation was this: The position of the planets was given, when Rama, the hero of an Indian epic poem, reached his twenty-first year. That period was found by calculation to be 961 years before Christ. None of these positions could be traced more than 1800 years before Christ, or long after the time of Abraham, and it was clearly settled that the *date of the system* was only 700 years since! Yet, the reader should recollect, that this very book was dated by the Brahmins some millions of years since!

This was the most plausible, and apparently the most irresistible argument ever advanced against the accuracy of the Christian chronology. It proves that even a *forged science* is inadequate to overcome the supremacy of truth. A brief account of these investigations will be found in Dr. Wiseman's Lectures, a work which contains some knowledge not easily found in any other book, and which should be possessed by every student who would understand the relations between religion and science. Those relations are most beautiful and most mysterious. It required the power, the metaphysical or moral power, which the influence and studies of Christianity communicated to the human mind, in order fully to develop the laws of science; but when those laws were developed, they shed a retroactive and radiated light over the foundation truths of our holy religion.

of duration in human transactions. It was then the stars became the measure of time, and were placed in the firmament for signs, for seasons, and for years!

LIGHT AND ITS THEORY.

The second great practical use of astronomy is also indicated in the book of Genesis. After it was said, that the stars were to be a measure of time, it is further said, that "they shall be for lights in the firmament of heaven to give light upon the earth." In truth, the first astronomical observation made by the eye, must have been that which determined the fact, that the sun and stars were the source of light, and that when they disappeared, even for a time, there was darkness visible. A succession of these observations also proved, that light and heat were also connected; and again, that on these great principles depended the germination, growth, verdure, and fruit-bearing of every plant and tree upon earth. Even the solid elements of earth seemed to owe them allegiance. Life was traced to light, and light to the stars. Thus they were supposed to hold influence over the spirit of man. The dark astrologer, in a darker age, naturally enough traced the lines of human destiny on the map of the stars, and by his theory made human life to ebb and flow with their motions, as science has since proved the tides to do with those of the moon. Light was the one great germinal element of nature, as much identified with every sun and planet, as mind with every intelligent man. Hence the progress of astronomy was almost identical with progress in knowledge of the laws and uses of light. The history of one is almost the history of the other.

It was in the pursuit of the theory of light, that some of the most remarkable and most brilliant phenomena of the heavens have been explained by the direct laws of astronomy. It was observation on the different appearances of the sun and stars, rising and setting, which discovered and demonstrated the theory of atmospherical *refraction.* By this was explained the wonderful phenomena of twilight. It told *why* the rays of the departed orbs of heaven continued, like the works of immortal genius, to linger round the world they had left; *why* they continued to fill the horizon with cloud-built palaces, beautiful as the visions of hope; and painted them, like imagination, with many colored hues!

It was the sun whose slanting rays, falling upon the dropping rain, produced the attractive curve and inimitable colors of the rainbow. It was observation on these which resulted in the development and demonstration of the principles of reflected and refracted light, upon which the arch was formed.

It was in perfecting the telescope as an astronomical instrument, while he was grinding lenses, and while yet a young man, that Newton discovered the *refrangibility* of light; by which he separated its rays, transformed them into the prismatic colors, and recomposed these colors back into light! Finally, it was these discoveries in the nature and power of light, themselves introduced by astronomical discoveries, which aided the astronomers in perfecting optical instruments, enabled Newton and Herschel to continue their discoveries, and which has brought our astronomical societies, emerging from the bosom of a new nation, into being; and which may enable them, in some future time, to crown the peaceful victories of republicanism with the laurels of science.

It is thus that light has illumined the works of physical creation, advanced the boundaries of knowledge, lit up the chamber of the human soul, and given to poetry its sublimest images. It was this LIGHT, which, in some glorious scene of the East, inspired the Grecian Homer to sing:

> "As when the moon, refulgent lamp of night,
> O'er heaven's clear azure spreads her sacred light,
> When not a breath disturbs the deep serene,
> And not a cloud o'ercasts the solemn scene;
> Around her throne the vivid planets roll,
> And stars unnumber'd gild the glowing pole,
> O'er the dark trees a yellower verdure shed,
> And tip with silver every mountain's head;
> Then shine the vales, the rocks in prospect rise,
> A flood of glory bursts from all the skies;
> The conscious swains, rejoicing in the sight,
> Eye the blue vault, and bless the useful light."

It is in scenes such as these, we realize that the

stars were placed in the firmament of heaven to distribute *light** on earth and in the universe.

ASTRONOMY DETERMINES THE FORM OF THE EARTH.

The third most obvious use of astronomy was in extending the knowledge of the *surface, dimensions, and composition* of the planet on which we live. With this knowledge was also extended the bounda-

* The term "distribute" is here used purposely, in order to avoid any controversy about the *source, origin, or duration of light.* The stars, as a matter of fact, do *distribute* light. Light apparently comes from them to us, whether it be a real emission from them, or whether it be reflected as coming from some common source or depository of light in the heavens. The origin and precise character of light will be the last discovery of science, if indeed it be ever made. Should natural philosophers succeed in identifying light, electricity, magnetism, and heat, as being *the same in principle, or as different modifications of the same pervading principle of nature,* then beyond a doubt another fact will be established: that is, that light, like heat, may be *latent*—that is, the principle may be existent and present without being, what we regard as the essential characteristic of light, *visible.* Its being visible may depend on certain modifications of other principles, with which we are totally unacquainted. The man whose sight is obstructed by the film called *cataract,* sees no light; but when the cataract is removed the light is visible. In this instance we know the cause. When the sun goes down and night comes on, we think we know that the sun gave light, and darkness comes because that light is obscured. But even if this be true, we know not whether the sun really gives the light, or whence it comes, or what is its elementary character. This is still a mysterious question. Philosophy has approached it very nearly, and doubtless some further discoveries are to be made.

ries of civilization, and the number of ideas included within the circumference of human thought. This grew out of the intimate connection between astronomy and geography. That connection is founded on the fact, that it is astronomy which teaches and demonstrates that the earth is a globe. It was from the properties of a globe in form and matter as thus demonstrated, was deduced the true idea of its nature and magnitude; it was this idea which gave courage to adventure, success to discovery, extension to commerce, dominion to power, resources to art, and, by the colonization of before unknown lands, *food* to unnumbered millions of the human race in the past, and unborn generations in the future! Why was it that to Thebes, and Rome, and Athens, clouds and darkness rested on two-thirds the surface of our earth? Could not the art which built the pyramids, the glory which flourished in the house of the Cæsars, nor that inventive genius which sparkled out from the hills of Attica, open up to the eyes of wondering men the sealed mystery of the ocean? Why was it that the Atlantic and the Pacific, with their embosomed continents and their ten thousand islands, were unknown to all classic fame? Why was it the Greeks talked of their lost Atlantis, but never found it? This grand fact of history can only be accounted for by the other fact, that the most intelligent men of science, even in the Augustan age, were so ignorant of the true form and magnitude of the earth and its astronomical relations to the face of the heavens, that curiosity remained unexcited, and no courage was given to the hopes of discovery. The Hindoo sacred books considered the foundation of the earth as something very much like a great pancake, out of which grew up, in some unaccountable manner, our land and its inhabitants! The Greeks, prior to the time of Ptolemy, viewed the habitable world as a circular plane, surrounded by the *River Ocean.* This idea Herodotus, the historian and traveller, contradicted by his own observations. In the trial of Anaximander, one of the earliest of the Greek astronomers, certain rough maps and nautical charts were made, by which the early Greek colonies established themselves in the islands of the Mediterranean. In this manner the progress of geography became nearly identical with the progress of astronomy.

In the Augustan age they had acquired the idea that the earth was a *globe;* but that idea was in its rude state. Aristotle proved that fact, by referring to the circular shadow projected by the earth on the moon in an eclipse. He proceeded to calculate from astronomical observations its figure and magnitude. The world had then, however, but a small body of scientific men, and it had no art of printing. Such ideas and demonstrations, therefore, made but slow progress; accordingly, by the mass of mankind this idea was not imbibed or believed at all. Subsequent to this period for many ages, science made no progress. It was enough that in the disorders and convulsions succeeding the fall of Rome it found any place of refuge ; it was enough that, like the light of a dark lantern, it could send its rays in any one direction through the almost impervious atmosphere around.

It was in consequence of this condition of society that the knowledge of the earth's sphericity remained for so long a period unimproved. It was a thousand years after the fall of Rome that the greatest of geographical discoveries was founded on the astronomical discovery that the earth was a sphere. It was when Copernicus was a young man, but before the publication of his works, that Columbus, by the direct conclusions of scientific reasoning, discovered America. It is true that Columbus had the compass (another discovery in navigation due to astronomy), but it was not the compass which induced the reasoning, in the pursuit of which he reached the shores of the western continent.

He argued, that the earth being a sphere, by sailing continually in one direction, he must eventually circumnavigate it. He argued also, that as the known land occupied but a small portion of the known surface of the globe, the equilibrium of matter, and the purposes for which the earth was formed, required there should be other lands in the depths of the Western Ocean. This was as legitimate a conclusion from the astronomical discovery and demonstration that the earth was a sphere, as any corollary is from any theorem.

Thus there is a complete sequence of ideas and

conclusions from the first demonstration deduced from astronomical observations that the earth was a globe, down to the final discovery of a new continent in the Atlantic Ocean. Who can estimate the value and the vast moral consequences of this continent, thus discovered, to the whole future life, dignity, and destiny of the human race!

To the eye of science, of Christian civilization, and of progressive humanity, it has emerged from the bosom of the seas perfectly and absolutely a new world; to the advancing generation of men in Europe and Asia, crowded in dense masses upon the old-settled portions of the earth, it acts as a new creation, inviting them to new conquests in the field of labor, to new investigations by the human mind, and to fresh hopes in the pursuit of happiness.

ASTRONOMY DETERMINES PLACE ON THE EARTH.

Astronomy has not only discovered new continents, but it has determined the *relations* of each spot on the earth to every other spot. In one word, it has enabled us to determine *where* any one place is, relatively to the whole surface of the globe. ***How***, without such knowledge, could the position of any town or place ever be described? The lines of latitude and longitude are the only means by which the locality of any spot on earth can be determined with any accuracy: they are the true basis of all other subdivisions. These lines are purely astronomical;

they determine place by mathematical conclusions drawn from astronomical observations. Thus, a *point* is fixed *relatively* only by the intersection of two lines: if we knew the position of one of these lines, and did not know that of the other, we should know that the point to be ascertained was in the known line, but *where* in that line we should not know. That point, however, which is at the intersection of two lines is palpably fixed, because it could not move without leaving that intersection. If one of these lines, then, be a line of latitude, and the other a line of longitude, it fixes the relative position of that place on the surface of the earth. This is what gives certainty to place on our maps, and gives a corresponding certainty to it in our minds.

To do this so that the idea of that place should forever remain fixed with accuracy in our descriptions of the earth, and not change with changing generations, was necessary to the truth of history and the durability of human records. It is done by taking as the basis of one of these measures, a line which is permanently fixed on the earth, by the very mechanism of the celestial universe. This line is the equator, or the intersection of the earth's surface with a plane, passing through its centre perpendicular to the axis of revolution. The revolution of the earth on its axis, then, determines the equator, and the distance of a place from the equator gives us the latitude.

The longitude is dependent on the same principles; it is the distance measured on the earth's surface between two planes passing through the axis of the earth. These two planes, then, one passing through the axis of the earth, and the other perpendicular to it, are both dependent on that axis of revolution for existence. Latitude is measured from one, and longitude from the other: these two determine place. Thus the exact relation, distance, and geographical position of every spot on earth is fixed, so that it will remain durably impressed on the pages of history, the lines of a chart, and the memory of the human intellect. This result is deduced from the axis of the earth.

This again depends on the revolutions of the earth; and these revolutions are observed and accurately demonstrated by astronomical science.

Nor is this all. The longitude, or difference between two meridians, is ascertained by the most vigilant and minute observation of celestial phenomena. To do this accurately, it is necessary to observe the eclipses of the moon, the eclipses of Jupiter's satellites, or the transit of some planet.

Thus does astronomy minister directly to one of the most common and useful branches of knowledge; thus does it determine distance and locality; thus does it make clear and beautiful charts of lands, seas, and islands, which, without it, would have existed in our minds only in a wild waste of confusion. No accurate measurement of lands, no true relations of distances, no correct charts exist, which owe not their accuracy and their being to those celestial orbs whose rays do not more surely descend upon matter, than does their mechanism give knowledge, suggestion, and aliment to the mind of the observer.

ASTRONOMY DETERMINES THE MAGNITUDE OF THE GLOBE.

Again: astronomy not only determines the relation of places to one another, but it has ascertained the exact *magnitude* of the globe itself—the limit of space assigned to mortal man in his abode on earth. By successive measurements of a degree on the surface of the earth, and its relation to the corresponding one of a meridian—measurements made by Picard, and various other astronomers—the precise diameter of the earth was calculated, and the quantity of its surface. Nor was this all: by the calculations of various arcs of circles on the earth, it was revealed that our globe was not precisely a sphere, but was what, in the language of mathematics, is called an *oblate spheroid;* that is, a sphere flattened at the poles.

This again gave rise to deep investigations as to the laws of gravitation, by which it is proved that the attraction is less at the equator than the poles, and that the earth could not be a homogeneous mass. By a succession of profound calculations, based on astronomical observations, was thus discovered and proved the laws which govern the irregularity of a sphere in motion, the magnitude of its surface, and the density of its mass.

ASTRONOMY DETERMINES THE MEASURE OF LANDS, AND IS THE BASIS OF THE PUBLIC SURVEYS.

After having determined the relations of *place* on the surface of the earth, and the quantity of that surface in the aggregate, there still remained a problem of geographical relations to be determined by astronomy, whose results entered into the business of every-day life. It was one of vast practical utility, and to no country more so than to that in which we live. That problem was, to give *exact measurement and precise locality* to those pieces of land distributed by legal title among the individuals of each particular nation. The solution of this problem has a direct and immediate value; it gives accuracy to the description of lands, and stability to the tenure of legal titles. In no part of the world has this been done with more strict method, with more harmony of parts, or with more symmetry of proportion, than in the survey of the public domain in the Northwestern Territory of the United States. The value of that survey to the public interests, the simplicity of its arrangements, and its immediate connection with the scientific history of the West, make it especially proper that I should make a brief statement of the astronomical survey of the northwestern states.

It was in May, 1785, now sixty-five years since, Congress adopted by law the plan of laying out the public lands *in six miles square, by rectangular co-ordinates*. In June, 1787, they passed the ordinance for the government of the Northwestern Territory. So it is the northwestern states which have been the chief theatre for the practical development of that system.

This ordinance for the division of the public lands, one of the most important in the history of the United States, was not the work of a moment, or adopted on slight consideration. It was wisely planned, and deliberately considered. It was before Congress, and fully debated during three months. In the debates, a motion was made to strike out the clause relating to this mode of surveying and subdividing lands, and the motion received the support of four states. This plan was, therefore, an act of deliberate wisdom.*

---

* The following brief history of the origin of the present admirable system of land surveys, adopted by the United States government, would be out of place here, but that it is a part of the history of the country very little known, and which reflects honor on the men of science, and the education of this country during the last generation.

The ordinance for the sale and distribution of lands in the Western Territory, preceded the ordinance of 1787, for the government of the Northwestern Territory, and was in fact the *first great movement* made after the cession of Virginia, for the future settlement of the northwestern states. A brief history of this ordinance is not altogether disconnected from the subject of Astronomy.

March 4, 1785, "An Ordinance for ascertaining the mode of locating and disposing of lands in the Western Territory," was read the first time in Congress.

March 16, it was referred to a committee of one member from each state. This committee consisted of Mr. Long, Mr. King, Mr. Howell, Mr. Johnson, Mr. R. R. Livingston, Mr. Stewart, Mr. Gardner, Mr. J. Henry, Mr. Grayson, Mr. Williamson, Mr. Bull, and Mr. Houston.

The connection of this mode of surveying with astronomy is obvious. An exact meridian line for

---

April 14, this committee reported an ordinance for "ascertaining a mode of disposing of lands in the Western Territory."

April 20, 21, 22, 23, 26, this ordinance was discussed. On the 26th, a motion was made by Mr. Grayson, to recommit the ordinance, which failed.

April 27 and 28, the ordinance was further discussed.

May 2, 3, 4, 5, and 6, various motions were made as to the mode of offering the lands for sale, and they were debated.

May 19th, the ordinance was again taken up, and on the 20th of May, 1785, it was finally passed, having been amply debated during nearly three months. This ordinance contains the following paragraphs:

1. The surveyors, as they are respectively qualified, shall proceed to divide the said territory in *townships of six miles square, by lines running due North and South, and others crossing these at right angles*, as near as may be, &c., &c.

2. The plats of townships, respectively, shall be marked by *subdivisions into lots of one mile square, or* 640 *acres, in the same direction as the external lines, and numbered from* 1 *to* 36, &c.

The first of these, it will be observed, is the system of *rectangular co-ordinates.* The second is the system of *sections*, as the land is now sold by.

This system, however, was not universally approved of, because its tendency was to delay the sales of public lands till they could be correctly measured, and the title perfectly ascertained. By this very procedure, so favorable to the people generally, and to the public prosperity, *speculation* in land warrants, and the irregular surveys and locations afterwards adopted in Kentucky and in Virginia lands, was prevented.

In the Madison papers, vol. 2, pages 637 to 639, Mr. Madison says, that the Eastern States favored the plan adopted, while the southern people were for "indiscriminate locations." These indiscriminate locations were precisely the evil which was sought to be avoided. In any given spot is determined by astronomical observation. Through this spot is drawn another line at right angles. This last line is parallel to the equator, because that also is perpendicular to the meridian. Here, then, we have two fixed astronomical lines at right angles to each other. The first of these is the meridian line, and the second is called the base line. They make the two standard lines from which all others in the survey proceed. From these, lines are run, at any required distance, by the common compass. The intersections of these lines determine the locality of every spot in the immense surface covered by the northwestern states. The result is, that the whole country is divided into squares of any size which the government or the holders of lands may choose.

In carrying out this plan, it was not enough to declare, as in the ordinance of 1785, that the lands should be surveyed in certain described squares of townships and sections. It was required that astronomy should be called in to determine the standard lines, and fix, with permanency and certainty, the true meridians, and the latitudes of certain principal

---

Kentucky they have occasioned endless litigation, while the lands of Ohio and Indiana, surveyed by the United States, have been comparatively without any legal difficulty.

At the period Mr. Madison wrote (1787), about six hundred thousand acres of the public lands had been surveyed under the ordinance of May, 1785.

points. In the year 1803, the late Colonel Jared Mansfield was appointed Surveyor-General of the northwestern states and territories, by President Jefferson. He was not appointed for the purpose of practical surveys, as they are now carried on, but for the purpose of determining astronomically certain lines of latitude, and the principal meridians on which the surveys were thereafter to proceed, and in fact have ever since proceeded, with precision and scientific exactitude.*

* In Niles' Register, volume 16, page 363, is a letter of Mr. J. Meigs, the Commissioner of the Land-Office, in which he describes the *principal meridians* that were run by the Surveyor-General, on which to base *systems* of surveys. *The first principal meridian* passed through the mouth of the Great Miami, and extended to the northern boundary of the United States.

The *second principal meridian* commences at a point five miles southwest of the confluence of *Little Blue River* with the Ohio, and extends to the northern boundary of the United States. At thirty miles from its commencement it is crossed bythe base line, a parallel to the equator.

The *third principal meridian* commences at the confluence of the Ohio and the Mississippi.

There are other meridians surveyed since. Mr. Meigs says, that "the principles of this system have governed the public surveys in Alabama, Mississippi, and Louisiana, and will unquestionably be adhered to until the public surveys shall reach *Astoria*, at the mouth of Columbia River, in longitude 48 degrees west of the capital."

In volume 12, page 97, of Niles' Register, will be found another letter from Mr. Meigs, in which this species of surveys is particularly described. In the same volume, page 407, Mr. Meigs thus speaks of the *authorship* of what may be called the ASTRONOMICAL SYSTEM OF SURVEYING; (for the reader will observe, it was one thing to divide

Official documents show that astronomical observations were a part of the duties of the surveyor-general in that early settlement of the Ohio valley. He was directed, if possible, to determine the southern extremity of Lake Michigan, the western extremity of Lake Erie, the confluence of the Ohio with the Mississippi, and the western boundary of the Connecticut Reserve. For this purpose astronomical instruments were necessary. Mr. Jefferson, who was a warm friend of science, directed the purchase out of the *contingent fund* of the President of a transit instrument, a telescope, an astronomical clock, and a sextant.* They arrived in Cincinnati in 1805 or 6,

---

the country into squares of townships and sections, and another to base that system upon *astronomical lines accurately determined:*) "A plan of survey was therefore devised by that valuable officer, Colonel Mansfield, the then Surveyor-General of the United States, which not only avoided this perplexity and comparison, but remedied the defects of the old system, which experience and reflection had pointed out to be considerable. His plan is the same that is described in my last (see Niles' Register, vol. 12, page 97), and is the same that is pursued in all the public surveys since executed under the direction of the Surveyor-General."

* A portion of these instruments are now removed to West Point, and placed in the philosophical department of that institution. They were removed after the appointment of Col. Mansfield as professor of philosophy. By means of the government instruments, his house near was from 1806 to 1812 a real observatory. Very recently the Cincinnati Observatory has been founded, of which Professsor Mitchel is the director. Celestial observations are there recorded, by means of magnetical machinery invented by him, with a rapidity unknown, I believe, to any other observatory.

were placed in the house of the surveyor-general, and constituted, as I believe, the first real observatory erected west of the Alleghany Mountains.

There, during a series of years, numerous and interesting astronomical observations were made. The orbit of the comet of 1807 was calculated and recorded in the transactions of the Connecticut Academy of Arts and Science: eclipses of various kinds observed, the longitude determined, and all other observations made which the nature of the instruments and the early settlement and rude state of the country would allow.

The meridian first surveyed with scientific accuracy was called the *second principal meridian*, and is that which commences at the confluence of Little Blue River with the Ohio, in the state of Indiana. This meridian is continued to the northern boundary of the United States, in its whole length, 580 miles. By this meridian and the principal base line at right angles to it, nearly the whole state of Indiana and a portion of Illinois were surveyed.

From the form of the earth meridian lines approximate, and in a great length of line that approximation would throw the townships which were intended to be squares into parallelograms. Hence, in surveying the public lands, a new base line, a perpendicular to the meridian, was run at intervals of thirty miles, and the errors of the meridian corrected.

This may be called the *astronomical system of*

surveying. The whole subdivision of lands, surveys in the northwest states, and those west of the Mississippi, with very little exception, is made in this manner, and depends on mathematical lines connected by astronomical observations. It is not merely a beautiful plan, but it is the best possible security to titles, and the surest prevention of litigation. In reference to this great utility of scientific surveys, Mr. Meigs, Commissioner of the Land-Office, remarked, that " man brings the heavens to the earth for his convenience. A few geographical positions on the map of the public surveys being determined by astronomical observations, it is with little difficulty that the latitude and longitude of every farm, and of every log hut and court-house, may be ascertained with precision."

While science was thus introducing civilization into the bosom of the forest, that forest covered nearly all the vast extent of the western plains. From the Miami to the Wabash was an uninterrupted wilderness. The face of the white man was more rarely seen than the fiery eyes of the implacable panther. The red man filled the woods with his war-cry. To him science had never revealed the mysteries of nature—

" ———— ne'er taught to stray
Far as the solar walk or milky-way."

To him celestial phenomena were the terrors of superstition. In the sun eclipsed he beheld the funeral pall of the earth; in the distant comet, the messenger of destruction; and in shooting-stars, the arrows of heaven! The warrior of a hundred battles bowed himself to the earth, and his red face grew pale with fear. The scene is changed. But a single generation has elapsed, yet the savage and the panther have alike disappeared. Civilization has built rich cities on the site of the wigwam and the hut. The dark ignorance of savage life is gone, and now science comes to erect her temples on our verdure-crowned hills.

The frown, once severely placed upon the brow of nature, is removed. The stars no longer shoot terrors across the horizon: the sun no longer veils his face in anger. *We* stand upon the vantage-ground of *knowledge*. We look to the firmament as upon the face of a friend, whose countenance is known. We trace the lines of his features: we go back to his great original. Light smiles out from every wandering orb, and eternal beauty rests on all the works of God.

I have now shown that astronomy, directly or indirectly, has produced vast practical consequences to other sciences, to knowledge, and to business. It has given us all our knowledge of time: it has taught us the sphericity and magnitude of the earth: it has furnished us with the only mode of accurately determining place: it has given us the only exact measurement of lands: it has given us the reasoning by which new continents were discovered in the bosom of the mighty deep. It has done more. It has dissected the sunbeams; converged them in lenses, and applied them through the telescope, by the hands of Galileo, of Newton, of Herschel, and now of Rosse, so that the realities of vision exceed the boundaries of imagination, and fancy herself, so long a wanderer wild, is startled at the leap which science calls her to make!

INFLUENCE OF ASTRONOMY ON THE HUMAN MIND.

Our next inquiry is, what effect has the study of astronomy produced by its direct action on the human mind? There are two modes by which the mind is improved by the study of science. The *first* is by increasing the quantity of its actual knowledge; the *second* is by extending the *range* of its inquiries, the *elevation* of its thoughts, and the *magnitude* of its conceptions. For it is obvious to any observer of intellectual action, that two minds may have nearly the same amount of acquisition, and about the same energy for all common affairs, and yet one may exceed the other a thousand-fold in the circumference of the sphere of its intellectual views. The one is limited by the horizon of things just around him—the other, disciplined by science, taught the powers of nature, and aided by a vigorous imagination, ascends from hill to hill, from mountain top to mountain top, till not a summit interrupts his vision from border to border of the physical universe.

In this grand result of added knowledge on the one hand, and of increased circumference and sublimity of human conceptions on the other, no science has equalled astronomy. Many of the discoveries made in consequence of astronomical observations I have already enumerated. There is, however, another extensive group of discoveries which were even more directly the consequences of astronomical inquiries.

These are the instruments, the means, and the mathematical analysis by which the problems of the celestial phenomena were solved. Before the time of Galileo, the means of observing the heavenly bodies were scarcely better than the smoked glass used by boys to look at eclipses. One of the greatest discoveries in mechanical knowledge produced by astronomy was that of the telescope. In the hands of Galileo, and while yet in its rude state, the surface of the moon, the forms of the planets and their satellites, were perfectly observed. Then commenced the unfolding of that vast field of starry orbs which has continued its development from Galileo to Herschel, and from Herschel to Struve and Rosse. The telescope was followed by the microscope, the pendulum clock, and various other mechanical inventions applied to astronomy. Step by step the mechanics of science were enlarged and improved by that very theoretical research whose inquiries they were destined to aid and advance.

Then came the discovery of the composition of light, of which it has been aptly said, that "Newton untwisted all the shining robe of day, and made known the texture of that magic garment which the God of nature has kindly spread over the surface of the visible world."* Great as were his other discoveries—his decomposition and recomposition of light remains the most brilliant gem in the earthly crown of Newton.

Beautiful and almost incomparable as these visions into the mysteries of nature were, abstract mathematics considered in regard to itself was to receive a greater than either. This was the introduction of the geometry of infinites; the mathematical analysis now known as the Calculus, or Fluxions. This is the Infinitesimal Analysis, and is that peculiar calculation which determines the laws of curve lines. It was the instrument invented by Newton, previous to his astronomical demonstrations, and used by him, La Place, and others, in calculating to their utmost limits the powers and forces involved in the mechanics of the planetary system. Then the domain of mathematical science was extended in every direction. Professor Playfair said that "these problems are connected with the highest attainments of wisdom, and the greatest exertions of power. They seem like so

* Playfair's Discourse.

many immovable columns erected in the infinity of space, to mark the eternal boundary which separates the regions of possibility and impossibility from one another."

Such were some of the additions to knowledge made in the search after the mere *means and instruments* by which the astronomer should ascend the stairway of the visible creation, enter the midst of its mechanical machinery, and direct the chariot of science through the throng of revolving worlds!

But these newly discovered elements of knowledge —various, beautiful, and wonderful as they are—were but a part, and the smallest part, of the effects produced upon the human mind by the pursuit of astronomy. Beattie, in his Essay on Truth, says, that the mind partakes of the character of the natural scenery by which it is surrounded. The mountaineer is the child of liberty; and virtue dwells amidst the pure air of his lofty hills. If such be the effect of natural scenery on the surface of the earth, what must be the sublime conceptions of him who, even in imagination, passes behind this earthly atmosphere, ascends the beams of the evening star, reaches the zenith of the firmament—

> " ———— riding sublime
> Upon the seraph wings of ecstasy,
> The secrets of the skies to spy!"

It was a sublime idea to conceive the infinitesimal analysis. It was a vision, exceeding all the bounds of poetry, to take the rainbow colors from the white light of the sun, to recompose them again, and make their colors resume the transparent beams whence they were taken ; but these were inferior acts in the drama of science, to that which finally solved the problem of the planetary system, and which accounted for all its movements, its relations, its irregularities, and its phenomena.

THE PROBLEM OF THE CELESTIAL BODIES.

In order to know what the human mind has accomplished in this respect, we must state, and understand, if possible, the exact problem which was presented for its solution in the phenomena of the celestial bodies. It involves no technical terms, but may be understood by a statement of common facts, and of what reason obviously requires to solve those facts.

In the sixteenth century, the era of Tycho Brahe, the celestial phenomena to be accounted for were these :—*it was known* the earth was a *globe,* and hung in indefinite space ; *it was known* that in the firmament around it were innumerable other globes of light: they too were hung in indefinite space. Between all these globes, or between any two of them, there was no communication. Some appeared to be in motion, and some appeared to be stationary. Man was placed on the surface of one of this host of globes; the only element common to him with them, was light—the only fact in their constitution which could be observed, was motion. Even this motion deceived him, for its appearance was often contrary to its reality.

These were the facts, and no other aid was to be had than what reason could furnish. These distant bodies were intangible to human hands, unapproachable by any means of conveyance, immeasurable by any instrument. There was no matter in their composition to be analyzed; no airy vessel which should carry tidings, like electro-magnetism, on the wings of thought. The mind alone was to furnish all that could hereafter be known of these unknown worlds. It was a draft on the immortal spirit, to go where only spirits could go!

The problem which these facts required man to solve, if it could be solved, was this:—

1. That he should invent and use such mechanical instruments as would observe the minute motions of these distant bodies, and measure accurately the element of time or the relations of motions, the only one which could be calculated.

2. Next, it was required that he should calculate from these relative motions observed in space, the figures, or trace, which these bodies made in the firmament.

3. Thirdly, it was required that he should discover and demonstrate the laws of that motion by which a body in space would describe that figure; and that

he should also discover what kind of compound forces would move a body in that curve.

4. It was next required that he should discover some general force or attraction of universal nature, which should keep all these bodies in their several relations to each other, and, combined with the original impulse, keep them in the curves in which they actually move; and that he should demonstrate this to the satisfaction of every reasoning mind.

5. When this was done, it was required that the theory of planetary motion and attraction, thus proposed and demonstrated, abstractly, should in actual observation account for all the motions, all the phenomena, all the irregularities, the most minute or the most distant, which then occurred, or hereafter should occur, in the history of the celestial mechanics. It must leave not one unsolved fact in all the motions and attractions of the heavenly bodies.

6. Lastly, it was required that, by the knowledge thus developed, the astronomer should become a prophet, and predict the future evolutions of the heavenly bodies; tell when the planets should cast their shadows upon each other; when their orbits would intersect; when the wandering orb should return from its mission to unknown and unvisited worlds; and thus, when the mortal body shall long have been returned to the dust, the immortal spirit should record its glorious victories, and fasten its memory on the dial-plate of creation!

This was the all-comprehensive, apparently impossible problem presented to the inventive genius of science; this was the problem which, if the human mind *could* solve, it might be said to have demonstrated its own immortal powers, and to have taken its sublime flight victorious over time and space. It required more of mathematics than all the philosophers had learned, more of optics than the world had discovered, and more of chemistry and mechanics than all the artisans had then attained; yet this problem *was solved*—solved in a little more than a century, chiefly by three minds. One was Galileo, who commenced the discoveries made by the telescope; another was Kepler, whose Three Laws of Motion, written without name, date, place, or circumstance, constitutes the simple and sublime epitaph on his monument; and the other Newton, whose theory of gravitation gave form, symmetry, beauty, and truth to all the discoveries preceding him.

The effect of these vast achievements on the human mind was not confined to the philosophers and savans who pursued the walks of astronomy and mathematics; it was not confined to the solitary student at the midnight lamp: it announced new and extraordinary facts to every intelligent mind in the civilized world; it disclosed *means* by which these facts were attained, exceeding any thing the human understanding had ever conceived of the powers of abstraction and the acuteness of reasoning. It made this power of abstraction and this acuteness of reason common to all instructed intellects; it gave the sublime thoughts and demonstrations of Newton to every pupil in a college-hall; it invited them to enter the chambers of the skies; to draw aside the curtain of the firmament; to walk with Galileo through its star-paved halls, and read with Newton the character of its history, so dim, so dark, so mysterious, and so inscrutable to patriarchs and prophets, to Greeks and Romans. This was the vast acquisition, the sublime flight which astronomy gave to the human mind.

THE STUDENT OF ASTRONOMY STUDYING THE HEAVENS.

And now, in this later day, when all lights of former days concentrate upon us, let the young student of science, with the Bible in one hand, and the brief volumes which record the discoveries of Kepler and Newton in the other, commence his walk through the heavens. He dissects the light; converges its rays in the telescope; and ascends with multiplied power of sight beyond the ring of Saturn, beyond Orion and the Pleiades; he passes in thought round the circle of the sun; ascends the slanting beam of some wandering comet; penetrates the dim atmosphere of the milky-way, and wonders to find each particle a living star! Again he beholds some new meteor emerging from the firmament, assuming new colors, changing them like chameleon hues, and again disappearing from sight! He examines the clustered nebulæ; separates them into single orbs, and, returning to the narrow closet in which his body is placed, writes all these mysterious phenomena down in his catalogue of human knowledge!

He ascends again; passes sun, stars, and nebulæ, till, standing on the verge of distant creation, he sees with the eye of the spirit this whole system of ours, sun, planets, and satellites,

> "hanging in a golden chain,
> This pendent world, in bigness as a star
> Of smallest magnitude."

He has begun with the earliest discoveries of astronomy; he has ascended by a series of successive elevations: each advance has been but a platform by which to ascend the next. The summit has still faded before him and still allured him on, till what seemed once the highest flight of the human mind is now but a single step in its progress!

This ascent of physical science through the material world from planet to planet, sun to sun, and star to star, has been but the *type* of the ascending flight of the human mind through the realms of knowledge. It is the conquest of spirit over matter: the spirit has gone forth, unrestrained by the attractions of earth, unlimited by the passage of time, undaunted by the vacuity of space, chainless as the mountain winds, free as the beams of morning light!

And now, when the student stands in his spiritual presence on the verge of this creation, there is something in his soul which moves him to inquire, where is the Spirit which has placed this immeasurable creation in this infinitude of space? where is the centre of these orbs and their motions? what hand sustains them in the emptiness of space? This student sees them attracting one another, and sustaining the motions of one another, as they wheel through the void immense; but what upholds in that immense this entire sidereal heavens?

He feels that he has sent his own spirit forth through created worlds a conqueror over matter; and he feels that nothing less than the power of an Infinite Spirit is equal to the task of upholding them in that infinity of nothingness, to whose extent neither human language nor human imagination can reach.

He hears the wild Indian speak of the Great Spirit beyond the hills; he hears the Assyrian worship him before the altar-fires of Baal; he hears the glorious harp of Homer chanting the Jupiter of Mount Olympus; he feels that the Infinite Spirit is confined neither to Indian hills, nor Grecian mountains, nor Baal fires. He turns to that Bible which is in his hand as he takes his walk through the material universe, and reads of Him who bowed the heavens and came down. No more he walks solitary in gloomy doubt through the jewelled halls of the skies; no more he turns to the cloudy Jupiter of the Greek Olympus; no more he finds pendent worlds hung centreless in the infinitude of space! He finds the golden centre in Him who is the Creator of nature, and the Redeemer of man; in Him who alone is immutable amidst the mutable things of a finite world!

He hears the declaration of St. James, that in the

Father of Lights, whether they be in the world of matter or of mind, there is no parallax of light, no shadow of change; and he feels that he can say with Spenser, in the Fairy Queen:

> "When I bethink me on that speech whylear,
> Of mutability,—and well it weigh;
> Me seems, that though she all unworthy were
> Of the heaven's rule; yet very sooth to say,
> In all things else she bears the greatest sway.
> *   *   *   *   *
> Then 'gin I think   *   *   *
> Of that same time when no more change shall be,
> But steadfast rest of all things, firmly stay'd
> Upon the pillars of eternity,
> That is contrayr to mutability:
> For all that moveth doth in change delight,
> But thenceforth all shall rest eternally
> With him that is the God of Sabaoth hight."

CHAPTER VIII.

THE UTILITY OF HISTORY.

"Now all these things happened unto them for ensamples; and they are written for our admonition, upon whom the ends of the world are come."—1 *Cor.* ch. x.

"History is philosophy teaching by example."—*Bolingbroke.*

The definition by Bolingbroke has received the assent of society, by its universal reception without denial. But history is extended even beyond that definition. As time advances, the laws of social growth and decay begin to assume the regularity of a science; and the divine government is developed in the same order and uniformity, in human action, as in the movements of the material bodies.

Science, too, has extended this instruction, by example, much beyond the boundaries of mere human transactions. It has shown us *history in every thing*. The tree, it is said, records its own age by the successive strata of its growth. The stars also measure the spaces of time, and there is an astronomical history which goes back to the morning of creation. The very elements and affinities of matter have undergone changes, and there is a record of them written on the features of nature. The fountains of the great deep have been broken up—islands have been cast up by fire out of its waters, and the memorials of its secret history scattered on the mountain tops. Chemical agencies have been employed, till the living animal and the decaying wood, petrified in stone, preserved in caverns, or imbedded in rocks, remain, and shall forever remain, historical monuments to the changes wrought by Almighty power, as well as to the *unchanging* truth of his word.

But *man* is at last the chief subject of history; for *his* restoration to a lost estate were the fountains of nature broken up, and that very registry of time, kept by the bright orbs of heaven, is a ministering agent to the record of human events.

Yet upon all this history of man, mutability, apparently the most wayward and destructive, is written with a pen of iron. Philosophy, viewing it as a *dis-*

connected series, has made little out of it; and the good and the wise have turned with sorrow from what seemed a dark picture of depravity.

While, however, there rests this apparent uncertainty on the great mass of human history, there stands out the fact, that there is no evidence of uncertainty found in the *relations* of the social system. Human nature has fixed principles, and when we observe it in society around us, we never doubt that the same effects will follow the same causes: and the legislator, as the author of the spirit of laws, never fails to derive lessons of instruction from the relations of institutions to society, and of manners to institutions. Hence it is only when we view events *without* principles that history becomes confused, and uncertainty rests upon its results. We conclude, then, that as human nature has a constitution, and as the physical world has laws, so the social system has not moved on through ages of various being, under organized forms, without principles proper to itself, and without acknowledging the relation of cause and effect.

To trace out these principles, and to establish this immutable connection of cause and effect, as they have been developed in the successive modes of human society, constitutes what should properly be called, the science of history.

1. Our *first object*, now, is to show what this science of history *is;*

2. And our *second*, to show its *uses*.

WHAT THE SCIENCE OF HISTORY IS.

Science is *systematized truth.** It is built up by three several processes. 1st. The observation of facts. 2d. The deduction of principles from the continuity and uniformity of facts. 3d. The classification of these principles into systems of *laws* having reference to some common object. *Facts* are first observed; next, it is observed that a certain class of facts or phenomena always occur under a *fixed condition* of things; this condition being observed, it is proved by experience or demonstration, and henceforth set down as an immutable principle: new facts are observed, and new principles deduced, as time and observation extend: at length these principles are classified, and a *system* is formed, based upon a common class of objects, which takes its form as a *science.* There is first the *particular facts;* next the general fact, which constitutes the *principle;* and lastly, a *system of truths.*

In this manner are all sciences begun and finished; so geometry was built up in Grecian antiquity; so chemistry has been formed within the last two centuries; so political economy is now forming; and so history, to be valuable as knowledge, must be a system of principles drawn from the phenomena of social life, observed and recorded during accumulated ages.

---

* For a more extended definition of science, see chapter 5th.

To know what the system of truths is, which is asserted and illustrated by history, we must note the fact that it comprehends the whole progression of the human race, physical and intellectual. Indeed, the very universality of its topics has caused its uncertainty, and will cause it to be the last subject which philosophy brings into the circle of the sciences, and reduces, as it has done more tangible things, into the simplicity of demonstrative systems. History has usually been regarded as relating to nations or eras, in the entirety of their multifarious transactions; but this is not the philosophy of history, and does not exhibit the progress of mankind at any period of its existence. It fixes the eye upon the tumults of human passion, as the mariner looks out in the storm upon the billows of the ocean cast up by the tempest, but leaves out of view that distant influence which rolls a tide through the affairs of men, as it does through the waters of the deep: and it contemplates man from wrong points of view; for, while twenty dynasties have risen and fallen, and a thousand battles been fought without changing even a boundary, some poor journeyman has invented the art of printing; some Florentine merchant has poured the dews of wealth upon the parched plants of literature; some Descartes has improved the mathematical analysis; or some Whitney introduced a new staple into the resources of nations. Thus the great moving causes of social progress lie beyond the mass of confused events, and must be sought for in the depths of society, as the diver goes through turbid waters to bring up the pearl of the ocean.

Again: when we consider eras and nations with respect to outward events, or partial standards, we arrive at *wrong results*. Thus while the human race has been steadily improving, it is notorious that the majority of nations and of persons, and those, too, frequently the most brilliant in the opinion of mankind, have been retrograding. It was during the height of the Roman empire, while history spoke through

> Tully's voice, and Virgil's lay,
> And Livy's pictured page—

that corruption—dark, fetid, and malignant, as painted by Juvenal—was already hurrying her backwards in the tide of time. Yet it was at that same hour, when admiration was fixed upon the eagles of Rome, that the primitive Christian—patient, faithful, and suffering—by prayer and by faith, struggled against adverse waves to save the lamp of life: and he did save it; and it became the light of nations when the darkness of destruction had gathered over those eagles of Rome. It was also during the ignorance of the middle ages, when the historian found nothing but lamentations for the people of Europe, that the wild Arabian became the cultivator of genius and learning; arts, sciences, and the muses clustered around the standard of the false prophet, and Medina presented the most brilliant scenes of the modern world.

It is not then by contemplating any one nation, or any one period of time, or the general events of history, the change of dynasties, or the splendor of arms, that we can discern the chain of cause and effect which, extending from the garden of Eden to the last men, has brightened as it lengthened, and, ascending link by link, has carried forward the human mind from conquest to conquest. This relation of cause and effect, though always connected *with,* is never dependent upon persons, nations, or events. Its only dependence is the development of truth. It sometimes leaves one nation to give glory to another: it leaves Charlemagne to dwell with Friar Bacon; quits the Delta of the Nile to pour splendor over the barren hills of Attica, and the plains of Chaldea to illustrate an island of the ocean. The science of history then is the development of the human mind, as is demonstrated by the experience of mankind. Its duty is to state that development, as it is exhibited in the various forms of civilization, and to investigate the causes by which its progress has been advanced or retarded. It is most evident that this is a study which could have no existence in the early ages of the world, because history had not then been written, or if written, could not have contained a thousand branches of knowledge and forms of society, which have been the result of invention, discovery, experience, and increased population in modern times.

It is also most evident that its importance has increased with the increase of experience and of knowledge. The power of knowledge is a multiplying power, and as society advances the problems of history are solved with tenfold readiness. Multitudes of questions might have been asked in Egypt or Greece upon the results of certain states of society which time had not enabled them to answer, but which the student now looks upon as among the certainties of knowledge. These questions are constantly solving, and leaving less for solution. The social sciences are thus rapidly accumulating, acquiring stability, system, and certainty.*

THE USES OF HISTORY.

Our next object is to show some of the *uses* of the study of history.

---

* The greatest works which distinguished the last two centuries (not on physical sciences), were the foundation of certain branches of social science; for example, *Montesquieu's Spirit of Laws* is the foundation work on the science of political law. So, *Locke on the Human Understanding* is the foundation work on practical metaphysics; so, also, *Adam Smith's Wealth of Nations* may be regarded as the original of the modern science of political economy. Neither of these sciences is completed; but they are begun and are growing. There are numerous other branches of social science which are scarcely yet begun, but which will in another generation grow into vast importance.

The first of these is its favorable effect on the *taste for literature.* The love of the *narrative,* and of the pictures of social life connected with it, is almost as universal as the love of novelty itself. It is this love of the narrative, deep seated in human nature, which is the exhaustless patron of the great mass of fictitious literature, whether in prose or poetry, which has been poured like a flood upon the reading public, increasing with the increasing power of the press.

The poet does not long support his flight without it, and the noblest of poems, the epic, owes to this principle its entire interest. The novel has no being without it, and in most cases contains nothing else. It is made the conduit for all the sentiment, principle, taste, or views contained in that great body of literature, which is created and nourished by the imagination. In our time, none can doubt that it has been abused to licentiousness. It has been made to scoop the kennel for characters, to clothe the viler principles in the most beautiful garments, to exaggerate truth into falsehood, and substitute an affected sentimentality for the noble hardihood of virtue. In fine, the literary standard of the age has been lowered by its tolerance, through its love of the narrative, of deformed facts, exaggerated truth, perverted sentiment, and vicious principles. The literary coin has been debased; the stamp is right, but it has been alloyed at the mint. A mighty principle of human nature has been made to contain a thousand follies, if not a thousand crimes, as the strong oak contains imprisoned sap. This principle *cannot* be eradicated: it would be most lamentable for human nature if it could, for no spring of the immortal spirit has poured a more fertilizing stream over the waters of human life; flowers and verdure have sprung up under its influence; sweet fountains have been opened upon the arid plain, and the heart of the wayfaring traveller made glad, upon whose journey even hope had ceased to shine.

The principle being irradicable, may we not use it for useful purposes? The true philosophy of correction in literature, as well as morals, lies not in destruction, but in reform. There is no principle of human nature implanted for evil purposes, and none which the power of man can destroy. A system which aims at either destroying or enslaving the natural tastes or faculties of the human mind, will as certainly end in its own destruction and ultimate ridicule, as that the spirit shall survive the body.

This love of the narrative is one of the earliest principles seized upon by skilful instructors to convey knowledge to the opening mind; and observation teaches us that it loses nothing in strength or freshness as life draws on. The last romance, filled with mystery and marvels, is often bent over with as much interest by declining age as it is by the blooming girl, who, at midnight hour, starts at the picture which imagination has drawn. And if, indeed, some sober utilitarian, or some recluse in orthodoxy denies himself these pleasures, he is sure to make amends by recounting with tenfold aggravation the particulars of the last shipwreck, or gazing with blood-shot eyes at the wonders of the last moon hoax.

A principle which is thus enduring and efficient, should be made to strengthen the power of truth, as it certainly gives energy to falsehood. As it is used in the beginning, so it should be used to the end of education. Let the power of the narrative be united *with*, instead of *against* the power of truth. Let it gather up the images of the right, the beautiful, and the glorious, as they lie scattered up and down the scene of life, and weigh them against its idols, its dross, and corruptions.

In this nature assists truth, for it has become a maxim, that there is nothing in fiction equal to the reality; and all who reflect will readily acknowledge the fact. The imagination has never painted baseness so deep, as that to which human nature has voluntarily sunk; nor has it in its highest flights been able to conceive of the strength or nobleness of the spirit, either in its trials of duty or its powers of achievement. It has never painted a scene, in depth of tenderness, or agony of suffering, or complication of misery, of beauty in virtue, of the heroic in conduct, or the terrible in crime, which has not been a thousand times more than equalled by the pencil of nature. And how can it be otherwise? What materials has imagination which the world has not furnished? And how can her abstracted colorings equal in depth or brilliancy the hues which real feeling throws around its objects?

Hence it is that the novelist has seldom succeeded in heightening the interest of any great historical character or remarkable event. Indeed the very contrary has generally been the case, while he trod on strictly historical ground. It is only when he assumes the vantage ground of a continuous, connected, and unencumbered personal narrative, which history from its multifarious circumstances cannot take, that the novelist succeeds in imparting to his historical characters half the interest of the original. Compare, for example, Walter Scott with Hume. There is no character of Scott stronger impressed upon the minds of his readers than the brave, stern, cruel, uncompromising royalist, Graham of Claverhouse. Yet who will compare him to the Viscount Dundee, following with bigoted, yet devoted heroism the fortunes of his master, when deserted by his own daughter, till victory meets him in death at the pass of Killycrankie? Who will compare the Mary of the Abbot with the fascinating royal beauty, who drew around her the circles of France, and the knighthood of Scotland? Who shall compare the Elizabeth of Kenilworth with the maiden Queen of England? In fact, wherever we go, we find a depth of interest and a splendor of scenery around real characters and events which no invention of the novelist has ever been able to exceed. What in pathos can surpass the massacre of Glencoe, or the speech of our Logan?

Who shall describe a more eventful life, or a more beautiful character, than that of Alfred? Who, from the Arabian Nights to the Mysteries of Udolpho, shall find a drama more terrible in interest, more gorgeous in scenery, or more strange in catastrophe, than that last great tragedy in which the Corsican figured, from the plains of France to the dark rolling Danube, and from the vale of the Arno to the sands of Egypt?

It is not, then, *want of interest* in historical subjects, which should exclude them from the body of our literature. On the contrary, could they be united with a continuity of personal narrative, they would far exceed, in that respect, any invention of fiction. Indeed, no youth worth having ever commenced the history of Napoleon Bonaparte, and left it off: night and day will he follow the army of France, from the field of Marengo to the plain of Smolensk; and when, at an after period, he has come to understand something of the changes of nations, and the mutability of human affairs, he will wonder *why* it was that nations have risen and sunk; that laws have varied; and that such men as Cæsar and Bonaparte have swept over nations with the besom of destruction. His love of inquiry is excited; he pursues the history of the human mind; he finds it progressing in spite of the wrecks around it; out of ruins it builds new structures; out of ashes its fires revive; he sees that the history of nations, of dynasties, and of men, is not the history of human nature; he finds that when these, and all that is external in the forms of society, have perished, the social principle remains, the treasury of knowledge is not exhausted; and that mind, passing through a chrysalis state, assumes a new form more beautiful than the last, ascends to new regions of discovery and invention, and though, like the bird in the tempest, often baffled, holds on its course with tireless wing.

It is at this point that he returns to history, as a science: the only science which can unfold this development and demonstration of the powers of the human mind.

The commencement of this investigation, we have said, was the love of *the narrative*, which begins with the personal narrative of history, and ends in elevating the literary taste by elevating the objects of its pursuit. As an example, we are told of a remarkable man, who is at the head of the literature of France, if not of Europe, a man of mingled romance, poetry, and politics, who has a large library without a single work upon any other topic than history.

We have said that the love of narrative was to the full as much interested in realities as in fiction. But how is it to be excited? By using the same means to cultivate a taste for truth, which we do for fiction: by placing well-written, lively, and personal narratives before the mind, when the world is a novelty to it, and every new fact a marvel. Language and facts are, in respect to knowledge, the business of boyhood; to use and digest them, the business of manhood. Every picture of history is as much a new world to youth, as the opening glories of nature to the child.

HISTORY THE DEVELOPMENT OF HUMAN NATURE.

Having now considered the use of history as an instrument of literature, we come to consider the science of history as a development of human nature.

The basis of sound philosophy is said by Bacon to be *experience;* and if the experience of an individual is the basis of knowledge with him, surely the experience of the human race, as a social mass, furnishes the true means of deducing the laws of social conduct in that mass. It is in this respect that the science of *statistics* becomes collateral to that of history: it collects and compares the experience of nations upon definite topics, and verifies the results with the accuracy of mathematical calculation; and it is not till this is done thoroughly and extensively, that the legislator and the educationalist can make any safe estimate upon the mutual influences of mind and matter as developed in the social system. If the commerce, the religion, and the science of England have done much to enlarge her empire, her improvements in the arts of agriculture have not done less: they have enabled her to feed fourteen millions of persons upon ground which a little time before supported but six. It is thus we see that the physical acts must be counted and weighed, before we can tell what powers propel the wheels of society. He who shall count that society arises wholly from the action of mind, or he who shall assume the reverse, that mind is dependent upon matter, will find himself in either case mistaken. The movements of society are results produced by the combined action of both the physical and intellectual conditions. So, too, we shall find that human nature itself is modified, by the mutuality of attraction in society, into forms and results different from those at which it ever arrives in isolated individuals.

Ignorance of human nature is said to have been the cause of half the crimes and follies of mankind: but where is a knowledge of human nature to be found? It is plain it is not confined to one's self; for, important as is the knowledge of ourselves, there are vast fountains of sensation, great reservoirs of mind, mysterious agencies, which could never be known to an individual, and are only put forth through the channels of society. One may discover within himself the conscience and the intellect of the spirit, but must look out of himself for all that concerns its connections with human mind. He may contemplate himself for a knowledge of his powers and his character; but, as a member of society, he is one of a mighty mass which moves on by laws as fixed as those of the stars, resistless as the tides of the ocean, and swift as the currents of time. The knowledge of human nature, then, as it is manifested *in society,* is not the knowledge of one person, like a brick taken from Babylon as a specimen of the city, but is a knowledge of social action—the laws which regulate the aggregated whole.

This is that knowledge of human nature which is valuable to the human economy, by affording the only just basis of right conduct, wise legislation, or true methods of education. All that we can hope for from science in aid of humanity, is to be derived from this source; she has yet to develop the machinery of social movements, and teach the application of the new and tremendous instruments she has furnished to the elevation of the soul and the increase of ultimate happiness. The mechanical arts are aiding the science of political economy; geology is ministering to history; statistics are rapidly searching the general laws of both physical and intellectual humanity; and the study of language is discovering hidden analogies in the roots of all language; whilst the traveller and the scholar have disentombed the monuments of Egypt, and interpreted the mysterious records of deep and dark antiquity.

We thus see in what mode history and its collateral aids are developing a science of human nature which shall contain a body of principles, in relation not only to what is strictly human, but to the forms and results of associated action, to the effect of the sciences, the arts, and modes of government upon the character and condition of men.

Whenever a system like this shall be formed, as in time it will be formed, it will commend itself to the universal assent of the intellect with as much certainty as the truths of geometry. Of the great value of such principles, and the interest with which they are received, we have examples, in respect to personal feelings and conduct, in the universal assent given to the apothegm of Solomon, and the almost universal sympathy with some of the proverbial passages of Shakspeare. These apothegms and passages are universal truths, drawn from human nature, and entirely abstracted from particular applications; hence they derive, even in Shakspeare, little aid from the narrative. Most of the quotations from the drama, made by orators, are entirely impersonal; they are made on account of a principle or a sentiment, and not on account of the character which utters them. Shakspeare himself derives reputation as much for his skilful analysis of human nature as he does from the splendor of his poetry, and much more than he does from any skill in narration.

Here, too, history has the same advantage over the drama in the extent of its instruction, that it has over biography in the extent of its jurisdiction.

HISTORY IS DRAMATIC.

History is both dramatic and biographical, but it is not special and particular in either. The personal drama is, perhaps, the most interesting form of the narrative; yet it leaves us amused rather than instructed. No one looks among his friends and neighbors for Richards and Falstaffs; for he knows he will not find them: still less does he expect to see Calibans, Ariels, or the witches of Macbeth. He knows that the drama, whether prose or poetic, has its license. Nearly all its characters are extreme cases, and extremes make the exception and not the general rule. Indeed this difficulty holds true of nearly all fictitious characters, from Shylock to Sir Charles Grandison: and we are at no loss for the reason; for if a drama was made up of a dozen just such persons as we see about us every day, it would no longer be interesting. It is the very *ultraism* of fictitious characters which constitute their charm. The appeal is to the excitability of the imagination, and not to the soberness of reason. Hence if we learn human nature from such pictures, we learn it only through those general truths, which, as in Shakspeare, are put into the mouths of the speakers, independent of their relative positions.

Reality, as we have seen, has its interest; an interest higher than any which fiction has been able to attain. Yet this would seldom be the case, if it were confined to a very small circle of persons in the quiet scenes of peaceful avocations. History reaches it, by being able to include within its gallery of pictures, as well the peculiar and touching scenes of real life, which have been created by an extraordinary concurrence of events, as the magnificent drama of ages and of multitudes, which have been unfolding since the dawn of time.

It is this *unfolding* of human nature, as it is now seen in the social laws of those ages and multitudes, and now in the personal characteristics of those great leaders in arts and arms whom fame has made the impersonation of their times, which makes history the science of human nature. As such it wants neither interest, truth, nor dignity.

It has the interest of a drama, of which *the world is the stage, and all the men and women in it the players,* whose action begins in deep antiquity, when solemn mystery cast darkness around, and

> "———— gorgeous Tragedy
> In sceptred pall, came sweeping by,
> Presenting Thebes, or Pelops' line,
> Or else the tale of Troy divine."

A drama of which

> "The four first acts already past,"

we may look back and examine the artificial machinery of its enactment. The player has long since dropped his heroic garb; the pasteboard scenery has disappeared; broad daylight has been let in upon the stage, and nature claims her own. There we can see all the little wheels, as well as the great moving power; all the miserable stimulants which have excited the actor, as well as the nervous energy of his action; all the episodes of the play, as well as the great catastrophe towards which its characters rapidly hasten; and there too, truth has pencilled, by the pen of prophet, poet, and philosopher, the motive and the moral of this drama of humanity. It is well to turn for a little while from the part we *are* playing to the part that *has been* played; to turn the eyes from the strong light of orbs which now touch to the meridian, to the milder glow of those which have passed beneath the horizon.

NATIONS ARE REPRESENTED IN HISTORY.

On this great stage of the world nations have been substituted for persons, and masses of men for individuals. Hence the philosopher has deduced laws from history, which were true of all mankind under the same conditions, instead of those partial laws which are true only in extreme cases, and are seldom applicable to real life. Take, for example, the influence of specific institutions in perpetuating conditions, as exhibited in the castes of Hindostan, in which learning is confined to the Brahmins, while labor is imposed on other trades, and where ages on ages have rolled away without ever changing or improving the condition of the people; or, as in the English feudal system, where an overshadowing aristocracy has been built up and perpetuated by the laws of primogeniture and entailment; or the influence of laws on morals, in the destruction of the known domestic ties by the terrible laxity and yet cruelty of its institutions, and finally the *reaction* of those poisoned morals in the destruction of the state; for we find that the Emperor Augustus had a whole code of laws enacted to encourage marriage, in which great rewards were offered to those who married and great penalties to those who did not, and yet the Roman knights were so corrupt that they insisted upon its abolition; hence it was well said, that the Roman empire was destroyed before it was invaded by the barbarians.

In furnishing examples of these general laws of human nature of which history is the development, the statistics of modern times afford powerful aid and instruction. Mankind are now in the crucible of analysis, and the laws of social action will as certainly be systematized and demonstrated, as that the violation of them has produced half the miseries of the race. Take, for example, the law in respect to the formation of opinions; *ignorance* of that law, a recent writer has remarked, has to answer for the atrocities of religious wars, the horrors of the inquisition, and the too great severities of the penal code. Creeds and confessions have been handed to men at the point of the bayonet; and if there was no virtue in kind words, there was supposed to be much in the sword. Yet whose opinion has *force* ever changed? Whom did persecution ever convince? On the contrary, has it not become a maxim, that persecution assists the persecuted? and that even a fool or a villain, or a most fallacious creed, may be raised into consequence by uncharitable and violent attacks? Here the principle deduced from history is the same with that laid down in the gospel, that the true mode of persuasion is by kindness and charity.

Again, we have an example of another principle illustrated in the history of the penal law of England, that when a punishment is disproportioned to the offence, however grievous and calamitous that offence may be to the community, society will not enforce the law. In a commercial community the crime of forgery is one of the highest which can be committed, because it attacks that commercial confidence which is fundamental to a commercial community. Accordingly in England they punish it with death, and no one fairly convicted has been known to be pardoned. Yet society, believing this disproportioned to the offence, very seldom convict: witnesses disappear, and juries find loopholes of escape. And when we attach death to a still smaller crime, *theft*, the government itself steps in to commute the punishment, and not one of a thousand criminals receives the punishment awarded by the law. Law, then, to be successful, must conform to the equity of society.

Again, we may refer to the established historical principle, that wherever mind and commerce are least restricted, there the social progress is the most rapid, and the mind most active; whether we cite positive examples in Athens and the United States, or negative ones in China and Spain.

Further, we might deduce the utility of knowledge from the statistics of modern society, in the fact, that crime and vice have diminished as education has increased in those countries where accurate returns could be had.

The illustrations we have now given, whether from the dramatic scenery or the aggregate facts of society, all tend to show that in history, aided by its great adjunct, statistics, we must seek the true science of human nature. She has taken the gauge and dimensions of humanity; she has descended into the caverns of the earth to describe the half-fed savage, and has ascended the heavens to "unsphere the spirit of Plato;" she has left no extreme of the race unvisited, and no principle of its nature without illustration.

In respect to this view of human nature, we may cite an extract from a recent article on statistics:

"To know human nature is to know the general laws of human action; to ascertain the general course of man's physical and moral faculties. Previously to all observation, it might seem that human actions would, if registered, present as vast a variety as the caprices of the will, and that to discover any thing like a law in their production would be more absurd than to investigate the rules of the wind, or the regulations of the whirlwind; yet when we pass from individuals to masses, we find even in those actions which seem most fortuitous, a regularity of production, an order of succession, that can arise only from fixity of cause. *Thus* were a man always to examine only individual drops of water, he could never conceive the beautiful phenomenon of the rainbow; it is only when the drops are aggregated in masses and placed in a position favorable for observation, that he can contemplate that glorious arch spanning the horizon and seeming to connect earth with heaven."

HISTORY IS THE RECORD OF GOD'S PROVIDENCE IN THE GOVERNMENT OF MAN.

The next *use* of history is derived from its being the record of that *providence* by which *God administers the moral government of mankind.*

That *there is* a system of compensations by which crime is made to produce its own punishment, at some time and in some form, enters into every scheme of religious belief, whether of savage or civilized, Jew or Gentile, disciple or skeptic. It was a fact legibly written in the constitution of men, and upon the works of nature. The true philosophy of the human mind taught it from the days of Socrates to the present time; the Bible teaches it both in the prophecy and the fulfilment of those tremendous desolations, which visited the iniquities of men and nations through their distant posterity; and it may be expected that history will teach the same lesson as she calls up, in long succession, the awful shades of departed nations. She will call them up from ancient graves, from ruins long unvisited, from monuments just discovered by the traveller, from pools where the bittern dwells, from mighty rivers and from desert plains; she *will* call the spirits of once glorious, long punished nations,

To vindicate the ways of God to man.

In illustration of this truth, we shall take but two or three remarkable examples. As a principle, *Provi-*

dence invariably attaches to corruptions of morals in a people, the destruction either of the people or their freedom. Scarcely a people ever existed, whose history has not borne testimony to this invariable fact of their social existence. The corruption of morals destroys public strength, which thus invites conquest from abroad, while its licentiousness imposes the necessity of a despotism at home. It is not the refinement, but the corruption of *manners*, that enervates the spirit, destroys the courage, and dries up the aspirations of a nation; it was thus when the despotism of the Cæsars was founded on the ruins of the Roman republic; and it was still further thus, as described by all its writers, when that despotism itself, with the empire over which it ruled, disappeared before a dark, yet uncorrupted barbarism. So also, it is truly said by Montesquieu, that when the people of England had actually reconquered their liberties from the tyranny of the Stuarts, they had not virtue enough to establish a republic; a fact which we can well understand when we reflect upon the account given by Baxter of the English pulpit in his day, or upon the abandoned licentiousness of the court of Charles the Second.

A still more glaring and fresh example, that a people cannot escape, even under all the forms of liberty, from the effects of their own corruption, is found in the history of the last century in France. A people already licentious destroyed a government already despotic. Freedom unlimited was in possession of the people. The original elements of government were opened to all the formations of which constitutional liberty is susceptible; experiment upon experiment was made upon them, but no experiment was able to bring out of the crucible a principle strong enough to make liberty and corruption consist together. Over and over again did the whole French nation swear solemn fealty to successive constitutions; and as often did they fade away into empty air. License itself must have an end, and the pirates must have their laws. The army came in to put an end to anarchy. The First Consul of the French republic appeared on the plains of Marengo, and the First Emperor of the French received his baptism under the sun of Austerlitz; and at length when the laws of nations restrained the flood of conquest, the same nation received back the same profligate Bourbons whom they had thirty years before expelled; and when, in another revolution, they exiled one branch of that house, it was only to place upon the throne the hated family of Orleans, which had furnished to the French Revolution the most detested of all its terrible characters. Such is one of the stern lessons in which Providence has taught that liberty is inseparable from virtue, and that corruption shall be its *own destroyer*.

But we have a nearer and a more illustrious example of that Divine Providence, which leads nations through the wilderness as it did the Jews, in the history of our own country; and it is the more remarkable and the more unanswerable, as it stands exactly in juxtaposition, both in time and civilization, to those examples of corruption punished which have been cited from the two most polished nations of Europe.

At the very time when the tyranny of the Stuarts became established in England, and the church became corrupt, the colonies of Plymouth and Jamestown were founded; and as it became clear that even the commonwealth could not be sustained, and that liberty of conscience could not be secured, emigration to America increased. So too in South Carolina, early settlements were made by that Huguenot emigration which were driven out of France by the persecution of the Protestants. Thus we see that Providence laid the foundations of this republic out of the very materials which the corrupt governments of the old world had expelled from their borders. *The very acts* which in their execution left England and France to the self-producing punishments of a dissolute tyranny, were made by Providence the means of founding, in a new world, a nation from whom they, by its reflective influence, should derive reform and liberty.

But this was not all. When England had twice changed her government, and when the family of the Louises, after desolating wars, and exhausting extravagance, and private licentiousness, had exhausted the moral energies of the French, the colonies planted in the wilderness had grown up in hardy strength, passed through a victorious revolution, and formed for themselves a written constitution setting forth and defining the great principles of human rights.

Who can look upon such a scene and not feel the moral sublime? Who was there that stood among those glorious events, and did not feel himself sustained by an arm mightier than his own? Of all the soldiers of the Revolution, there was hardly one who did not look upon Washington as sent from heaven. He was to them as the pillar of fire by night.

And of all the great chiefs and statesmen of that day, there were few who did not look upon the American Revolution as an extraordinary event, brought about by Providence for its own purpose. Many proofs from authentic records might be cited of this; but we shall take one only from the letters of one of the most powerful and distinguished men of that day.*

Patrick Henry, in one of his letters says, "that the American Revolution was the grand operation which seemed to be assigned by the Deity to the men of this age in our country over and above the common duties of life. I ever prized at a high rate the supe-

* The history of the United States has been written by various hands: among the older writers, *Ramsay* is probably the most accurate; among the school histories of the United States, *Mrs. Willard's* is preferable, on account of its method and the spirit of patriotism which pervades its pages. *Bancroft's* is highly praised as a general history of the United States.

rior privilege of being one in that chosen age, to which Providence intrusted its favorite work."

Such has been the course of Providence heretofore in building up and spreading out the strength and the glory of the American people. But of the future the indications can only be gathered from the lessons of the past. Let us take one from the most splendid era of antiquity.

Two thousand four hundred years ago, the Prince of Babylon walked in the palace of that mighty city. Its hundred gates of brass were spread around, and the vast plain about was filled with magnificence. Beneath, rested in silence that city whose foundations were laid at the flood; and from the cloudless heavens shone the same bright stars upon which the first astronomer had fixed his gaze. The beauty of the Chaldee's *excellency* was there. The Prince walked upon those battlements, saw that splendor, looked upon those countless orbs, and gave not the glory to God. Upon the plains of *Dura* he had erected a golden image, and his decree went forth for all nations, and people, and tongues to fall down and worship it. And now as he walked abroad and meditated in his heart, he said: "Is not this great Babylon that *I* have built for the house of the kingdom, by the might of *my* power and for the honor of *my majesty?*" And while the word was yet in his mouth a voice from heaven came, "Thy kingdom has departed from thee;" and he was driven out from among men: he ate grass with the beasts; his hairs grew like the eagles' feathers, and seven long years was he wet with the dews of heaven.

His understanding returned again, and he sent forth another decree, that he praised the God of heaven, " whose works are truth, and his ways judgment, and those that walk *in pride* he is able to abase."

But the Providence which ruled in that nation was to be written in a still more terrible and enduring lesson. Another prince rose up who made new idols. He drank wine in the presence of a thousand lords, and called upon nobles and ladies to praise the gods of gold and silver. In that same hour the bolt of destruction was hurled from heaven, and the glory of the Chaldees departed forever.

Long time has passed since these scenes were enacted on the plains of ancient Asia; but history has treasured them up in her deepest memories; poetry has clothed them in numbers; painting has transferred them to the canvas; and true philosophy would grave them on the human heart.

But *these* examples of human folly and of divine wrath are not alone: they are units among millions. History is filled with monuments; earth is strewed with ruins. Stranded wrecks lie up and down the highway of nations, that those to come may profit by the example. But if history be full of terrors, she is also full of hopes. In every storm there has been a light ahead; green islands have emerged from the watery deep, and new continents acknowledged the dominion of mind. Amidst all the desolations of the external world, *humanity* has progressed; and alike from history, from prophecy, and Providence, it has the *promise* of progress — of progress till restored to its lost estate; when wisdom and knowledge shall be the stability of the nations, and the spirit of man go forth as spotless in beauty as it is immortal in being.

CHAPTER IX.

THE SCIENCE OF LANGUAGE.

"And the whole earth was of one language."—*Genesis.*

MAN, the last and noblest work of creation, was made the possessor and ruler of the earth. To him was given the dominion.* This implies, in itself, the power of *announcing commands intelligibly.* It includes the power of *designating* the objects upon the earth; and it includes the greater power of intellectual *communications* between mind and mind. The means by which this is done easiest and best, is *language.* Accordingly, the Scriptures say, that when God had created man, he "*commanded* him, *saying;*"† a phraseology which implies the use of language, and that it was naturally and spontaneously understood

* Genesis, ch. 1, v. 26.

† Genesis, ch. 2, v. 16.

by Adam. So, also, God brought the living things to Adam to see what he would call them, and what he called them, that was their *name.*

This is all we really *know* of the origin of language. But it is enough to characterize it as one of the highest talents of man; at once an instrument of reason, of history, and of progress.

LANGUAGE AN INSTRUMENT OF REASON.

It is not my intention here to enter into the controversy respecting ancient and modern languages. Language is a *universal* element, and its great principles can be studied in any tongue which is not absolutely barbarian. It must be admitted, however, that the most perfect model of language is that in which it can be studied to the most advantage, and which will give the most accurate conceptions of universal Grammar. It is this principle which has probably retained the classic languages in our universities long after the period in which they had ceased to be used, except as a means of education. Assuming that we take the language of any civilized nation as the model or subject for the study of language, let us consider it as a *science,* by means of which the mind is to be developed. Here the first thing to be remarked is, that this study develops an entirely *new class of reasoning powers.* Heretofore we have considered physical science only. In language we begin the metaphysical; for language is in fact the *bridge* which leads from the physical to the metaphysical world, so far as reasoning goes. So true is this, that the greatest part of the controversies in metaphysics have arisen from the use of different *terms* to express the same idea, the various interpretation of the same terms, and the want of terms to express a precise idea.

The science of language, therefore, develops faculties of the mind, which would otherwise lie dormant. It leads to the designation and separation of ideas independent of matter. It leads to criticism. It leads to observation upon the relations of mind with matter, and of mind with mind. It leads to the classification of objects, in terms distinct from matter. In fine, it leads to a higher philosophy, embracing objects of contemplation without and beyond the material world. Let us consider for a moment the process of *reasoning* which is developed in the study of language. Language, to one who has never thought of it as a study, must appear a *chaos* of words. It has come to him naturally—his mother-tongue—to use these words to designate certain things; but he has never dreamed that they stand in fixed scientific relations to one another, and the whole language itself was but a sort of defined picture of his own mind! He has employed a certain sound, or combination of sounds, to designate objects; and then, by a certain flight of the imagination, he has symbolized certain other things with these. Thus, he has called a species of bird an "*eagle*," its dark color, "black;"

and, observing that this is a war-bird, he has called the war-chief of his nation the "Black Eagle." The first terms were the simple *designation* of objects by terms applied to them: the last was an abstraction of those terms to symbolize very different objects. The first seems to be the result of a simple impulse of man to *name* things: the second is the exercise of a higher quality—imagination. From the moment this second step is taken, mind has begun to ascend, although it be only that of an untutored savage. It is thus that language is constructed by the development of the mind, the very soul of man itself. The higher the growth, the more extensive the elements of civilization, the more perfect and extensive will be language. This is the process by which it is formed: a process of observation, of imagination, of reasoning, and of philosophy.

When, in a nation of high civilization, this process has been carried on till its language has become various, extensive, classified—embracing all the subjects of human study, and the finest specimens of literature—then the structure and relations of that language become a science: a science which leads us into the realms of metaphysics, which leads through refined processes of reasoning, and contemplates the highest objects of philosophy.

CLASSIFICATION OF LANGUAGE.

In reasoning upon this science, we must take it in its perfect state and *invert* the order of its formation.

To the unlettered and uninstructed mind, this vast array of words is but a chaos. It is like the material of the lofty mountain; stones, rocks, minerals, earth, water, trees, thrown together, without apparent form or object. But the geologist or mineralogist, like the mathematician, gives every thing a name, a place, a class. Then all these confused objects assume a beautiful order. The reason detects the utility of every thing. The mind is charmed with these new evidences of beauty and harmony in the method of creation.

Language is of later date, and being created, in a great degree, by the growth of man himself, is more imperfect. But, in reasoning upon it, we take the same mode, and are charmed with the same kind of results.

For example, we may *analyze* thus, independent of any special form of grammar: suppose we would *classify* the words of language as a *universal* element, we might arrive at the following results, as an illustration of this species of reasoning.

1. How many *universal classes* of words are there? This leads us to consider how many *objects* of words there are, or what is their classification. First, we have the *state of being*, whatever that is. The first idea of the human mind, if it think at all, is *existence*. The word which expresses that idea is essential to all language. But as the state of being may be in different ways, the words which express the state ot being may be very numerous, and thus we have the

first class of words in those which express *the state of being*, whatever that is.

2. Every object, whether material or merely intellectual, must be designated, or else that object must float loosely in the mind, without any means of identifying it. Hence, the next class of words are those which *designate* objects, or *words of designation.*

3. All objects have different qualities, not merely attached to their substance, but also as to time and degree. The next class, therefore, of words, are those which *qualify* other words, or *words of qualification.*

4. These classes of words, in order to constitute sentences, or express more than a simple idea, must be *connected* by other words, which serve to express the *kind* of connection they have. The next and last class of words, therefore, is *words of connection*—connectives.

Thus, however complicated or however simple a language may be, we conclude, by reasoning from the nature of mind, that language must contain four entirely distinct classes of words. 1. Those which express a *state of being;* 2. Those which *designate* objects; 3. Those which express a *qualification;* and, 4. Those which *connect* other words.

Now, however various (from the rudest to the most perfect) are the grammars of different languages, yet grammarians are everywhere obliged to adopt this general classification, just as the geologist is obliged to adopt general classes of stratification for the elementary earths. Then, too, a circle or a square will be the same things to a mathematician wherever he finds them, or in whatever language they may be called.

The *state of being* is the same thing in language, whatever may be the particular *word* which expresses it. In English we say, "I am," and in Latin, *Sum;* but the idea expressed is the same. Thus we arrive at the idea of universal grammar, or the philosophy of language. Then we come to the great truth, that it is the soul itself—the mind within—which gives form to language; and although it applies that language to the rock and the tree, yet the language expresses the idea of the mind, and is classified by the mind itself. As the mind grows and enlarges, its language becomes more abstract, more refined, more metaphysical, expressive of that higher philosophy and those nobler objects to which it has arrived in its continued expansion. As in the beginning, so now the soul holds dominion over matter, and makes its language the expression of its thoughts.

Pursuing this train of reasoning on the classification of language, we find that the word which expresses the *state of being* may express either a state of *action* or a state of *passiveness.* Thus we have two forms of the same word, and two orders of the same class. Again: the *condition of being*, whether active or passive, may be either a *limited* or an *unlimited* existence, a *positive* or a *conditional* state, &c. Thus we have different *modes* of existence expressed by forms of the same word. Then, in looking a little further, we find that a word of the same class, the same order, and the same mode, may be in different periods of *time*, and used by different *persons*. These, again, afford many new varieties of the same word. In highly finished languages, such as the Latin and Greek, these varieties are expressed by different terminations of the same root. In the Latin verb *amo* (love) there are one hundred and eighty varieties or terminations of the same original root! Thus we find by this analysis, that language is continually expanding to meet the exigencies of thought and the progress of the human mind.

The *reasoning* upon language thus becomes an *analytical examination* of the composition of thought through the composition of words, by which it is expressed. It differs from the analysis of quantities by being the analysis of ideas abstracted from quantity. The utility of the study of the science of language consists largely in furnishing the student with a new method of reasoning, and calling other faculties into exercise. It is for this cause that the study of language has ever been considered, and is really one of the most solid foundations of a sound and thorough education.

THE SCIENCE OF LANGUAGE IS AN ILLUSTRATION OF HISTORY.

The language of any one civilized nation, critically studied, will illustrate in a very striking manner the intellectual history of that nation. On language, as much as on any element of human society, is marked mutability: this is a necessity of its existence. From what I have said, it seems obvious that language grows with the growth of a nation, and receives an increase of words with an increase of ideas. But the language of a people also suffers great changes from political shocks. A foreign invader introduces new men, new laws, and new customs, which in time engraft on the language new words expressive of these new ideas.

No language is a better study in this respect than the American. It is almost identical with the English, having an addition of some words local and peculiar to America. The changes in the structure and vocabulary of this language express to a critical student all the great changes which the English and Anglo-American people have undergone. If, for example, we take specimens of our language in each one hundred years since the Christian era, we shall find that in each hundred years it has received additions, or undergone changes, which decidedly modified both its words and idiom. If we look further into the periods when the most marked changes have occurred, we shall find that they have been greater or less, just in proportion as the changes in society have been greater or less. Thus, the greatest change in the language occurred from the thirteenth to the sixteenth century, when English society was emerging from the ignorance and rudeness of the middle ages to the brightness of the Elizabethan era.

But when we come to examine the vocabulary of

the Anglo-American tongue in reference to its roots, we shall find still clearer evidence of great historical changes. Political shocks have impressed themselves on the language. The vestiges of all the English revolutions are there; volumes of words have been introduced by conquest; while the classic student, like Milton, has been compelled to supply the defects of his own vernacular, by borrowing largely from the storehouses of ancient literature.

An examination of our language by the most learned men shows that nearly one-third the words are derived directly or indirectly from the Latin; that another large share (and those the words in most common use) are what is called Anglo-Saxon, or Germanic; that another portion are Norman-French; that others are Danish; and that there are many of the ancient British or Celtic.

From these facts one might *infer*, almost by a strict demonstration, the historical changes which the people had undergone. Thus the first and greatest conquest of Britain was by the Romans, the remains of whose works and fortifications are scattered over the island to this day. The Roman conquest directly, and the Norman conquest indirectly, and finally, the prevalence of Latin literature during the middle ages, introduced our large stock of Latin words. The next conquest was by the various invasions of the Teutonic tribes, the Angles, Saxons, and Danes, making an entire revolution in the country, and establishing the prevalence of the Saxon tongue and people. Hence we have the Anglo-Saxon language for a long time predominant in the country. Next came the Norman conquest, and for a time the Norman-French was the language of educated people. It was not till the thirteenth century that the English tongue began to assume any regular form; and it was not till three centuries after, in the days of Elizabeth, that it took the form in idiom and structure which it now possesses. The Lord's Prayer, as written and used in each successive period, has been preserved, and makes a very good standard of the changes which have taken place in the common language.*

LANGUAGE IS THE RECORD OF SOCIAL PROGRESS.

The science of language, properly studied, affords the very best record of human progress. This will appear evident from the consideration of two very plain principles.

1. It is manifest that if a people have no knowledge of a given science, or no ideas on a given subject, that then that people can have *no words* to express the terms or ideas of that subject or science: it is a blank in fact, and a blank in language.

2. If a people, at any period in their history, begin to acquire knowledge of a subject, and think upon it, then they also begin to acquire a corresponding

* Sharon Turner's History of England has a very good history of the progress of the English language.

language. They will have words to express their meaning. Thus the accession of new words and phrases proves conclusively the accession of new knowledge and new ideas. The American language affords a fine illustration of this progress in the growth of the public mind. By reference to Webster's American Dictionary, and an analysis of terms, ample proof will be found to sustain, as illustrations of the principle, the introduction of entire classes of words, in consequence of the introduction of a new branch of knowledge. Thus, take the following examples:

1st. The Greek words in our language are almost all terms of art or science, introduced because that art or science was introduced from Greece. The science of medicine has taken almost all its terms from the Greek, because the knowledge of medicine as a *science* was derived from Greece; *physic*, *physiology*, *osteology*, &c., are Greek words, and so of a very large number of medical terms.

2dly. The *terms of the art of war* are derived chiefly from the French, because the French have been the great cultivators of what may be called the science of war; the terms were introduced into England with the study of this science. For example, the words *fort—fortify—bastion—glacis—parapet*, &c., are introduced from the French.

3dly. Terms connected with the art of *printing* have been multiplied since the invention of printing. The word to *print* is derived from the French *im-*

primer; but most of the words connected with printing are derived from the Latin, and used in a figurative sense.

4thly. Terms of *steam navigation* are now rapidly increasing, many of which are entirely new, and introduced within the present generation. Thus the words *steamer—steaming—wooding—fire-up,* &c., in the manner in which they are used, are all new. Such words must rapidly accumulate, till they form a numerous class.

5thly. Terms derived from the construction of railroads are also numerous; for example, *locomotive—freight cars—the train—the conductor,* &c. Many of these words were already in existence, but the application of them is entirely new, and we thus give them a new meaning.

6thly. Terms of *politics* and *law* are also rapidly increasing, and have meanings which they could not possibly have had before the present century. Of political terms we have such as these: *caucus—clique—ballot—congress—convention—quorum—legal tender—test-act—stump-speaking,* &c., &c. The vocabulary of politics has been immensely extended by a class of words which could have no existence before the formation of democratic governments; there are many of these peculiar to America; others are peculiar to England, such as the word *hustings,* &c. The law terms were mostly introduced by the Norman conquest, when, for a time, the language of the law courts was the Norman-French. But there are numerous terms introduced since, and which mark great and important changes in the elements of society. For example, we have *jury—grand-jury—parliament—indictment—impeachment*, &c., indicating that the government of England has been completely changed since the days of William the Norman.

7thly. Another and very numerous class of words are continually introduced by the new ideas and moral changes created by the action of religion and society. Christianity makes a new mark with each new generation, and continually develops its irrepressible energy and its dominant influence. Thus we have *missions—missionaries—tracts—colporteurs*, and hundreds of words, brought out by the Christian action of the last half century. Society, too, gives names to its changes, its doctrines, its new sects, and novel ideas; thus we have *Mormons—Mormonism—Socialists—Socialism—strikes—radicals*, and a host of terms, which originate in some new movement of society.

Thus we see that language records in its vocabulary and embodies in its own substance the revolutions of society, the increase of knowledge, the inventions of genius, and the progress of art, society, and religion. It does this, though no historian should make up the record; though no poet should sing the praises of glory achieved; though man should leave no monuments to perpetuate his growth and greatness. If the language lives, it carries in itself the record of his acts and his improvements.

Language is, therefore, the record of PROGRESS, as I have already shown it to be the instrument of reason and the voice of history.

It is the science of language which develops these facts, and by analysis, the comparison of vocabularies, and the philosophy of structure, demonstrates these beautiful truths, and exhibits language as the *expression* of the soul—as clothing itself with this delicate, elastic, and refined garment, in which to appear in the visible and tangible world.

Among the languages accessible to an American student for the purpose of an American education, none can be superior to our own. Other languages, such as the Greek and Roman, have been far more perfect in their form and structure; others have been more homogeneous; others have been more musical; but the English-American is superior to them all in strength and copiousness. It contains within itself the best words of the Latin, the Saxon, and the French; its vast vocabulary affords an almost boundless range of words and phrases in which to clothe almost any shade of thought, or adapted to any new form of ideas. Accordingly, we find the most splendid diction of modern literature in the classic authors of England. What can surpass the magnificent dress in which Milton, and Bacon, and Shakspeare clothed their admirable thoughts? Well may an Englishman boast that

"Chatham's language was his mother-tongue!"

CHAPTER X.

LITERATURE A MEANS OF EDUCATION.

"——There studious let me sit,
And hold high converse with the mighty dead;
Sages of ancient time, as gods revered,
As gods beneficent, who bless'd mankind
With arts, with arms, and humanized a world."—*Thomson.*

LITERATURE is the written *expression* of human thoughts embodied in various forms of composition. Hence it includes all of learning, except what is contained in books of science and books of business. These last are indeed compositions; but are the expression of *fact* rather than of thought or fancy. Hence, too, literature embraces history, poetry, criticism, essays, novels, stories, biographies, travels, and, in fine, the whole body of those books which constitute the reading of a people. Now, to that part of the people who are educated at all, this makes the chief, and perhaps the most influential, part of their education; yet this great teacher—literature—is allowed to instruct his pupils hap-hazard, or perhaps not instruct them at all! I think that nearly all the youth of the country are left entirely to chance in the direction of their reading, and allowed to read or not read—to read this or to read that—as their own discretion, or rather taste, may select. This indifference to what is read in the course of education arises, I think, from too low an estimate of the general influence of literature on the character of the mind. It is not so much the *fact* as the *shade of thought* expressed in a book, which does good or evil. An important and serious truth may be stated in two books; but the first states it with a reverence and a tone of sincerity, which shows the writer's conviction of its weight and verity; the second states it in a tone of levity or irony, which shows that the truth is not believed, though the writer may directly state it. In the second case there can be no charge of falsehood upon the book; but he who reads it cannot divest his mind of the skeptical sneer which accompanied the announcement even of the most positive truth. His spirit will on that subject be poisoned with the subtle influence which the mind can so readily throw even into words the most simple and innocent; so the gay and licentious poet throws a repulsive dress over virtue, and clothes with unusual charms and seductive graces the form of vice, which, if seen naked, would be hideous to all eyes: electricity itself is not more subtle in its motions, or more vivid and striking in its effects, than is *thought*, insinuating itself into the most unsuspected language, and fascinating in the most brilliant pages of literature. It is to show, in a brief sketch, the importance of this element of education, that I write this chapter.

LITERATURE AN EXPRESSION OF THOUGHT.

I have already defined literature as the *written expression* of thought. But what is thought? It is not a mere fact; that fact may exist whether we think of it or not. It is not a mere truth; that truth will exist, whether we think at all or not. Thought is made up of all those ideas, images, fancies, spiritual operations, which fill up, and furnish, and inhabit the vast regions of the spirit. How vast, how tenanted, how multitudinous, or how solitary—how brief in time, or how far wandering through the chambers of eternity, no science and no history can disclose. They make up the volume of that great mystery which shall never to this mortal world be opened!

The spirit, being gifted with a language which can be understood by its fellow-spirits on earth, and having sympathies which long to go forth and be understood, UTTERS its voice in written language, discloses voluntarily a part of its *thoughts*—a small, broken, vista-like picture of that internal world of images, idealities, visions of the day, and dreams of the night, which have been wandering to and fro through his soul! The poet utters his fancies in the melody of verse—

> "Presenting Thebes' or Pelops' line,
> Or the tale of Troy divine."

The philosopher seeks to unsphere

> "The spirit of Plato, to unfold
> What worlds or what vast regions hold
> The immortal mind that hath forsook
> Her mansion in this fleshly nook."—

The novelist rears castles in the air, fills them with imaginary beings, moves them like the puppets of a show, and causes them to weep or to rejoice in fancied woes or fancied joys. Thus, some wizard SCOTT fills the bright world of ideality with stories

> "Of tourneys, and of trophies hung,
> Of forests and enchantments drear,
> Where more is meant than meets the ear."

But it is not the writers of visions who alone picture forth the internal world of thought. The historian weaves round the most naked facts the most beautiful dress which his own brilliant intellect can produce. The bleakest rock of the world's cold realities rises before you clothed with the softest verdure of his own spirit. It is thus that literature is the continual utterance of voices from the internal world; and this is the reason why the brightest, but most sensitive spirits, like to steal time from the world, to retire in some secluded hour from the delusions of actual life, to commune with these spirits of the past —to hear these voices from invisible societies, and call around them the great souls of the mighty dead!

In the unperverted state of the human mind, when the tastes are not drawn away by sensual pleasures, when nature presents nothing but objects of delightful contemplations, there can be no doubt that to a mind having the elements of intellectual education, the pleasures of reading are the most attractive among those which originate in human society. The beauties of nature are enhanced by a knowledge of the observations and discoveries of others; while a world of new visions, the dreams of other minds, the utterances of other voices, the travels of other spirits, the pictures of other lands—come over the young dreamer, as if the veil had been drawn from the face of a new and even more beautiful creation. The kaleidescope does not present with its fragments of glass and beads, more broken, distorted, and partial views, than does our literature of the human mind. Yet neither does the kaleidescope present them half so brilliant, half so various, or so beautiful. It is the panorama of a world, where, in distant glimpses, the spirit catches for a moment an idea of the eternal and the immortal!

All that we have preserved of this ideal world is written. It is literature. It is "thoughts that breathe and words that burn," in Tully's voice and Virgil's lay. This literature is, therefore, in fact, the *written expression of thought.* Let us now consider briefly what this literature actually does in forming and educating the human mind.

LITERATURE IN FORMING STYLE.

In any use of speech, either by conversation or writing, there is a manner of expression called *style.* This might be called, in mathematical terms, the general *formula* which the mind assumes for the expression of thought in sentences and paragraphs. It is not, indeed, exactly the same in every instance; but is the outline to which the writer adapts the expression of his thoughts. Thus every distinguished and eminent author has a *style* of his own—a style which distinguishes him from most, if not all other authors. This *style* is the creature of literature. It is a combination of both art and nature. In a high state of civilization we might as well think of dispensing with the ornaments of dress, of furniture, and of houses, as to dispense with that ornament and refinement of style which is the creation of high artistic skill.

There are two things to be considered here, in reference to the formation of style: first, the advantage of a good style, either in writing or speaking; and next, the influence of literature in forming style.

Style is like dress or manners. It is that which adorns and sets forth in pleasing colors the original thought, however barren or meagre that thought may really be. The power of dress in making an ugly form agreeable is well known. The still greater power of elegant and pleasing manners to conciliate antipathies, to disarm jealousy, to charm the simple, to overcome prejudice, and to attract all beholders, is well illustrated by all observation and all history. Great as these charms may be, the charm of style is even greater. It is almost impossible to over-estimate the effect of the eloquence of style on the mass of readers; it is almost impossible to conceive how much meagreness of matter it has concealed; how much rotundity it has given to slender thoughts; how much evil principle it has draped in magnificent robes; how it has imparted the melody of music to the beatings of a drum-head, and given to vapid vaporings the solemn gait of wisdom. The world little knows how much more is due to the art of authorship than to the genius which is supposed to dwell in that eloquent page so praised and so admired! The reader of elegant literature is seldom suspicious: he pursues his literary walk for pleasure. He asks not what qualities of life or death may be found in the blooming flowers of orange and crimson which overhang his head: he asks not whether it be the pine or the hemlock which sheds this dark and solemn verdure, so soothing and so calm, in this his quiet path. This solemn shade of verdure, this brilliant bloom of flowers, this garniture of all rich and magnificent foliage, alarms him no more than if this had been the Eden of the first creation.

As I have defined literature to be the *expression of thought*, it may be said that there must at least be thought, and that thought must be obvious. It is true, there must be thought; but what *proportion* there may be of thought to expression, and how much more of the latter than the former, and how much more of beauty there may be in the style than in the thought, are very different questions. Every reader knows that a thought may be distinctly expressed in a single sentence, and that it may also be spread over an entire page—appearing more beautiful than in its merely isolated annunciation. In the last case, the thought is connected with brilliant epithets and pleasing metaphors. It is very easy to illustrate the influence of style in magnifying small thoughts, or gilding the most vicious sentiments. Unfortunately, all literature, ancient and modern, is full of most striking examples of this literary vice. I will briefly cite two of the most popular specimens of English literature. Take, for example, Pope's beautiful poem, "Eloisa to Abelard," purporting to be a poetic version of Eloisa's letters. It is difficult to find any composition more filled with music than this, or more filled with the beauties of style, yet the number of ideas in it are very small; almost the whole piece is the expression of a single feeling—her passion for Abelard—and that passion is represented by herself as gross and animal. The piece is a signal example of the attractions of style and melody in poetry. In the midst of her lamentations, Eloisa exclaims—

> "How oft, when press'd to marriage, have I said,
> Curse on all laws but those which love has made!
> Love, free as air, at sight of human ties
> Spreads his light wings, and in a moment flies.

Let wealth, let honor, wait the wedded dame,
August her deed, and sacred be her fame;
Before true passion all those views remove;
Fame, wealth, and honor! what are you to love?"

For sentiments like these, some modern reformers, who may have borrowed them from this poem, have been made infamous. The world has rejected this theory of love, and the eloquent language of Eloisa may now be quoted to point a moral and adorn a tale. The poem is an illustration of the effect of style; a small amount of sentiment, and that bad, is made beautiful by the splendor of diction and the melody of verse.

Another example may be found in the famous letters of *Junius:* it is true that there is vigorous thought in them, that they appealed to principles of liberty, and that they seized upon some public abuses; but suppose that all that is either fact, principle, or sentiment in those letters, had been written in plain, unpretending style, would they have lived beyond the day of publication? It was the pointed antithesis, the bitter irony, the apt metaphor, the personal malignity, which was worked up and polished into the most powerful style, that excited the wonder and admiration of the reader.

It may be thought that few persons need style, because few will be called on to write. If this idea be true of other countries, it is not true of the United States; here every educated person is, in some form, called to use the pen. Take, for example, the vast number of political documents, resolutions, essays, &c., which are every year prepared by large numbers of persons; then consider how many persons are in a few years engaged in public affairs—how many are obliged to prepare public writings. Nothing can better illustrate the value of a literary education, than the sad figure which some of our high state functionaries have been compelled to make in public! The messages of some governors, the reports of some state officers, and the speeches in our legislatures, are many of them so coarse in language, so confused in style, and so absurd in their statements, that it is well they are soon lost in the mass of ephemeral rubbish, and cannot be quoted as specimens of American literature. On the other hand, many of our public documents are among the most beautiful specimens of literary compositions; and it is in these, chiefly, must be sought the true American literature. Jefferson, De Witt Clinton, and John Quincy Adams have scarcely been surpassed in strength, beauty, and elegance of style, by any modern writers.

It is obvious, from what I have said, that the art of writing in a clear style is of great practical use, especially in this country, and this art is necessary to a large number of persons.

The second remark to be made on this subject is, that this art is to be acquired as much by the example of the best authors, as in any other mode. Literature furnishes the best models of style; and it is a familiar acquaintance with these authors, and particularly a critical examination of their works, which will best exhibit to a student the art of composition. I say the *art;* for it is unquestionably true that the *value* of a composition will depend on the *matter* which is in it, rather than the dress in which it is clothed. It is equally true that, at last, every writer will have his own style, because it is a property of each individual mind to think in its own way. It is somewhere said that when Gibbon was preparing himself to write the Decline and Fall of Rome, he sought to acquire a *style* fitted to the dignity of the subject: he preferred the simplicity of Hume, but said he could not imitate it; he next admired Robertson, and thought he could model himself upon his style. The result was, he had the style of neither, but formed to himself a peculiar and yet more gorgeous drapery of language. Beyond doubt, however, he studied style, and gained much from the example of others.

Our conclusion, then, must be, that literature is an expression of thought, but the *mode* of expression may be very various; and that a finished and refined *style* is an achievement of art.

LITERATURE THE GUIDE OF IMAGINATION.

IMAGINATION is the most excursive, the freest, and, if we may so speak, the most *originating* faculty of the human mind. It is that faculty which, at the instigation, or rather *permission* of the will, wanders forth to gather up or to discover, or to frame out of its present materials, new *images* of things real or unreal, of things possible or impossible, the creatures of a visionary world. The objects of ambition, of future fortune, fame, glory, happiness, so continually presented to the mind of aspiring youth, are creatures of the imagination; they are the images of the future, called up to excite the intellect and impel the energies; they may be realized, because there are such realities, but at the time they thus float in beautiful array before the spiritual vision, they are *but* images. These images are innumerable, and the power of the imagination to call them up is most beautifully described in the Castle of Indolence: one of the tenants of the Castle is represented as passing his days in sauntering about, and often musing amidst twilight shadows:

> "Yet not in thoughtless slumber were they past;
> For oft the heavenly fire, that lay conceal'd
> Beneath the sleeping embers, mounted fast,
> And all its native light anew reveal'd.
> Oft as he travers'd the cerulean field,
> And markt the clouds that drove before the wind,
> Ten thousand glorious systems would he build,
> Ten thousand great ideas fill'd his mind;
> But with the clouds they fled, and left no trace behind!"

This faculty of the imagination, wild, lawless, and originating as it is, is not so lawless and so original as to be wholly unlimited or irresponsible; on the contrary, there are two great intellectual facts to be recognized in reference to the imagination, which are of vast importance in forming a just view of the means of education, and just views of the constitution of the human understanding

1. The imagination does not *create* any new *materials* of thought, but it constructs new *forms*, or various and strange images, out of the materials it already has; it *combines* these materials in air-built castles, but it creates nothing but forms and images. If the imagination could *create* a single new idea in substance, a something of which the mind had previously no element, then we should continually live in a new creation, and no finite limit could be placed to the power of the human mind. If there be any such thing as new materials, or in other words, absolutely new ideas, furnished by imagination, they will probably be found among the poets, who have dealt most largely in the dreams of fancy. Let us take Pope's Rape of the Lock as an example: the great feature of this beautiful poem is the creation, as it is called, of the race of sylphs and gnomes, aerial spirits, who are represented as the guardians of the fair. The following passage gives the idea of this creation, and its uses:

"Ye sylphs and sylphids, to your chief give ear;
Fays, fairies, genii, elves, and demons, hear!
Ye know the spheres, and various tasks assigned
By laws eternal to the aerial kind:
Some in the fields of purest ether play,
And bask and whiten in the blaze of day;
Some guide the course of wandering orbs on high,
Or roll the planets through the boundless sky;

Some, less refined, beneath the moon's pale light
Pursue the stars that shoot athwart the night,
Or suck the mists in grosser air below,
Or dip their pinions in the pointed bow,
Or brew fierce tempests on the wintry main,
Or o'er the glebe distil the kindly rain;
Others on earth o'er human race preside,
Watch all their ways, and all their actions guide."

The poet has exhibited as beautiful an array of sylphs, fairies, and gnomes as can be found in the range of literature; and yet, in the idea, what is there new? The whole idea of his fairy creation is resolved into the simple thought that there are "attendant spirits;" and this idea is not only very old, but it is expressly affirmed in the Bible. Thus we see that the imagination of the poet has formed a succession of beautiful combinations out of old ideas; it is a beautiful picture formed out of the materials which were pre-existent. The poem is an original one: all I mean to say is, that the imagination seizes and combines, but does not really *create* the materials of its airy fabrics.

This principle is all-important; for if imagination does not create, but simply *calls up and combines* the elements of thought, then arise the important questions, upon what principle, by what guide, under what authority, does it thus call up, and combine, and array these images and pictures? Must we admit that the imagination is the dominant faculty of the soul, wandering forth without restriction, and liable to no recall by superior authority? If we did this, we must also admit that the human mind is incapable of moral sanity. Reason does not dwell in dreams; conscience is not wounded by imaginary pictures; the will, that mighty leader of energies, would lose control of its natural subjects, and the human being cease to be a responsible agent; the soul would be a wreck, in wandering mazes lost. It is when the imagination does, in consequence of some invisible disorder, gain this ascendency, that insanity commences, and we have all the phenomena of a mind in ruins. In walking through lunatic asylums, we find kings, princes, lords, and heroes enacting their several parts, and happy in their visionary state; the imagination has become predominant over all other faculties. The conclusion, then, is, that the imagination is controlled by some other faculties.

2. The WILL can control the flight of the imagination, and the REASON can select the objects of thought upon which it shall dwell. I shall not stop to demonstrate this by any other argument than that included in the above illustrations. To me, it is self-evident that the sane mind cannot be deluded by the imagination, or left to follow its vagaries, unless by the *assent* of the will, and the *disuse* of reason. It is on this principle that man is accountable for the *abuse* of the imagination; and that to this abuse may be traced the largest share of the wickedness upon earth. The Bible states the fatal consequences of a perverted imagination, and the moral accountability of intelligent beings for that perversion, in the clearest and

most forcible terms. It was on the eve of the deluge when God declared of the wickedness of man, that "every imagination of the thoughts of his heart was only evil continually." The will had voluntarily allowed the thoughts to select topics of contemplation, and the *images* called up were evil continually; images of evil actions, of unrestrained desires, of impure thoughts, of allowed falsehood, of violated law, of fraud, of violence, of unhallowed ambition, of earth desecrated, and heaven despised.

This, says the Scripture, was the imagination of the thoughts; and for this imagination man was held *accountable.* Hence it is assumed, as a matter of fact, that these imaginations *could* be restrained: they *might* have been directed otherwise.

I have arrived, now, at *the direction and government* of the imagination, as one of the processes of education. I affirm, that literature acts on minds having the elements of education, as an excitant of the imagination, and that it excites those images and thoughts which are genial to the spirit of the author.

If the imagination, however fanciful its visions, must use *pre-existent materials,* then it must find them in nature or literature; it must find them in the *state of things* as they are, or in the *representations and records of the human mind* found in the pages of literature; that is, these must contain the suggesters and excitants of thought. If, also, the selection of the topics of contemplation and the direction of the imagination can be controlled by the will, then it follows, as an inevitable conclusion of reason, that an intelligent and responsible being should select the subjects and works of literature in reading so as to furnish images of the good, call up visions of the beautiful, and lead the mind, step by step, in the ascending scale of being. In this, literature offers a great variety of choice. There are those who represent the darker side of humanity, like the moon in dim eclipse; and there are those who represent it as yet the subject of divine light, like that same moon when she turns her "silver lining" up; there are those who give us dark fragments of a glorious but distorted intellect, and those whose minds seem, like some peaceful lake, reflecting the images of the heaven above; those who delight in hateful and hideous images, and those who dream of all that is lovely and loving.

When a young mind takes the works of different authors, they thus become guides of the imagination. The images formed by the author are called up, and lead to others of a kindred nature. Thus, literature really becomes a guide to the imagination.

It is impossible to analyze precisely the effect produced upon different minds by the reading of different species of books. The mind is too subtle an element to detect all the influences upon it: its operations are invisible; but, as the thoughts are engaged on pre-existent materials, and as the utterances of the mind are the outgoing of the thoughts, we often learn by these utterances what are the materials on which the mind has previously been engaged. It betrays itself. In this manner it has been demonstrated, that some minds have lost their balance and become insane, under the influence of an ill-regulated imagination, excited by reading visionary books—books of romance, or books of wild and delusive theories. Undoubtedly these were weak minds ; but the fact is enough to prove the powerful influence of literature, acting upon the imagination, in forming and directing the mind. If it is thus powerful over weak spirits, it must have much influence even on the strongest. The world is now filled with the worst species of literature—that which does not merely deal in imaginary creations, but fills that imaginary creation with beings, professing to be portraits of living nature, who indulge the worst of passions, pursue the grossest pleasures, mock the holiest of duties, and represent men as only a race of intelligent beasts !

There is a great and vital distinction between merely *imaginative* literature and that which is both imaginative and *passionate*. For example, Pope's Rape of the Lock is an *imaginative* poem, filled with beautiful images, but excites no passions, calls up no gross thoughts, and leaves the mind, after its flight of fancy, with no evil impressions ; on the other side, the recent French novels are imaginative also, but the characters profess to be *real*—they come, as men and women, from real life. In this character, they are represented as the creatures of passion and pleasure. One indulges the gross and animal passions. One, with a more decent exterior, circulates through the gay life of fashion, but when the exterior of civilized manners is taken off, is nothing but a naked profligate. A third has high intellect, but without the slightest notion of religious responsibility. A fourth is filled with *sentiment,* and deals largely in love, and honor, and poetry, but seems to have no actual idea that there is such a thing as truth or religion upon earth! These are, in reality, pictures of the worst part of human society in a state of civilization, and for that reason far worse than such works of the imagination as the Arabian Nights' Entertainment. The poetic fictions of the Arabian poets deceive no one. They present no examples for imitation. They lead us through a world of marvels; but no one imagines that he can ever become one of the wonderful genii who perform these marvels. It is a vision of pure, unreal imagination. But when a writer of genius makes a hero of a robber, a lady of a courtesan, or a moral exemplar of an atheist, he not only treats with contempt the duties of religion and the faith of Christians, but he presents vicious examples of society, and administers a powerful excitant to an already depraved imagination.

If literature, then, is to be made a *salutary* means of education (and a means of education it *is*), it must be, like other branches of education, read, received, and administered, under the supervisory care of the wise and good teacher. There is no need—there never was—that young men should taste of all the poison-plants of the field, in order that they may be nourished by salutary fruit.

LITERATURE AN EDUCATOR.

Literature is read, not studied; hence it is only in rare exceptions that this reading, as to time, manner, and quantity, is at all considered as a serious thing. To the lover of reading, it is a pleasure: to the seeker for knowledge, it is pursued in that direction where the kind of knowledge sought may be found: to the mere student by necessity, reading is a labor, and he reads just what is necessary, and no more. In almost all cases, literature is read for pleasure or necessity, with scarcely a thought of its general influence as an educator. To nearly all persons, the great mass of books on the shelves of libraries and bookstores look like an undigested *chaos*, from which order can never be brought, and to read or even look over which would consume the years of Methuselah!

If the attainment of all the best thoughts, or the acquisition of all the useful knowledge contained in those volumes, required that they should all be read through, the task would be interminable, the labor beyond human endurance, and life exhausted in the vain attempt to perform such an immense labor; but, happily, this is not the case, and intelligent minds soon learn that, by reading one volume, they may attain all that could be got by reading a thousand other volumes. The history of human learning, philosophy, and even poetry, proves that the standard of excellence is attained by slow degrees, and that, as a general principle, the books of the last age are, in reference to that language in which they are written, the best. It is self-evident that the authors of each century must, in one particular, be superior to those of the preceding. They must, if the book be on any branch of knowledge, have as much more information in it as the last century has learned. For example, if a traveller had, a century since, told one half of what is now known about Egypt and its monuments, his book would have been a marvel. The same is true of all the books which contain a knowledge of the earth, of science, of history, and biography; for it must be recollected, that our knowledge of ancient history and ancient men is, like our knowledge of science itself, greatly enlarged by modern discoveries. Hence, of all the books which have been published in a thousand years, not one in a hundred is of any value, however meritorious they may have been at the time of publication. They have been superseded by later and superior information.

It is works of *sentiment and fiction* only, of which it cannot fairly be said, that the last is *probably* the best. These admit of infinite variety. Some new combination in an epic poem, and some new style of novel, may attract the world's admiration, and prove a superior model of literary art to those which have preceded, or those which for centuries will follow it. If the number of models of this sort were very numerous, it would present great difficulties in the choice of reading, and greatly increase the labors of the student; but, happily for the student, if not happily for the world, the class of *model works*, in poetic or fictitious literature, is very small: the models are very rare. There is but one Homer, one Milton, one Arabian Nights, and one Walter Scott. It seems to be the characteristic of the fine arts in literature, as in painting and sculpture, to produce but few really great works.

We have thus got rid of one of the great obstacles to the proper and systematic study of literature. Books no longer present an interminable mass of unsystematized volumes, through which no life, and no patience, is sufficient to wade. There is no longer a chaos. The modern works of systematized knowledge give us a luminous and distinct view of the whole circle of science and information. The works of high poetic art and invention are but few. Thus, we have brought within the reach of a few years of time and an energetic industry, all the books which are necessary to inform, dignify, and refine the mind of any intelligent inquirer.

Having in this brief analysis shown the influence of literature in directing and forming the mind, and that the immense number of books does not present a real obstacle to the acquisition of whatever is valuable in them, I have but two or three other suggestions to make. *Reading* acts as an educator in two different modes. In the first place, it gives positive ideas or facts, in the way of knowledge; in the second place, it acts as a continual *exciter* and *suggester* to thought. Unquestionably, the last is the most valuable effect. Positive, actual knowledge, is invaluable to one who knows how to use it. But of what value would be a storehouse of goods, if one could not put them to use? There are men whose memory is very strong, but whose reason is little cultivated. These often acquire a great variety of knowledge, and are minute in their recollection of facts; yet this knowledge seems little available to them. The truth is, if the reason be active and strong, the knowledge of minute facts is of little use, provided the repositories of books and information are accessible. It follows, then, that a course of general reading, systematically undertaken, would be far more useful, if it was accompanied by an *analysis* and *review* of the subjects read. This is rarely done, and it will not be done, unless by the advice and assistance of a judicious parent or teacher. The conclusion I draw is, that youth should not be so restricted in reading, that it ceases to be a pleasure; but that the teacher should select a systematized course oı the best authors, pursuing a regular order in time and topics; and that the young reader should be questioned and examined on what he has read. The mind should be gradually accustomed to analysis; to the connection between cause and effect; to the philosophical sequence of events in the moral world; to the artistic effect of style; to the use of figures; to the illustrations afforded by the natural world; and thus learn to consider and reason upon all that great range of subjects which connect physics with metaphysics.

LITERATURE—HOW TO BE SELECTED.

If a series of books is to be selected which comprehend the substance of what is necessary to know in literature; if this series is to be critically analyzed, and if it is to be salutary in its effects, then it is important to inquire upon what principles and method this course is to be selected. It is in the selection of books as it is in what *appears* (to the uncultivated mind) as the disordered materials of nature—that, at last, there is in this apparent disorder, method, sequence, law. Literature, I have said, is the expression of thought; books, therefore, written in each period, must express the thoughts of that period. Literature must, therefore, from age to age, present us with serial pictures of the progress of the human mind; but the last picture in the gallery must present a perspective of the whole series. Here, then, we have the first *principle* in the selection of books. The works of history, biography, art, &c., whoever may be the authors we select, must be such and so many as will present in the whole series the history of man, his mind, his action, and his progress; this must begin at the first syllable of time, and proceed in the order of time to the present day.

Observing the movement of the human race, again, we see that it has sometimes moved by a *leap, per saltem;* and that in a single age more progress has been made than in ten common ages: here we have another principle of reading. We must stop at these passages in time, and take authors who have made it a special study, and present it in a picturesque style; we can afford to spend more time on such an era. Thus, we can afford to study the modern illustrations of Egypt, because Hebrew and Egyptian history are intimately connected, and they mutually illustrate the first great period of civilization. So we may stop to dwell on the Athenian era, the period of a rapid and powerful intellectual development; on the downfall of Rome, produced by internal decay; on the Arabian literature, on the Reformation, and on the English Revolution. Thus, by proper attention to the choice of authors, we may get the most minute views of important periods, drawn by the pencil of accomplished artists.

A third principle is, in the departments of poetry and invention, to select always the model writers, and make them a critical study. Take the Homer of the Greeks, the Horace of the Latins, the Spenser, Shakspeare, Milton, and Pope of the English; there are but few such models, and the time required in reading them, for the sake of criticism as well as pleasure, need not be long. A hundred volumes will contain all of poetic or fictitious literature it is worth while to read in a systematized course; even half of this amount will answer for most persons. The three principles of systematic reading I have indicated are these:

1. That books of history, biography, &c., should be selected so as to give a serial view of the entire progress of human action and the human mind.

2. That the history and view of important periods should be dwelt upon more at length; and that for this purpose, the more minute and picturesque accounts of particular writers may be read.

3. That in works of poetry and fiction, the model writers should be preferred.

I think that if an older and experienced mind were to select for a class of youth such a series of works, were to persuade them gradually to commence it with a proper spirit, and were to excite their minds by inquiries and comments, that the result would be astonishing; that this reading would soon become the greatest pleasure; that a great amount of information would be acquired in a short time, and that the young students would soon become good critics in the highest branches of literature.

What I have written here is suggestive only. Confident that no one has yet estimated high enough the influence of literature, by reading, on the character and mind of the reader, I have here recorded some of my own thoughts on the subject, and offer them as suggestions to others.

CHAPTER XI.

CONVERSATION—AN INSTRUCTOR.

"Though nature weigh our talents, and dispense
To ev'ry man his modicum of sense,
And conversation in its better part
May be esteemed a gift, and not an art,
Yet much depends, as in the tiller's toil,
On culture, and the sowing of the soil."

Cowper.

"Who is a wise man and endued with knowledge among you? Let him shew out of a good conversation his works, with meekness of wisdom."—*St. James.*

Conversation is the exchange of thoughts; therefore, the announcement of a fact, or the recital of a narrative, or the communication of intelligence, by one person, is not properly conversation; it is an important use of language, but is not an *interchange* of ideas. The true idea of conversation is, the communion of two, three, or more persons in the interchange of thoughts which arise at the moment, without set order or form of words. Its great advantage over all written forms of expression or studied statements is, or should be, the truth and freedom of its utterance; conversation occurs usually between friends, in private retirement, without fear or restraint, and it brings out, more than any other action of human life, true pictures of the inner mind. How much the minds of the greatest and best may have been developed by conversation of which the world has never heard, we cannot know; but one thing we know, from the observation of every individual, viz., that conversation is not merely a communion, but also an *experimental process*, among intelligent minds. Who is there, whose mind has any vitality of spirit, that has not questioned the origin, laws, condition, and future of his own being? Who has not questioned the uses of the stars, and the beings that may inhabit them, or whether they are inhabited? Who has not inquired of what lies beyond the horizon of being—of what existences fill up the immensity of space? Who has not looked with wonder upon the minor beings of this earth? What limits, or does any thing limit, the myriads of living creatures who inhabit the leaves of flowers and the skin of fruits? Where does the world of life end, and where does life itself begin, or go? What are the laws which bind the lightnings, which pour forth the rain, which cause plants to vegetate, men to flourish, and this wide world of being to pursue its ceaseless round of motion? Thus questions man of himself, and of all that is visible and tangible in the visible universe. His questions are often far beyond the limits of the human intellect to comprehend or answer, perhaps presumptuous in the eye of Heaven; but in the midst of these are questions which concern those laws of nature or of society which may be comprehended, and are within the proper range of human inquiry; his thoughts dwell on that verge of the known and unknown where something may be discovered; his imagination, excited by some previous discovery, hits upon some new step, and, without knowing its truth, utters his thoughts in some friendly conversation. A circle of scientific friends thus communicate their ideas; experiments are made, and in some future years the world learns the results of these thoughts, these conversations, these experiments, and that reasoning by which new discoveries have been brought out. I said, therefore, that conversation was often *experimental;* experimental by bringing out and comparing the thoughts of different minds. The *effect* is often like that of bringing the opposite poles of electricity together—a spark is elicited, a flash is seen, and minds are startled and excited in a way in which no one could have been by its own action; knowledge is communicated, wit flows, genius pours forth its vivid fancies, and the spirits of the parties, thus mutually exciting and excited, are made happier and brighter by this delightful communion.

UTILITY OF CONVERSATION.

Man is social. Human society is not only made up of individuals, but each individual in it feels that society is necessary to himself; it is an original desire.*

* Dr. Brown, in his Philosophy of the Human Mind, thus speaks of speech used for society, and the desire of society: "We use speech, indeed, in its vulgar offices, to express to each other the want of bodily accommodations, which can be mutually supplied by those who know

Solitary confinement is the severest punishment to which a human being can be exposed on earth, and it has been known to occasion insanity. This continual impulse to society, and this constant dread of solitude, which make the general law of human beings (though there may be some rare and sad exceptions), demonstrate that happiness lies largely in the communion of souls; that human kind have faculties specially adapted to that communion; and that, properly

---

each other's necessities; and as a medium by which those wants can instantly be made known, it is, in these vulgar offices, an instrument of the highest convenience, even though it were incapable of being adapted to any other purpose. But how small a part of that language, which is so eloquent an interpreter of every thought and feeling, is employed for this humble end! If we were to reflect on all those gracious communications, and questions, and answers, and replies that in a little society of friends form for a whole day a happiness which nothing else could give, the few words significant of mere bodily wants would perhaps be scarcely remembered in our retrospect of an eloquence that was expressive of wants of a very different kind—of that social impulse which, when there are others around who can partake its feelings, makes it almost impossible for the heart, whether sad or sprightly, to be sad or sprightly *alone*, and to which no event is little, the communication of which can be the expression of regard. In that infinite variety of languages which are spoken by the nations dispersed on the surface of the earth, there is *one* voice which animates the whole; a voice which, in every country and every time, and in all the changes of barbarism and civilization, still utters a truth, the first to which the heart has assented and the last which it can ever love—the voice of our social nature, bringing its irresistible testimony to the force of that universal sympathy which has found man everywhere, and preserves him everywhere, in the community of mankind."

used, this communion must be a mighty instrument in that ascending progress of which the consciousness makes so great an element of happiness. When Adam was alone in the world, God condescended to commune with him; and when the Almighty called him up, like a child, to see what he would name things, the very use of speech was the creation of knowledge, an act of progress. And thus, from the first man down, by angels and by men, the voice in its uttered speech has been the expression, the herald, and the evidence of a communion of spirits through the wide universe of being! From the garden of Eden to the plains of Mamre, from Jacob to Moses, from the prophets of Judah to the disciples of Jesus, men, and angels, and ascended spirits have, by the utterance of the voice, showed forth the intercourse of all spirits with one another throughout the world of intelligences! These communications have not all been by conversation; but all spirits have exhibited their capacity for, and their pleasure in, this mode of communication.

Conversation, then, must be regarded as one, and perhaps the very mightiest, instrument in the cultivation and expansion of the human mind. It is almost the only mode by which childhood acquires knowledge, and it is the last in which old age delights.

The necessity or utility of conversation, as a means of education, will abundantly appear from two or three very obvious reflections. In the *first* place, the *rapidity and ease* of conversation enables an intelligent person to communicate information, or suggest ideas, or direct attention, with a readiness and a velocity which it is impossible to do by reading. *Secondly*, it may be done more *fully* and more accurately, because there is an opportunity to ask questions, to express different shades of thought, and to illustrate in different ways. *Thirdly*, conversation *suggests* rapidly numerous ideas, which can only be expressed in a very limited manner by written instruction. *Fourthly*, such instruction may thus draw out a *sympathy* of minds, by which the pupil is enlivened, is led forward without labor, and ascends, enlarges the circle of ideas, loves the pursuit of knowledge, and inquires into the reason of things, without ever suspecting that a task has been put upon him. Beyond all doubt, this is the natural mode of instruction—the mode which prevailed in the primitive ages. Books have been resorted to only as helps and aids to the teacher. In this regard, they are absolutely essential; because the great mass of children and youth, who in darker ages were wholly neglected, have now to be taught. The consequence is, that teachers must economize their time; must instruct by classes, at wholesale; and hence, pupils must employ much of their time on their text-books. This seems, at present, to be a necessary part of our system; but while we admit this, we must not forget to use and properly apply that great natural method of teaching and of harmonizing society which God made for the benefit and blessing of mankind—oral teaching. The sympathy of spirits will ever be, while mother and child, philosopher or friend, remain on earth, the most powerful instrument of communication with the human mind.

CONVERSATION—HOW DIRECTED.

I have described conversation as free and spontaneous. So it is; and in this is one of its greatest charms. But it must not, therefore, be assumed that all possible conversation is right, and tends to instruction and improvement. On the contrary, the Scriptures inform us, that the very thoughts themselves must be restrained; that the imagination must be chastened and corrected; and that thought, and the communion of thought, must be regulated in conformity to the pure and holy law of God. This restriction, however, still allows the mind an almost illimitable range of subjects, a variety and expansion of contemplation, which is more than sufficient to fill the most august of human souls, through the ages of eternity.

In the choice of topics, the persons conversing have the same rule that I have laid down in relation to reading. It is the WILL which directs the mind; it is the Reason which guides its choice. Hence the individual always has a self-governing power to direct both its reading and its conversation. When the Apostle describes, in his energetic language, the powerful attributes of the *tongue,* he shows by his conclusion that, notwithstanding the intractableness of this fiery instrument, yet at last, we are accountable for its use. Let the wise (said he) show out of a good conversation his works, with meekness of wisdom.

That all conversation, even among the good and wise, should be always just, right, and instructive, is not to be expected of the imperfect condition of human society. Nor is it to be supposed that grave and important subjects must be always the theme of conversation, when the very intention and beauty of it is to give a light and airy play to the fancy; to enliven with the sallies of wit, and indulge the dreams, which flit like spirits through the intellectual vision. No; human nature must be allowed its natural recreations in the conversational play of minds. The news of the day must be told; the death of friends must be lamented; the last marriage must be talked over; the last joke must be circulated; and gossips must secretly tell all the little events of the neighborhood!

But, having allowed full room for all these natural topics, there comes often a time when intelligent minds meet together for the higher play of intellectual interchange of ideas, or when youth are in company with their superiors, or when accomplished women grace the circle, and minds begin to commune and circulate in higher ranges of thought —here such topics should be conversed upon as involve the most important social problems: the nature and destiny of spirit; the last discoveries in science; the probable course of governments; the tendencies of the times; the changes which manners and customs undergo. No place is so proper for the discussion of social problems as the social circle; for there the solutions of these problems are to produce effect, and there are the individuals upon whom these changes are to operate. In the conversational intercourse between old and young, few persons seem to be aware of the vast amount of influence and information thus communicated. Young persons of intelligence listen with instinctive veneration to the words of the old, and every word so told them is recorded on the leaves of an imperishable memory. Happy is the Gamaliel who can find some intelligent youth to instruct, and happy the youth who can find a Gamaliel whom wisdom has informed, while age has made him venerable!

In the direction of conversation, then, when minds begin to discuss more important things than the casual gossip of the day, let the thoughts be turned on all those problems of society, of nature, and of human improvement, about which some discoveries may yet be made, and on which the intellect becomes interested, and the suggestions of several persons mutually excited may elicit some new experiments, or new results. It is thus that conversation will aid inquiry and the activity of the mind be kept up, and its energies strengthened.

CONVERSATION—HOW CARRIED ON.

As conversation is free, confidential, and in a great degree spontaneous, it seems absurd to suggest any rules for its conduct. So it is; but as Cowper has thought it not beneath him to write a poem on this subject, I may venture barely to state two or three *hints*. Most of what may be said on the subject of conducting conversation must be negative; for most of the errors of manner in conversing arise from doing what ought not to be done. I will state what I think conversation *is*, and what I think it is *not*.

1. The proper manner of conversation has been defined by some one to be "a ball, which is thrown from player to player without being allowed to drop, and thus keeps each one in play." This figure certainly represents what the manner *ought* to be.

In a circle of friends met for mutual converse, no one is so humble that he should be neglected; no one so high that he is entitled to engross all attention. When people meet together, as superior and inferior, to be measured by station, strength, or talents, all conversation, as such, ceases. That beautiful play of fancy, wit, and sentiment, which often beams from a young girl with more brightness than from the most learned sage, is lost. The timid girl shrinks within herself; the youth stands abashed; the diffident part of the company refuse to speak; and thus the party is chilled with an icy reserve. This is a great mistake on the part of those whose exclusiveness has brought it on. Conversation, to be conversation, must be shared in by all; and it should be a duty as well as a courtesy, on the part of those who have the highest place, and talk with the greatest ease, to bring out the minds of all the others—to reflect the lambent rays of those who shine the least, and allow an unclouded brilliancy to those small but bright stars which are visible only when greater ones retire.

In fine, conversation must be this continual play · this perpetual motion of the ball from hand to hand, in order to make it genial to all the company, to bring out all minds, and to make it that free, gladsome communion of spirits, which makes society here seem sometimes like a picture of the ideal heaven.

2. Dogmatism is *not* conversation. When any one in company, whether having just or unjust claims to superiority, assumes an air of consequence, and deals out a succession of dogmatic assertions, it not only offends the sensibilities of the other members of the circle, but absolutely puts an end to any free intercourse of sentiment. It is an oracle, and not a gentleman, who speaks. There may be much information conveyed, and that, too, of value; but it is seldom received with any feeling but that of disgust by the hearers.

3. Debate is *not* conversation; it is simply an argument to maintain opinion. It is not an interchange

of ideas: it is not an inquiry: it is not sentiment; it is only an argument. Cowper says—

> "Ye powers who rule the tongue, if such there are,
> And make colloquial happiness your care,
> Preserve me from the thing I dread and hate,
> A duel in the form of a debate."

4. An harangue is *not* conversation. If any man feels himself impelled to *harangue* others, he should choose a larger audience than a private circle. He should get a lecture-room, and invite his friends there on a stated occasion, when doubtless both they and he may profit by the exercise. But conversation is the *mutual* intercourse of several minds, and admits of no monopoly by any one of the party.

5. A mere narrative is *not* conversation, because it is all on one side; yet narrative and anecdote may be employed to illustrate the subject of conversation:

> "A story, in which native humor reigns,
> Is often useful, always entertains:
> A graver fact enlisted on your side,
> May furnish illustration well applied;
> But sedentary weavers of long tales
> Give me the fidgets, and my patience fails."

The general idea of conversation, as I have described it here, is that of a mutual *interchange* of ideas, sentiment, wit, and information; kept up, like a ball, by constant play, and never monopolized by one person. This shows what the leading members of a party or circle should endeavor to do, in order to accomplish this. They should direct attention to topics of common interest; they should draw out diffident and backward minds, and throw out ideas which may excite and enliven. Should any of the party still retire within themselves, and refuse to mingle in the general current, still the others should keep up the ball, and never let it drop from neglect.

THE COMMUNION OF SPIRITS AN EDUCATOR.

Why is it that great men have had either great mothers or great teachers? Or, in other words, as mothers are teachers, why is it that *mediocre* teaching does not produce great men? On the theory, that it is *genius* which makes great statesmen, great generals, great orators, or great workmen, then it is of no great consequence what sort of teaching they have, since it is a sort of supernatural genius which accomplishes these great results. But it is not so. This remarkable genius is almost invariably found accompanied with either great industry or superior instruction.

It is a *fact*, that most of those who have been remarkable for superior talents, have had either superior mothers or superior teachers. The source of this great influence of a great mind in rearing and nourishing other great minds, we readily discover by looking a little into the mode by which mind acts upon mind. If we were to go to the school of a man, many of whose pupils have turned out brilliant and successful men, we should probably find that he used the same text-books, and nearly the same mode of discipline which are used in other schools: we should notice nothing very remarkable in the general formula of that school; but if we were to hear him speak, we should soon discover that he had an active, vivacious, vigorous mind; that he was continually alert and enterprising; that with him life was in every thing; the world was revealed in beauty, and all creation bloomed and beamed in living light. In one word, he is a *live* man. He sees vividly, feels strongly, and judges sensibly. To sum the whole up, he is a man of quick perceptions and sound judgment, well informed.

Now the theory of his influence over his pupils, and the impulse he gives to their minds, is very simple. He hears them recite their books as others do; but when he *talks*, then he vivifies his young hearers with pictures of the living world; communicates his own ardent spirits; sends his own energy through their thoughts; directs their ambitious steps; and paints on the horizon of futurity glorious castles of hope, with lofty spires and golden domes!

This is the influence of mind upon mind: it is the communion of spirits by conversation: it is an inspiration which those whom God has gifted with great and noble talents, are able to diffuse on all around. Happy are they who are thus gifted, and happy those who, fallen within such blessed influences, know how to use and enjoy such inspiration with wisdom and with meekness.

CHAPTER XII.

THE CONSTITUTION—THE LAW-BOOK OF THE NATION.

"The unity of government which constitutes you one people, is also now dear to you. It is justly so; for it is a main pillar in the edifice of your real independence; the support of your tranquillity at home; your peace abroad; of your safety, of your prosperity; of that very liberty which you so highly prize."—*Washington.*

WHAT is the Constitution? The Constitution is the constituted *form of government.* It embodies in it all the powers and duties with which the nation has thought proper to invest the administrators of government. It is *the fundamental law;* the regulation which determines the manner in which the authority vested in government shall be executed.*

There are certain great principles of national organization which are as necessary to national life in a state of civilization, as the structure of the body is to its motions and functions. The administration of the civil laws is absolutely essential to the order, peace, security, and harmony of society. Civil law, however, must have its limitations; it will not answer to intrust the administrators of law with discretionary powers; for such a government must soon become a despotism, in consequence of the abuses which the ambition and selfishness of public officers

* Mansfield's Political Grammar—Definition 4.

would create. The imperfection of human nature shows itself in nothing more palpably than in matters of government. Hence it is necessary to define and restrict all grants of power. There must, therefore, be a *fundamental frame-work* of what powers the people grant; what functions are to be performed; what duties are required; and what penalties and tribunals are provided to maintain the law. This frame-work is organic; but it is *only* organic. As the circumstances and wants of the people change continually, there must be special laws adapted to their condition, which may be enacted and repealed from time to time. There must, therefore, be legislative bodies under the Constitution, and subsidiary to it: there is, therefore, in the Republic, the major and the minor laws, the organic and the functional.

The organic law is the Constitution. This contains all the essential and elementary principles of republican government; it is, therefore, a fit and most useful part of the studies in an American education.* Our CONSTITUTION may be termed the last and best result of all the experiments upon govern-

* In the year 1834, I prepared the "Political Grammar" for the use of young men, and to encourage the study of our organic law in the colleges and high-schools of the country. At that time it was an *experiment*. Since that period, this subject has been steadily advancing in the educational institutions of the country. The "Political Grammar," which is an outline of the theory and practice of our government, has been widely circulated, and is now in market. It is published by *Truman and Spoffard*, Cincinnati.

ment since the creation of man. It would be ridiculous to look into antiquity for forms of government; it would be equally ridiculous to look to Europe for examples of government, when all its institutions are tottering and tumbling. What one country of Europe is there of which it can be affirmed with the least probability, that its political institutions can last a single century? It is in the elementary principles of our own country that intelligent men in every nation look for a final solution of the difficulties in government.

THE NATURE OF THE CONSTITUTION.

The Constitution is the organic law, and therefore defines and limits the functions of government. Now these functions, in their nature and action, constitute a science, just as much as the anatomy and physiology of the human body, or the geometry of matter. Government is, in its very origin and nature, a system of principles, and there is no government, however despotic or however much abused, which does not in some measure exhibit these principles. Government may be a tyranny; but it cannot be a chaos: the moment it becomes a chaos, it ceases to exist. Society must be recognized, and must re-institute its political institutions.

The functions of government commence in the family; for that is the primitive society. There originates every institution which is valuable; there we shall find the germs of government. For example, take what we may suppose to be the condition and manner of the family of Abraham: he was a patriarch, with a large number of persons under his control. He commands, that in their journey through the land (not unlike the recent emigrant movements through the centre of this continent), certain things shall be prepared, arranged, and done by his family and servants. This is the law: Abraham in this is a lawmaker. The law is made and declared. This is the first and highest function of government. But laws are dead and of no effect unless they are *executed,* administered; and this requires officers, functionaries. Thus Abraham made Eliezer of Damascus his steward, and no doubt had other subordinate officers. These executed the laws under his directions. But there comes a time when some child or servant disobeys the law; then there must be some mode of determining whether the law is violated, and if violated, how the violation shall be punished, and the law vindicated. This is the office of a judge. We thus have the judicial function. In Abraham's family this function was exercised by himself, as in reality were all the powers of government. But we see that these three great powers of government are founded in nature. They are part of the original elements of human society, as much as the forms of geometry are essential attributes of matter.

It is obvious, therefore, that there can be no knowledge of the science of government, and consequently no real freedom, while there is no just understanding of the nature, separation, and proper functions of the three great elements of government. The greatest discovery made in the theory of government is that of the natural and necessary separation of these great functions. In the head of a family we see them united; but there is little danger of abuse there, because all tyranny is restrained by natural affections. In a despotism we see them again united, and what is the consequence? Tyranny, oppression, and darkness. In a perfect republic only, are they entirely separated. There the legislator, the executive, and the judge, are respectively confined within their respective jurisdictions by the Constitution. The nature of a constitution of government, then, is to recognize, define, limit, and prescribe the duties of the three natural and fundamental properties of government. This is its nature and its office, as an organic law. Let us now see in what relation the people stand to this Constitution.

SOVEREIGNTY OF THE PEOPLE.

It is the sovereignty of the people which enacts a constitution. Look again at the family. Abraham was before his family, its founder and maker. To him, as prior to all family regulations, there was no binding law of human regulation; that is, he was the original sovereign, ruling by virtue of a prior and natural sovereignty. So there was a time when the people had no constitution enacted by themselves. In that condition, having granted to no one the natural powers of government existing in the family, each member of society, and consequently society as a whole, retains all the powers of a sovereign, in relation to all human regulations. This is what is called the sovereignty of the people. Perhaps there never was a time when any considerable body of people were entirely without government, and therefore no perfect example of a dormant sovereignty of the people. The sovereignty of the people, however, is prior to the constitution, and the constitution exists by virtue of that sovereignty.* This *fact* brings us to consider the citizen as exercising this power.

---

* M. de Tocqueville remarks (chapter 4—Democracy in America), that "In some countries a power exists which, though it is in a degree foreign to the social body, directs it, and forces it to pursue a certain track. In others, the ruling force is divided, being partly within and partly without the ranks of the people. But nothing of the kind is to be seen in the United States; there society governs itself for itself. All power centres in its bosom; and scarcely an individual is to be met with who would venture to conceive, or still less to express, the idea of seeking it elsewhere. The nation participates in the making of its laws by the choice of its legislators, and in the execution of them, by the choice of the agents of the executive government; it may also be said to govern itself, so feeble and so restricted is the share left to the administration, so little do the authorities forget their popular origin, and the power from which they emanate."

THE CITIZEN A SOVEREIGN.

The citizen of the United States exercises the duties of a sovereign in all those functions which it is usual in modern days for a sovereign to exercise. He chooses all the ministers of power: he chooses the President, the governors, the members of Congress, the members of the Legislatures, and soon will probably choose all the State judges. He chooses, therefore, the legislature, the executive, and the judiciary. Indirectly, he carries on the government himself. It is true, that in a certain election he may be only one in ten thousand: alone he cannot control this mass, and every election may result precisely opposite to his wishes and his vote. Does this fact absolve him from his political and moral responsibility? There is apt to come over many minds, after political defeats, a feeling of discouragement; a feeling that, do what they may, there is an irrevocable and uncontrollable majority which does and will render their votes useless. They then say that they can do no good, and that they are not responsible for results, and will not vote. This seems at first plausible; but a very simple illustration will show its fallacy, and that it leads to ruinous results. Suppose that in certain party divisions there are 3000 voters one side and 7000 on the other, thus giving a majority of more than two to one. In the violence of party spirit, this ratio remains at several elections with very little change. The minority are hopeless:

they then cease to make opposition. The majority, because there is no opposition, fall off in their votes, success being certain. In two or three years, not half the majority vote. The minority do not vote; and it soon appears that out of 10,000 voters not over 4000 have voted! What happens from this? There being no attention paid to their political duties by the majority, the political power has fallen into the hands of the *minority!* Not only this; but the direction of this minority is in the hands of small *caucuses and cliques.* Thus the power of 10,000 voters has fallen into the hands of perhaps only a hundred! A *minority* governs; and the whole theory and spirit of republican government is perverted! But the minority may say, "This is no fault of ours; we should have been overwhelmed if we had voted." True; but is there no difference in the results, in fact and in morals? If the 3000 of the minority had voted, the whole 10,000 would have voted. The majority would have been *compelled* to exercise their discretion, and stand upon their responsibility. In one word, the minority would have held the majority to their duties, and it would be the *majority* and not a minority which governs. Minorities have power, and it is false reasoning—utterly false—by which any man excuses himself from political duties, or neglects the public responsibilities which in the course of human events have been cast upon him.

From these facts we come to the particular conclusion which concerns us in an American education. If, in the United States, every man is in one sense a sovereign, and has political duties inevitably cast upon him; if all these political duties, and the general scheme of government, are marked out and limited by a constitution, then it follows that this sovereign citizen ought to *read, study, and understand that constitution.*

Government is in its very nature a complex machine; and the republican form of government the most complex of any in its practical operation. It is by the separation of the functions of government, the divisions of departments, the checks and balances of power, that freedom is secured. Elections are very simple; but the rights, duties, and operations of the citizen, the public officer, the legislator, the judge, the army, the navy, the states, the municipalities, and the townships, are not simple, by any means. On the contrary, all these various functions of American government make up a very complex system; and there are few who have studied it in all its branches.

The sovereign citizen should, therefore, at least study and understand the constitution of his country.

A CITIZEN A SUBJECT.

The citizen is a sovereign; but there is an anomaly in his sovereignty which attends no other sovereign on earth. He is also a *subject.* To what is he subject? The law. His sovereignty is void, when it attempts to intervene between the law and himself. All other sovereigns can arrest the law, or pardon the offender; but the citizen cannot. When he has put his vote in the ballot-box, his sovereignty is exhausted: he has chosen his ministers by his vote; but he has voluntarily in the Constitution deprived himself of any power to interfere with the administration and operation of the laws. From that moment all goes on without him, and he becomes one only in a mass of human beings, among whom the law knows no distinctions, and over whom it rules with ceaseless sway.

There follows from this double relation a very curious and important consequence. It is, that *obedience* to the law as a *subject*, is the surest foundation of his power as a *sovereign*. If the law be supreme, then the political sovereignty which enacts the law is supreme; but if the people in their individual capacities can overthrow the law, then they overturn their own political power. In one word, law is the medium, the instrument by which the popular power in a republic is administered. If the people, who really have made the law, overturn it, they create a chaos. There is no longer government; there is no longer law; there is no longer liberty; for there is no civil liberty which is not defined and defended.

There follows another consequence from this creation of law and its obligations by the sovereignty of the people: that is, the public officers are the creatures of the law only. Their tenure is not held from any power independent of the people, which can enlarge or diminish their powers; but is a precise and defined creation of the popular sovereignty through the law. Hence public officers, in relation to the people, have precise and limited functions, which, if they transcend, their acts are void.

Thus, we have all the rights, duties, and obligations of the citizen, and all the powers of public officers, and the limitations of the law itself, traced up to the Constitution. The Constitution, therefore, is the political and legal guide of the citizen.

THE CITIZEN AN OFFICER.

Every citizen of the republic is liable to become an officer of the republic, in some of all the legislative, judicial, or executive stations, which require the performance of public duties. There are in the United States full *five hundred thousand public officers,* from school director up to the President. Probably there are more than even this great number. *One in six* of all the male white citizens of the republic are actually *in office.* But, as many are in office but a short time, there is a rapid rotation; so that probably *one-fourth* the voters of the Union are, at some time or other, called into office!

The performance of these duties, however small or humble, requires the officer to look into the law which regulates his duties. This law, again, has some reference to the State Constitution, if not to that of the Union. In a special as well as a general sense, the citizen is required to know something of the outline of the constitutional law of the country. I know how easy it is to say, that all that is required is to read the statute; that a great deal of information is got by political discussion; that newspapers are the great medium of intelligence; and that, finally, it is impossible for common citizens to be scholars, and learn law, and study constitutions. There is much truth in all this, but it is not the whole truth. Political discussions and ephemeral publications furnish a certain degree of information; but this information is partial, and often erroneous. It is superficial and inadequate. It may do for those who have no time to get any thing better. But, when we speak of *education*, we speak of those who *have* time to learn something better. We speak of those to whom schools, academies, and colleges are accessible. When we speak of the means of education, we speak of those to whom education is a possible thing. To say that there is any portion of the citizens of a republic to whom education is *impossible*, is to accuse the republic itself of gross injustice, and of fatal wrong to itself.

When I say, then, that *one-fourth* of all the citizens of the republic will be called upon to perform the duties of public officers, I assume that full that proportion of the citizens have time and means to make themselves acquainted with the organic law of the republic, and I give the best reason why they should acquaint themselves with it.

THE CONSTITUTION AN INSTRUCTOR.

To acquire absolute *knowledge* is, as I have shown in previous chapters,* very far from being the only, or even the principal object, in the selection of the topics of education. The chief object is to strengthen, discipline, enlarge, and in all respects improve the mind. But the mind has various faculties, or susceptibilities of improvement in various directions. Whatever this may be called, it is certain these faculties may be improved by different kinds of exercise. Thus the memory may be improved in a remarkable degree, while the reasoning is deficient. So, also, the reasoning may be exercised in different ways. I have exhibited mathematics and astronomy as educators in strict, logical reasoning; history as teaching social science; language as teaching the structure and philosophy of thought; literature as the written expression of thought; and conversation as the interchange of intelligent minds. But neither of these teaches that peculiar train of reasoning which is connected with the operations of civil society. They raise no questions in relation to law and government. Now, it is absolutely certain that

* The Utility of Mathematics, chapter 6.

the whole train and manner of reasoning, in relation to civil laws, is totally different from that called forth in the positive sciences. A new class of ideas is developed, and a dormant species of intellectual functions called forth. It follows inevitably, that the study of the best form of government will be a useful element in any well-adapted course of American education.* What is the best form of government? The Constitution of the United States is the only instrument which exhibits a perfect picture of republican government. That instrument is itself an outline of the science of organic law. It is a study for the wisest of men, and is to all young minds the geometry of law. It contains all the principles in their elementary form, which enter into the idea of government. Nothing, therefore, can improve the mind more than a critical study of that instrument. Nothing can be better adapted to bring out that kind

* I have seen it stated in a respectable newspaper, that these political studies of any kind ought to be banished from places of education, because the professor will thus indoctrinate his pupils with party doctrines! This is precisely of a piece with the objection to the study of the Bible, because it will teach sectarianism! This objection is fatal to the whole circle of social sciences, which must soon become the principal objects of study. Of course, these objectors would not have history studied, for that is full of both party and sectarianism! They cannot study the philosophy of light; for light is composed of the seven colors of the rainbow, and of course is *parti-colored!* In fine, the objection either amounts to nothing, or it is fatal to education.

of reasoning which is requisite to the perception and understanding of the structure and principles of civil society.

Nor need any one apprehend that the value of this study will diminish with the passage of time. The Constitution is an imperishable monument in the highway of nations. The waves which sweep away the ephemeral productions of human genius, will wash in vain its adamantine base. It is a durable structure. Opposition will cement its strength; age will make it classical; posterity will admire its beautiful proportions; generation after generation will repose in security under the protection of its lofty columns; the student of liberty will come a pilgrim to its portico from every clime, and its glorious form become a model to every nation.

CHAPTER XIII.

THE BIBLE—THE LAW-BOOK FROM HEAVEN.

"All Scripture is given by inspiration of God, and is profitable for doctrine, for reproof, for correction, for instruction in righteousness: that the man of God may be perfect, thoroughly furnished unto all good works."—*St. Paul.*

If the law-book of the nation be necessary to the furnishing of a well-educated mind, still more is that law-book from heaven, which is filled with all divine knowledge as yet communicated to man. Nay, if science, if literature, if language, if liberty itself were wanting, the Christian would still find an inexhaustible treasury of knowledge, of doctrine, and instruction, in the Scriptures, which would be alike his consolation and his support. Well has Cowper sung—

"——— there is a liberty unsung
By poets, and by senators unprais'd,
Which monarchs cannot grant, nor all the pow'rs
Of earth and hell confed'rate take away."—

It is of the Bible, however, as a means of education only, that I would speak. As a book of divine law, no one can think of the Holy Volume without awe. It seems as if we were speaking of the Inner Temple, where a divine presence shines on every object, and makes them sacred in our sight! This sacred book, however, has been made free and open to all inquiring minds. "Search the Scriptures;" for they are profitable for doctrine, for reproof, for correction, and for instruction in righteousness. These terms comprehend a wide range of knowledge, and are by no means confined to metaphysical doctrines or theological tenets. It embraces something of almost all branches of information, and on some subjects comprehends all that is known; while on the true nature and destiny of man, it contains *all* that we can know, because it is all that God has chosen to reveal. It would be absurd, therefore, to reject the Bible in a system of education, if it were considered merely as a book of literature or knowledge; but when it is considered as a book of divine law, inspired of God, to reject it as a means of instruction is not only absurd, but insane. It would be to shut out light and welcome darkness, for no reason but that man loved darkness better than light!

Let us glance at the reasons why the Bible should be studied as a book of instruction.

THE BIBLE THE OLDEST AND TRUEST HISTORY.

No human history whatever exists of the origin, being, progress, social organization, laws, science, or civilization of the human race for the first two thousand years of human existence. The Book of Genesis contains it all. In that brief, solid, condensed record, where every sentence contains the matter of a volume, is registered and delineated every fact, every principle, and every germinal idea which has governed and directed the entire family of man from the first to the last hour of time. There lies the origin of nations, the causes of their separation; the predestination of races; the seeds of prosperity and adversity; a world deluged with destruction, and a world restored with the hope of a glorious future. There we see the first man leaving the Eden of creation, and with the first mother, hand in hand, taking their solitary way; there we see the first murderer, the first shepherd, the first artificer, the first war, the first building of cities, the first colonies, the migration of tribes, the wandering of men away from civilization, and their alienation from the worship of the true God; there we see the most marvellous pictures of real things; there are patriarchs who lived for ages, angels who conversed with men, and men who communed with spirits. All was new, and fresh, and wonderful: the angelic host had not yet wholly abandoned the earth, and man had not yet learned to pursue his pilgrimage alone.

This history of more than two thousand years of the most wonderful period of the human race, belongs to the Bible. Strike the Book of Genesis out, and you can find it nowhere else. In vain you search the ruins of Egypt; in vain you dig up the foundations of Nineveh; in vain you search the boasted antiquities of Hindostan; in vain you read the pretended legends of China—all is darkness, or all is fable. Every history, every tradition, every philosophy, every book, however assuming authority, every science, and every art fails to discover the early history of man! Here only we have it. Brief, sententious, rapid in its survey, and yet picturesque, it is *the* history of man in his creation, his progress, his separation, his wanderings, and his civilization, during one-third his recorded life on earth!

If this history were lost, the entire foundation of human knowledge would be lost; for all that we know of the history and progress of the human race is connected with, bound to, and derived from this short record of its primitive age. Nothing can be gathered from ruins, from tradition, from conjecture, fancy, or philosophy. Here is all; and this history contains the axioms, definitions, and elements of all historical science. It is a solid foundation, around which the storms of time have beaten in vain.

Nor is it only in this history of the early ages that the Bible is valuable and peculiar for its historical information. All subsequent history is deduced from, and *dovetailed*, as we may say, into this Genesic record. The Bible continues to record the transactions in part, and the moral history entirely, of all the primitive nations during fifteen hundred years, since the patriarchal period. There are portions of the beginning, rise, prosperity, glory, and ruin of Egypt, Chaldea, Babylonia, Tyre, and Persia, in addition to the complete history of the Hebrews, in whom reposed for many ages the highest civilization on earth. This history also does what no human history can ever do: it verifies itself by a continual reference to existent facts, and by a continual consistency of each part with every other. The monuments of Egypt, the ruins of Nineveh and Babylon, the concurrent history of all nations, and the traditions of all people, so far as they relate to the same subject, have corroborated, and most wonderfully illustrated, the Biblical record. More wonderful yet is its own consistency, stating briefly, and yet most positively, the facts which must run through and govern the condition of a race or a nation through thousands of years; and while that fact, too, must be multiplied and ramified in thousands of channels, like the minute fibres in the root of some mighty tree; yet we find that all subsequent facts consist with the original statement, all subsequent history but serves as a verification of the original record. As time brings us nearer to the issue of the drama, the characters, principles, and plan of the divine history become more apparent and conspicuous. All is order, beauty, and harmony.

THE BIBLE IS A DELINEATOR OF HUMAN NATURE.

All discussions upon moral philosophy, intellectual philosophy, and metaphysical laws generally, at last depend upon, and centre in, two ideas, viz., the nature of the soul, and the nature of its obligations.

Now, the origin and nature of the soul and its obligations are fully stated in the Bible. Where is he who has added any thing to that knowledge? Where is the philosopher, the writer, the genius, the reasoner, who has been able to discover a faculty of the mind, or a source of moral obligation, which was not known to the prophets of Judea? If a man cannot add one cubit to his stature, still less can he add a new quality to his soul. Humbling as the thought may be, and ought to be, it is yet a truth, that while man has been endued with faculties capable of conquering matter and civilizing society, and out of all bringing glorious triumphs, he has been utterly unable to add any thing to the soul itself, or discover any thing of its nature beyond what is revealed in the Scriptures. That is a path in which faith, not reason, must be his guide and friend:

> "Dim as the borrow'd beams of moon and stars
> To lonely, weary, wandering travellers,
> Is reason to the soul; and as on high,
> Those rolling fires discover but the sky,
> Not light as here; so reason's glimmering ray
> Was lent, not to assure our doubtful way,
> But guide us upward to a better day."

It is true, that many philosophers have busied themselves with *systematizing* what is called intellectual philosophy, and *codifying* the laws of moral philosophy; but what iota of real knowledge has been added to the original stock? Much dangerous speculation has been engrafted on revealed truth, but no real discoveries made. These treatises may in some sense be valuable, by classifying the facts and phenomena of mind; but when we want simply to realize the actual powers and duties of the soul, they cannot give us any real addition to the knowledge revealed in the Bible.

The portrait of man, in his generic character, as given in the Scriptures, is a daguerreotype of his moral nature, drawn by the pencil of divine light. It is accurate in all respects. No human being has been able to read that description of man, and say—This is not my nature. No one has been so great, and none so low, that their likeness was not inscribed on the pages of Holy Writ: none have been so base, and none so noble, none so deformed, and none so perfect, that all his features, his peculiarities, his baseness, or his glory, have not been drawn so clearly, so strikingly, that through all the ages of time that character will stand forth, and those features be recognized!

The Bible is the only book which contains this portrait of human nature. It is the only one in which this branch of knowledge can be learned. If it be useful, then, for man to know himself (and ancient philosophers have said this was the most valuable of knowledge), certainly it is useful to study the Bible, which alone contains an accurate account of human nature.

THE BIBLE CONTAINS THE DIVINE LAW.

That there are certain impulses of feelings, and suggestions of uninstructed reason, which may be called the law of nature, and sometimes lead to right actions, St. Paul admits when writing to the Romans. But that this is an insufficient moral law, and totally inadequate to perfect any part of character, much less lead to the righteousness of faith, the same inspired writer, in the same epistle, proves, by drawing the darkest picture of human depravity, when restrained by no other law, which was ever exhibited to human eyes. It is a true picture of the Roman, in his highest estate of glory; and a true picture of man, unguided and unrestrained by a divine law, in every age and in every nation.

There follows, then, from this fact, that there is a need of a divine law. Because there was a need of it to perfect his announced plan of mercy, God revealed such a law. It was revealed, at first, in a dark age of the world, when the visible and tangible only could be understood by, and impressed upon the human mind. It was revealed, therefore, in the midst of all the sublime phenomena which could strike and astonish the wondering soul. It was attended by the visible presence of divine glory. It was given to men invested with supernatural power. It was revealed to a peculiar people. It was preserved by a succession of extraordinary acts. The spirits of heaven, and all the elements of earth, were made to conspire in preserving, extending, and glorifying this holy law.

Such was the first dispensation of the law, revealed in an age of darkness, but accompanied by types and shadows of a more glorious dispensation yet to come. For two thousand years, this divine law continued to be the only spiritual light visible amidst the darkness of antiquity. On Judah's hills and Syrian plains it continued to shine, invested with supernatural glory, guarded by supernatural power, and gradually extending its illumination over other nations and other lands.

This illumination was not confined to the peculiar people to whom the divine law was originally revealed. It was a light shining in a dark place, but a light which could not be hid. Through the midst of ancient empires some knowledge of this law extended. Daniel proclaimed it in the court of Babylon, and Jonah preached it amidst the palaces of Nineveh. Although unacknowledged and unobeyed, the traditions, history, laws, and even arts of the ancient nations, exhibit ample proof that they were not unacquainted with the sacred history and holy laws of the Hebrews. And thus the light of the first dispensation became diffused, in however faint a degree, through the civilization of antiquity.

This was the preparation of antiquity. At length the day of the second dispensation dawned from on high. It was in the midst of the most gigantic and the most corrupt nation which had ever been reared amidst the empires of paganism; it was at the height of its glory; it was in the zenith of its power—when its conquests overshadowed the earth—that CHRIST came to announce the second dispensation. The ERA OF CHRISTIANITY was begun. The world no longer dated time (*urbe condita*) from the building of the city, but (*anno domini*) from the year of our Lord. The calendar of time and the annals of history were both changed. Man commenced a new spiritual era. Figures and shadows were forever removed, and Christ revealed the second book of the divine law.

It is thus that the Bible, the HOLY BOOK, contains, in our enlightened day, both volumes of the divine law. It is thus that the figures, and shadows, and promises of the first dispensation have been opened up, interpreted, and made clear to our minds, by the full beams of the Sun of Righteousness.

This divine law is, to all who profess Christianity, the one fundamental law of life and action. Hence, there can be no Christian education without making its principles, its precepts, and its history a constant study.

THE BIBLE CONTAINS THE TRUE PRINCIPLES OF PROGRESS.

The evils of mankind are various in form, but one in kind. Departure from the divine law is the one universal evil; but its visible effects in deranging society, in rendering individuals unhappy, in disturbing the harmony of mind, and in creating moral insanity, among the most gifted and beautiful of the human race, manifested in thousands of forms, are the *special* evils against which philosophers and reformers have directed their attacks. In this they have endeavored to check the stream at its mouth, rather than its spring. But while the spring remains, the stream will flow. The ancient philosophers enumerated what they called the cardinal virtues. They were prudence, temperance, courage, and fortitude. Yet nothing is more certain than that a man might have all these, and be neither wise nor good. The savage has fortitude, the warrior has courage, the miser may have both prudence and temperance; but if all that savage, warrior, or miser have, could be united in one person, he would be neither lovely nor admirable without graces and virtues which the sages of Greece did not enumerate.

There are others, in more modern times, who think that if government could everywhere be constituted on certain principles; society modified in certain forms; industry organized to produce the utmost possible results; temperance be universally adopted; and all mankind instructed in the elements of intellectual education: that then the broken fragments of society would be moulded into a united whole; the disturbed spirits rest at peace; and all move harmoniously and beautifully in their respective orbits!

But this whole scheme fails exactly at that point where failure is fatal. All its arrangements are external or social. It would give a frame-work to society, an energy to industry, a system to effort, a prevention to drunkenness, and an instruction to intellect. All these are happy results; but do they, or *can* they, control the individual spirit? Will they arrest one passion? Can they call back one wandering soul from its dark imaginations? It is palpable —most palpable—that after all, it is the individual spirits, deranged and diseased, which cause all the mischief. The Bible states this fact, and then proposes a remedy, which, if adopted, will restore society to a beauty, harmony, and glory, beyond what the most vivid imagination has ever pictured to itself. Its doctrine, in regard to human evils and human reformations, is simple, direct, and positive. It states as a *fact*, that man has departed, and continues to depart, from the divine law: it states, that as a consequence of this, man has broken the relations which connected him with God on one hand, and with his fellow-man on the other. To reunite these broken relations, is in itself to restore harmony and peace to the human race. There are, then, given two general *principles* by which that restoration can be effected. The first is love to God; and the second, love to man. By the adoption of the first, the divine law will be perfectly obeyed with reverence and humility, because the subject perceives, admires, and loves the wisdom and goodness of the law. By the second principle, it is rendered impossible that man should do evil to man; for how can murder, or theft, or oppression exist in a society where every one loves his neighbor as himself? All actual evil becomes then impossible. This is the simple, direct, and easily understood theory of human reformation proposed in the Bible. It was Christ who announced this doctrine. He was standing in the temple, at Jerusalem, where the Mosaic ritual and observances had for ages been the law, amidst Pharisees and Sadducees, the philosophers of Hebraism—in the presence of those Roman conquerors who had subdued the earth—surrounded by all the splendors of that Roman empire, whose civil laws were carried to the highest point of legal art, when learning was the ornament and glory of the greatest men, and the brilliancy of Greece yet illuminated the nations—when He announced this simple and sublime view of the principles by which human society is to be reformed and restored. Has experience shown any other method by which it can be restored?

In these simple principles are contained all the elements of the most rapid and most powerful progress of which society is capable. They are not opposed to any thing not inconsistent with themselves. They are, therefore, not opposed to any partial or minor plan of reformation which may promise good. On the contrary, these great principles will energize and make effectual any partial and particular plans of good which human ingenuity may devise for human reform; but in those principles themselves lie all the elements of real progress.

THE BIBLE ANNOUNCES FUTURE GLORY.

Hope is the strongest excitant of the human mind. It is exhibited in various forms. We hope, not only for ourselves, but for others; for communities, for nations, for country, and for the world. Perhaps the brightest picture which ever floated before the human vision is that of a lost race restored a world in ruins rebuilt in all beautiful proportions; wandering orbs returning to their spheres; a discordant society made harmonious; a fractured harp made whole; and the air made melodious with its sweetly swelling music!

Such is the picture set before us in the Bible of a future condition of society upon earth. To the eye of faith this future is clearly visible. However near, or however remote, there are no clouds or shadows which can obscure its glorious certainty. The Christian of this day sees it, if possible, with even more clearness than did the prophet of Judah, when announcing it from Judah's hills. He sees now the fulfilment of long trains of prophecy; he sees the Jerusalem of the first dispensation perished; he sees the Messiah ascended; he sees the leaven hid in the lump bursting out through the earth; he sees the dark power of paganism crumbling away; he sees the leaves for the healing of nations scattered through the earth; he sees light rising in the regions of darkness; he sees that knowledge is increased; and he feels, with almost the strength of Daniel, that a glorious future is drawing near, and that the prophetic picture may soon be realized in all its beauty.

Leaving out the special hopes of individuals—so bright to the eye of faith—there is no doubt that the coming glory depicted in the Bible is an animating thought and exciting hope to multitudes of Christians. It stands out clear, and above all the obscurity of our present circumstances: it is the rising, not the setting star. Cloudy and tempestuous as may be the day of our pilgrimage here, yet to our longing eyes that light will remain the consolation of the past, the support of the present, and the hope of the future.

CHAPTER XIV.

THE EDUCATION OF WOMEN.

"So God created man in his image: in the image of God created he him; male and female created he them."—*Genesis*, i. 27.

"Male and female created he them; and blessed them, and called their name Adam in the day when they were created."—*Genesis*, v. 2.

"And did not he make one? Yet had he the residue of the Spirit. And wherefore one? That he might seek a godly seed. Therefore, take heed to your spirit, and let none deal treacherously against the wife of his youth." —*Malachi*, ii. 15.

NOT many years since women were exposed to sale in the market-places of Egypt and Turkey. The sale of white women is now confined to the houses of the slave-merchant; but that of black girls still continues in the open streets. At the time when Circassian, and even Greek girls, were yet the subjects of open sale, it was related by an English traveller,* that he saw, in a market for slaves, about twenty young *white* women sitting upon the ground half naked, awaiting a purchaser. One of them fixed the attention of an old Turk. The barbarian examined her shoulders, her limbs, her mouth, her neck, as minutely as he would have examined a horse. During this examination, the slave-merchant extolled the eyes, the elegance of form, and other personal perfections of the poor girl, who he said

* This story is taken from the work of Aimy Martin.

was an innocent of fourteen. In short, after a severe scrutiny, and a higgling for price, the innocent and beautiful girl was *bought* for one hundred and sixty-five francs! She was bought, body and soul; but the soul counted nothing in the bargain. Her mother, too, was there; and half fainting in her mother's arms, she shrieked for help to her sad companions. Alas! what could that avail? In that barbarous land all hearts were closed. The law made them insensible to the crimes it permitted. The affair was concluded. The girl was delivered over. Thus vanished for her, and thus vanishes for all women in that part of the world, all the future of a happy love!*

This scene was enacted eighteen hundred years after the advent of Christ, and to this hour such is the treatment and such the fate of women among the nations which number two-thirds of the human race.† But if such be the condition of woman, what is man? Can he forget with impunity that male and female, God created he *them*, in his own image?

---

* All of Africa, nearly all of Asia, and some part of Europe, are yet in that unhappy condition of society in which women are *really* if not nominally, slaves. The system of polygamy, although in practice confined chiefly to the rich, degrades the whole social condition of women; and the system of ignorance degrades them, if possible, still more.

† Some persons (whose minds seem capable of better reasoning) say that women who are slaves are not so much to be pitied, for, after all, they have all things necessary to their comfort;—they want

Can he, unpunished, rob one half the human species of their heaven-granted inheritance? Can he roam a freeman, while his copartner remains a slave? Divine justice has, in the constitution of things, made a punishment for every social crime. Man cannot overturn the divinely-constituted fabric of social order, and not fall in its ruins. The blows which one portion of the race inflict upon another, rebound upon themselves. The cries of one suffering being re-echo in the ears of another. The dark minds of mothers cast their shadows upon their children; and upon their posterity will rest clouds and darkness till the day dawns from on high.

In the wide and ancient Orient, the cradle of the human race, man has degraded woman; but *what* is man? Free born, he has no idea of liberty: a despot without a people; civilized without humanity; possessed of beauty which he cannot love, and a family without affections—he stands alone amidst slaves, and amidst ruins! Man degraded himself by degrading women. An eminent writer has said, that it is an eternal law of justice, that man cannot abase women without falling into the same degradation; and he cannot elevate them without becoming better. The last thought is as consolatory as the first is

nothing more, and are very happy and contented! This sort of argument excites in one a feeling of profound indignation. It is in itself an insult to human nature. It places the human being on a level with brutes. Have not the cattle what is necessary to their wants, and are they not contented with their condition?

painful. If we can elevate the future mothers of the race to a higher level, we shall thus erect a platform upon which to elevate the race itself. *How* can we do so excellent a thing? Let us contrast the degradation of woman in the Old World, with her greatly improved, but still imperfect, condition in the New. Let us turn from the Orient to the Occidental. It is in our prosperous, and, compared to the greatest part of the earth, felicitous country, that woman has attained both more freedom and more elevation of character, than has been attained by her sex in any nation of the earth. Splendid and beautiful examples of female excellence, heroism, and worth, shine out from the Hebrew commonwealth and the classic nations; but, like stars in a dark night, they but make more obvious the thick and profound darkness of the mass beyond. It is in the Republic of North America only that women have begun to take their proper rank in society. To this fact, our testimony might not be received by the world, if it were not confirmed and established by the impartial testimony of intelligent travellers in all nations. Among those who have given the strongest evidence in favor of the superior character of American women, and their influence on national manners, is M. De Tocqueville, who speaks of this element as one of the remarkable and peculiar characteristics of American society. One of the peculiarities noticed in the condition of women, is their great freedom, and therefore, greater *self-sustaining power*. But whence arises this greater freedom, this greater energy, this greater power? Simply and only because, for the most part, women in America are considered as companions, and neither slaves nor inferiors. But *whence* does this idea of freedom and of untrammelled personal responsibility arise? It is the one great moral and social idea in this country. It has extended to women the same liberty which is allowed in worship and government. It has given the individual liberty of action, and thrown upon him the *moral and social responsibility* for his acts. It is the same of women. It is the one universal idea of American liberty. If we inquire whence is the *origin* of this great idea, this idea which must soon fill the world, modify all government, and overturn all ancient institutions; if we inquire its origin, we trace it historically to the first colonists. In the first settlements there was no other idea. The women and the men went alone into the wilderness. Together they built the first house; together they erected the first church; together they provided food and raiment; together they were buried in the first green grave-yard—leaving behind them no hereditary titles; no entailed estates, to be possessed by an eldest son, to the exclusion of his sisters; no badge of that menial servitude which degraded in the old country the majority of men, and all of women. The green fields they had cultivated, went to their children, sharing equally; the society they had founded recognized their equal positions; the freedom of worship they had enjoyed was left to their posterity. In fine, by the act of exile, they became as peculiar a people as the Hebrews, when they crossed the Red Sea from the land of the Pharaohs. But why exiles? Why fly from the time-honored governments of the Old World? Religious excitement, or, in other words, the CONVICTIONS OF THE SOUL, are the only source of the English Rebellion, the colonization of the United States, the peculiar form of the first colonies, the severity of manners, the freedom of women, and that long train of political results which have followed, and must follow, through ages of time. And what produced these religious convictions? The reading of the Bible laid open to the people, and the inquiries which that reading suggested. For twelve hundred years after the advent of Christ, the people—the masses of the people—*read* nothing, much less knew any thing, of the Bible. For three hundred years more, but few read any thing. The Bible was a closed book. Then the Bible was opened, and the art of printing sent it round the earth: then people read and thought; they thought and inquired; they were convinced of certain great truths, and they acted upon them; they were repelled, trampled upon, and derided by the proud oppressions of the Old World; they fled to the wilderness, and nursed the child of Christian liberty, till it has become glorious in might and beauty—going forth a deliverer of nations.

Let history be searched, and criticism examine with microscopic view the minutest facts, and the most obscure records, and this at last is the simple sequence of causes by which American liberty and society are what they are. Take from human knowledge those views which the Bible furnishes of the nature of the human soul, of its functions and destiny, of its relations to God and its relations to society, and there is absolutely nothing left upon which to found the idea of a free society. There is no moral basis left for such a society. There is no reason left why the conqueror should not make the conquered a slave; or why women should not be regarded as inferior; or why hereditary monarchs should not be thought the natural, and therefore exclusive, rulers of mankind; or, in one word, why *power* should not be deemed the sole evidence of right. It is the idea of moral right, founded in the nature of the soul, and derived from the Bible, which is the sole foundation of republican government, and the sole evidence that women have equal rights in the social system, and are equal partners in whatever benefits society can confer.

Here, then, we start in the consideration of what is necessary in the education of women. It is, that in all moral and social elements they are equal before the law of God, and therefore should be equal before the law of man. In the physical system they are different; and in the political system, which is always an artificial arrangement, it may or may not be expedient to make them equal; but in both these, the *differences* relate to nothing which any education can influence. The education of men in all that concerns the use, strength, functions, and ultimate faculties of the mind, does not relate to sex. Why, then, should it do so in women? It is only after a young man has received the most valuable part of his education, and is inquiring how he can earn a livelihood, that there comes up any of those practical *applications* of knowledge or reason which may relate to his particular sex. In one word, it is practical *business*, and not *precedent studies*, which in the least relates to the question, whether the student be a man or a woman. It may be thought that I have stated the equal right of women to education in too strong terms. But I have turned the subject over in various ways, and can discover nothing in revelation, nature, or reason, which can absolve society from its moral obligation to give the mothers of its children the highest and best education which it is expected those children of either sex will ever attain. Let us consider separately some of the *facts* which demand this duty from society, and some of the *modes* in which it may be performed.

THE HUMAN NATURE IS ONE.

The human soul has no sex. Human nature is not two. I state in this proposition a broad fact, and which, if it be a fact, deserves to be seriously considered. It is not, philosophically, a necessary consequence from what we know of human nature, as it is known by observation; for all we know of human nature, as seen and tangible, is known of it as male and female only. But there are two species of evidence by which this fact is irresistibly established. First, we have a *consciousness* of a living and dominant spirit, which is, in fact, the real *being;* and we have, by mutual communion with others, a consciousness that the original and distinctive attributes of spirit are the same in men and women, and among all nations. This of itself would be conclusive that there is no sex in the soul. But, secondly, there is a stronger and an entirely decisive species of evidence derived from revelation. There are not two redemptions, nor two condemnations; there are not two standards of character, nor two modes of trial; there is one commandment, one baptism, one condemnation, one redemption, and one judgment. In all that concerns the existence and nature of the soul, the revealed law has made no distinction between the sexes, and acknowledged none in the world to come. This is enough: it is decisive; for all the purpose of the soul and of its future, human nature is one. Neither clime, nor race, nor sex, are recognized, as affecting the attributes of spirit, in the eternal law. Therefore, neither clime, nor race, nor sex should be recognized as a reason for denying to any part of the human race an education whose object is the improvement of the soul, and whose effects will last through eternity.

DIFFERENCES OF BODY DO NOT IMPLY DIFFERENT FACULTIES.

All the discussions about the relative value, and strength, and character of the sexes, have ended in confusion, and brought conviction to no one, because they have not begun at the beginning, nor ended at the end. There can be no clear convictions of truth when there are no clear ideas of elementary principles. When it is argued, that *because* women are, in the course of nature, mothers and nurses, and by reason of those offices, keepers at home, they are, from that fact, to be wholly engaged on inferior objects and inferior thoughts, and are incapable of the loftiest flights of the soul, it is a false conclusion. It does not follow from the premises. It is what logicians call a *non sequitur*. By way of testing it, let us apply a parallel argument to the avocations of men. At the same moment that women were ordained to become mothers in sorrow and suffering, man was also ordained to eat the herb of the field, and in the sweat of his brow to eat the bread of his labor. Suppose that, in conformity with this ordinance, man is assumed to be the peculiar and only laborer, and therefore, that his mind is never to ascend above the avocations of mere labor: he is never to inquire into the phenomena of the natural world; he is never to search the laws of motion in heavenly bodies; he is never to weave out the beautiful creations of fancy; never to wander through the regions of philosophy in search of the causes, operations, and laws of that vast world, whose mysteries and harmonies delight his wondering spirit! Would this inert and unproductive existence be a just conclusion from the *fact* that he was ordained to be a laborer, eating his bread in the sweat of his brow? Surely not. Yet it is, logically, as correct a conclusion as that women are incapable of the highest intellectual efforts, because they are ordained to be mothers and nurses. The truth, I suppose, is, that the character and powers of the human soul —which is *the* being—do not depend upon avocations.

Men and women have been compared by the forms of their bodies, and by their special avocations and employments. In these are found varieties and differences — differences which are undeniable and important. But these do not necessarily imply any difference in the fundamental character of the soul. To think, to inquire, to sympathize, are the same functions of life and spirit, whether exhibited in man or woman. What constitutes, then, the highest character, must, in its essential elements, be independent of sex or condition. It must depend on the strength, the culture, the direction, and the government of the individual soul. It is the soul which is the living being, and it is its immortal capacities which are to be developed in thought, feeling, sentiment, and principle—in all worthy culture, fitting it for a better life here, and immortal life hereafter.

THE EDUCATION OF MOTHERS.

I have now established two *facts* which are preliminary to any system of female education. The *first* is, that human nature is one; and the *second*, that differences of body do not imply differences of faculties. It is absolutely certain that on the question of whether these are or are not facts, must depend the whole system of female education. If these are *not* facts, then woman is essentially an inferior being, and her education should be adapted to that inferior condition; but if these *are* facts, then her education should be essentially the same, in all that relates to the culture and strengthening of the SOUL (which includes both the intellect and the affections), as that of man: that is, that the elementary, fundamental, and philosophical part of education which relates to the development of the faculties, and is independent of avocations and professions, should be the same, in reference to all individuals, according to their time and opportunities, in the order of Providence. I have protested in another place (Chap. II.) against the *conclusion* that, because the mass of mankind must be engaged in daily labor, that, *therefore*, they must not think of attaining the higher and nobler branches of education.* For the same reason,

* There is probably no impediment to general education greater than the popular idea, that education is not necessary to the great mass of people engaged in common pursuits; and the popular idea,

I protest against the conclusion, from the domestic employments of women, that, *therefore*, they are incapable of attaining or enjoying a superior education. The existence of one Newton does not prove that all mankind can become Newtons; but it does prove that human nature has powers capable of such sublime exhibitions of strength and learning. Newton came into the world with the very feeblest of all bodies—the candle of life just flickering in the socket, and kept alive by the assiduous care of a wise and tender mother. How many other Newtons and how many other mothers may the world hold, whom such care and such culture would have reared to such illustrious powers!

So the existence of women remarkable for learning and intellectual eminence, does not prove that all women are capable of attaining that eminence; but it does prove that there is nothing peculiar in their nature and constitution which renders such eminence and attainments naturally impossible. The existence of Mrs. Somerville, of Miss Herschell, or of that Italian lady who was one of the most distinguished mathematicians of her age, does not, indeed, prove that all women may become astronomers and mathematicians, any more than it proves that such would be

---

also, that women not being legislators, divines, lawyers, and doctors, do not require a high education. Nothing can be more false than this idea, and if it remain among the masses of the people, we cannot hope for universal knowledge, or the perpetuity of freedom.

the most profitable employment for them; but it does prove that they are capable of such studies and acquirements. It comes to this, then, that women have the same faculties, and are capable of the same culture and acquisitions as men; they are not inferior, or opposite, or totally different from men in the essential elements of character.

We come now to the practical application of this principle. What *reason* is there why women should be highly educated, or as highly as the circumstances of their condition will admit? The first thing we observe is, that women are the mothers of mankind. As such, they are the *first teachers.* This fact cannot be avoided. There is no substitution possible. If an infant is taken from its mother, it must still be committed to a woman. For the first five years of its life, at least, and generally much longer, its sole teacher is a woman; but, in nine cases out of ten, so as to constitute a permanent law of the social condition, the mothers guide and influence their sons, as well as daughters, through the whole period of youth. Nay, their influence passes far beyond this, so as indirectly to direct, in no small degree, their pursuits in life. If they do not teach or influence the studies of science and literature, or govern in the selection of employments, they do what is more important: they impress their passions, their prejudices, their views and coloring of life and society on their children, with a strength and durability which all subsequent education and experience can scarcely efface. The tree inclines as the twig is bent; but, with few exceptions, it is the mother who gives that bent to the twig. Her influence and her teaching is like the silent dews of heaven: it falls on the soft soil of the soul, and every young and tender plant springs up to meet it. If there be but one blade of grass, it grows the greener; if but one bright flower, it takes new colors from its parent stalk. In fine, both by the sympathies of nature and the principle of imitation, the mother is the model teacher of the child. She trains its instincts; she implants its principles; she points the way; she inspires the spirit; and, in fine, when that child has gone far out of sight in the wayfare of life, and she herself is descended to the tomb, this natural, but mysterious, influence remains: it hovers round the child, even when his head is silvered with the locks of age; it lingers in the mind, like a spirit of the dead come with grave manner but gentle looks to watch and judge the actions of the living!

This ever-present, yet gentle and almost invisible, influence of the mother is the greatest single influence which inclines and directs the minds of men in their young and forming stages. Hence, we find the mother—in fact, though she should never formally instruct her child in a single lesson—the *earliest and most powerful teacher.* Every mother may not be so. There are exceptions; but this is the general and natural rule. Hence arises, at once, the question, What kind of teacher is this mother? How is she qualified for this task? She cannot put it aside; she must perform. If she were to do nothing, she would still be powerfully teaching that nothing is necessary to be done. But this inertia the natural instinct will not allow. She is unnatural who does not teach her children all she can teach, and procure done all that she thinks useful to them. What, then, can the mother do? Here we arrive at the beginning of a perfect system of education, viz., the EDUCATION OF MOTHERS. With these facts in regard to the condition of women and their relation to society before us, we come to inquire what shall be the practical elements of Female Education.

SCIENCE FOR WOMEN.

If women have the same faculties with men, and if they are the first teachers of men, and have the domestic care of families, then it follows that their reason and judgment should be strengthened and cultivated, in order that they may be able to discriminate, judge, and teach in the best manner. This is an inevitable conclusion, from the premises I have laid down. But to strengthen the reason and the judgment requires the study, analysis, and discussion of some of the graver sciences. To this study and discipline, however, among women, there have at all times been raised certain popular *objections*—objections which, undeniably, have existed among the most intelligent men, as well as among almost the entire female sex. If these objections prevail, it is in vain to attempt a high order of education for women; for the very best kind is that which brings out and strengthens the reasoning powers. Let us, then, look at these objections a moment, to see if they really present any insuperable obstacles to the study of science by women, who have time and means for thorough studies. The very first *objection,* though expressed in a hundred different ways and in very polite terms, is, in substance, that women are *unequal to the task;* that is, in plain terms, they are inferior to men. One gentleman says (and it is printed in books) that women are governed more by *instinct,* and men more by *reason!* What does this mean? It can only mean, that women *have* more instinct, and men more reason; for, if they have not, then the one or the other cannot be governed more by the one or the other quality. God, then (according to the theory), has given men more reason and women more instinct. This is contrary to all observation and all experience. Has the drunken Indian, roving like a beast in the forest, any more *reason* than his dark-minded but peaceful wife? Reverse the case. Has the young squaw, who with pleasure, and even pride, becomes the second wife, sharing with the first in the household of a great war-chief, any *instinct* that this polygamy is unlawful? Go to any people, savage or civilized, and there is no example that *instinct* has enabled women to see any truth, which reason had not taught or God revealed to them. The distinction is idle.* Man is not a beast, to be governed by instincts, but a being, endowed with spiritual faculties, and held accountable for the use of them. The objection stated is completely met by the simple fact laid down in the premises of this discussion, that human nature is a unity, and the faculties of the soul the same in both sexes.

Another gentleman says (and that is printed in books) that man is the strong oak, towering upwards, and woman the tender vine which climbs around its trunk and delights in its shade! This poetic figure carries a very doubtful compliment; for it is the poison vine which most frequently climbs round the forest trees! The figure carries with it a certain degree of truth; but, when applied to education, utterly fails. When man is considered as stronger in body, as the conqueror of earth, and the builder of houses and cities, and woman a mother, engaged in domestic employments, it is figuratively true that she reposes under the shade of his labors. But what has that to do with the faculties of mind? It is difference of employments only. Does this difference show that either class of employments needs not the use of reason? Such an idea is absurd.

A third gentleman puts this thought in a different form. He does not like to see women *masculine!*

---

* The idea that there are some such *instincts* in women is still prevalent. Every one must see that to admit that women are governed by *instincts*, and not by reason, is to admit their inferiority.

He wants no *blue stockings!* He thinks that women should be beautiful, graceful, ornamental, delicate, a lily or a rose, perpetually blooming, perennially fresh, for ever smiling, uttering sweet words, and breathing soft melodies! Then he will be ready to exclaim with Horace:

> "Dulce ridentem, dulce loquentem
> Lalagen amabo."

There can be no objection to such a delightful ornament of society, provided she be really a woman, and a *reasonable* woman. But what can she do without reason? She cannot be merely ornamental without being worthless; and she cannot be useful without reason, and the stronger it is the better. This life is a reality; and no woman can be either wife or mother without finding it filled with realities, many of them both hard and sad. For all this she requires the more firmness of character, discrimination, and judgment; a certain strength and proper use of reason will enable her to understand better the compensations of her condition, and enjoy a new and higher class of pleasures than she could as one of the idle ornaments of society. Reason is no more masculine than feeling is feminine. If it be *masculine* to reason, then it is *feminine* to feel. Both ideas are absurdities.

Another objection, and a far more serious one, is that the domestic employments and early marriages of women do not leave them time for a more extensive and severe course of studies. This objection is met by the fact, that young women have no *professional studies* (so called) to pursue; or, in other words, their professional studies are those of their daily home avocations. Three years of time is thus gained to them; another year is gained by avoiding certain collateral and technical branches of university studies, which are unnecessary to women. If the time and studies of young women are properly ordered, they will have time for the most complete education in what is essential to either their intellectual, moral, or ornamental cultivation before they are twenty years of age.

The objections stated above may therefore be considered of no practical weight, when the object is to provide a solid, useful, and even elegant education to the young women of our country.

We return, then, to the cultivation of the REASON and the Judgment by the study of science. In this respect all education has the same object, and must be attained by the same means. To *strengthen* the understanding should be the main object in female education, however many accomplishments and graces may be also acquired. There is nothing more certain than, without a complete and ready use of the reasoning powers, no education is available in practical life. There have been men whose retentive memories have stored up an almost incredible amount of knowledge, and yet they were not able to apply it in any useful business; and so there may be women who have numerous accomplishments and much reading, yet who will cut a very poor figure as housekeepers or teachers. The difficulty lies in the want of that discrimination, power of comparison, and judgment, which result from a *mastery over the reason;* an ability to direct and use it at will, by making an analytical examination of every subject which comes before them for decision.

1. In intellectual instruction, the first thing to be relied upon is the study of MATHEMATICS. The rule is the same for women as for men. I shall not go over again the topics, which were fully discussed in Chapter VI.; but will only repeat, that the science of mathematics embraces the great system of natural logic, which is not so fully contained in any other science, and cannot be so well studied in any other way. Geometry contains one species of reasoning; algebra another; and the applications of this reasoning—as in descriptive geometry, mensuration, and trigonometry—teach the use of this logic in practice, and the modes in which theoretical principles become of vast actual value. If these elements of mathematics be thoroughly studied, the higher and more abstruse branches need not be undertaken. There will then be time left for some of those applications of science, which are, in fact, the most beautiful. Among these I would class the doctrine of perspective, of shadows, and of linear drawing.

2. The next subject of study should be chemistry, which is the first and greatest of the *experimental*

sciences. There is no branch of knowledge which so charms the mind with novelty—none which exhibits such striking and surprising phenomena. It is in one respect a more profound and interesting science than mathematics: its elements are deeper; it does not stop merely at figure, extension, quantity, and number, external qualities; but it passes into the interior of objects, and searches out their hidden characteristics. At every moment we are startled and surprised by new results. But the great advantage in the study of chemistry is, that *it draws out and exercises a new class of faculties.* Thus, in the pure mathematics, we assume certain truths, axioms, and facts; and from these we deduce, by logical reasoning, certain general laws. In chemistry, we begin and reason in a different way. We first *observe* facts; then we *compare* them, and deduce analogies, or draw general laws from universal observation; then we *experiment* on certain simple elements; then we analyze, and we compound, till a new class of general principles is obtained: thus we have observation, comparison, analogy, experiment, and general reasoning, all combined. We have excited even the imagination by new combinations: in fine, we have called out a new class of faculties; we have pursued a new process of reasoning; and, as we have pursued the path, we have charmed and excited the active powers of mind.

3. Natural philosophy, or that which describes the phenomena of nature, and the general causes and

laws thereof, should be the subject of study in physical science. There are certain obvious operations of nature which are continually occurring, and often before the eyes of all mankind. Among savage, and often among civilized nations, these are regarded as mysteries or miracles, entirely supernatural, and therefore, causing an unreasonable fear and astonishment.

Thus eclipses throw the North American Indians into terror. So, too, the phenomena of electricity, magnetism, light, all present operations which are marvellous to the ignorant, while they are beautiful and exciting to the intelligent. To describe, classify, and explain these operations of nature, is the object of natural philosophy. Here we have a new exercise of the understanding. There must be generalization; there must be more of memory; and there must be a more precise observation.

4. The next subject in physical science is mechanical philosophy. This is not, as some may suppose, the mere science of mechanics (which, indeed, is included within it), but is the science of force and motion, or those two elements which give life to the whole system of the material universe. Of this philosophy, that part which comes under the heads of dynamics and hydronamics are essential to an understanding of any part of the machinery of the physical world; but no branch of this philosophy should be neglected.

5. The next and highest topic of physical science

is astronomy. Of the elements and uses of this study I have already spoken at large in Chapter VIII., and here refer to it only as one of the special topics of study in female education. I must observe, that that part of astronomy which only is necessary in elementary instruction, is neither very abstruse nor very difficult; for it does not comprehend the long and intricate chains of demonstration by which Galileo, Kepler, and Newton arrived at the laws of the heavenly bodies. It is sufficient that in elementary education there is taught the general facts, laws, and principles by which the sublime system of celestial bodies has been developed and sustained. The great object of this study in women is to *enlarge* their minds and develop philosophical reasoning, by exhibiting the ultimate and grand results of all those sciences and principles which they had previously studied, and which they now perceive are coextensive with the universe. Here is mathematics in all the forms of matter, and the laws of quantity and relations. Here is chemistry in the composition of light and the affinities of bodies. Here are all the phenomena of natural philosophy, and the mechanics of creation! Here the student has ascended from the minute to the grand, from particulars to generals, from the light of a torch to the light of a thousand worlds, blazing and revolving around the throne of the Creator!

Let us now see, if we have pursued these studies aright, in what order, and to what extent, we have developed the faculties of the understanding. The following is a tabular view of the method we have taken to strengthen the understanding:—

Subject of Study.	Operations of Mind.	The Philosophy.
MATHEMATICS.	PERCEPTION, CONSCIOUSNESS, REASONING, DEDUCTION, ANALYSIS, CONCLUSION.	The Logic of Demonstration.
CHEMISTRY.	OBSERVATION, EXPERIMENT, ANALOGY, EXAMINATION, JUDGMENT.	The Logic of Experiment.
NATURAL PHILOSOPHY.	OBSERVATION, REFLECTION, CAUSATION, MEMORY.	The Relations of Cause and Effect.
MECHANICAL PHILOSOPHY.	APPLICATION OF PRINCIPLES, REALIZATION OF POWER, ANALYSIS OF FORCES, EXAMINATION OF MOTION.	The Relations of Force and Motion.
ASTRONOMY.	OBSERVATION, GENERALIZATION, SYSTEMATIZING.	The Generalization of Causes.

The above table may not be strictly accurate in its philosophical arrangement, but it is sufficiently so to show how numerous and various are the operations of mind which have been called into play by this course of scientific studies.

THE CULTIVATION OF LANGUAGE.

A woman has, in some respects, more need of the use and command of language than men; for she is known and is influential chiefly by conversation. The oral utterance of her thoughts is her principal mode of communion. Her expression should be fluent, and her vocabulary copious. To have this, she should study the science and art of language thoroughly. To this end, some one language should be selected, and made by the teacher the subject of critical examination and philosophical inquiry. Use, reading, and criticism, are the best means of acquiring a knowledge of the structure and philosophy of language. There is much difference of opinion at this time, even among educated men, as to the necessity or advantage of studying either or both the dead languages. This difference of opinion extends to the education of both men and women. It must be admitted, however, that if it were decided to take the most perfect language which can be found, and make that the subject of a purely philosophical study, that then no languages will compare with the Greek and Latin: they are refined, elegant, and complete; but the time required for their study is very great compared with the total time which most students can afford. In the case of young women, another objection is found in the fact, that one of the modern languages (in addition to our own) is generally considered necessary as an accomplishment. This question, however, is one of *expediency*, and may safely be left to the judgment of the teacher. It is enough to know, that a careful and analytical study of our own language, at least, is necessary for any well-educated woman. She should not be contented with any mere cursory glance at grammars and dictionaries: they are but *tools*. It is the actual use, power, and philosophy of language which is wanted. Take some English classic author — for example, Addison or Hume, Milton or Pope — and examine and compare sentence after sentence, and page after page. Thus the force and meaning of words, and the power and beauty of the language, will be understood. Here, as in the study of physical science, we shall have a new exercise of different faculties of the mind. We have *comparison, analogies of expression, variations of thought, the application of metaphor and figures.* In fine, we are in a new department of science, and acquire, as we proceed, new ideas. I have already given a sketch (Chapter IX.) of the use and advantage of this study. It is the last one which should be neglected in female education.

COMPOSITION.

Composition, or *writing*, is one of the very best exercises to acquire a knowledge of language. In fact, it is not possible to attain a complete knowledge of it without being expert in the use of the pen and the expression of thought. Women are not usually, in the course of their employments, led to write much of what is termed literary composition; but there is one department in which they are, or should be, supreme—that is, epistolary composition. A very large part of the correspondence of families falls upon them. Nor is this all. The correspondence of families makes a very large part of the history of the times. Letters are the documents to which historians now resort for the materials of history: they are also among the most pleasant and instructive modes of communion in society. Cast asunder, and often separted widely for years, kindred and friends have little other mode of keeping up their intercourse and friendship. It is a mode too much neglected. It is a duty of families, and office of friends, and a delightful exercise of mind, to keep up, by letters, a constant intercourse of those whom nature and affection should bind together. Unfortunately, there is a large part of those who are even well educated, who value at too low a rate the high privilege of epistolary correspondence. They estimate the *useful* consequences, also, at altogether too low a value. Among these, are not only the valuable exercise of mind to the writer, but the perpetuity and strengthening of friendships, which could in no other manner be kept up. Some persons, and especially many ladies, are averse to writing letters, because they think they do not *appear well* on paper. Now, the appearance of a person in a letter depends on exactly three things, which it is the office of a good education to give. These are, *thought*, *style*, and *handwriting*. I need say no more on this head than to make these suggestions. Fortunately, we have in the English language some of the finest examples of epistolary correspondence. The letters of Cowper are in the first class of English literature, and are beautiful examples both of style and refined feeling.

READING.

Reading is the most important means of acquiring that general *information* which is necessary to appear well in conversation. Of the different classes of reading, that of history is the most valuable. But a woman, in this respect, may be contented with a thorough reading of those authors which will give her a *continuous and distinct outline* of the history of civilized nations. Among these, the one upon which she should specially dwell is the history of England and America. The history of England, thoroughly studied, embraces the history of the last thousand years. In that time she has been mingled with the growth and progress of the whole civilized world. Her arms, her commerce, and her arts have grown beyond those of any other nation, and given a stamp to the civilization of mankind. The Anglo-American in the United States is but a branch of the same stock. We cannot separate our history from the history of England; nor can we deny what we owe to the parent family.

But, to a lady, reading should be extended to all the branches of polite literature. Poetry, history, essays, all that makes the body of English classic literature, she should read as much of as time and opportunity will allow. This is the great means by which (so far as knowledge goes) she is to refine, polish, and adorn her mind. Here, again, the mother and the teacher should be the guide, as far as guidance is possible. I may here suggest that a family library, if it be but a dozen volumes, should always be composed of the *best of their kind.* The want of *discrimination* in allowing all sorts of trash to come within the reach of youth, is the great evil in regard to reading. All temptation cannot be kept out of the way; but surely there is no need of bringing temptation with double strength into the family.

ACCOMPLISHMENTS.

It is said that a distinguished gentleman once took a young lady to be placed in a celebrated female seminary. He was asked what he would have her taught? "Dress and address," he replied. "It shall be done," said the lady teacher. Beyond doubt, both the lady and the gentleman estimated accomplishments too highly. The term "address," in its full sense, will, indeed, comprehend much of education; but it is that part which *appears* in society, and not that which gives strength to the solid qualities of the mind. After these solid qualities have been made sure of, then we should not neglect the graces and accomplishments. It may be safely admitted, that in women the accomplishments may be cultivated to a greater extent than among men. The feminine form and their softer dispositions seem to invite a culture of the refinements and elegancies of life. Where hard necessity has not precluded them from such advantages, there seems no objection to the culture of those arts and studies, in a moderate degree, whose object is to refine and adorn, rather than to serve the mere wants of life. In the *idea* of accomplishments, however, different persons include a great variety of things. I shall be contented here with some *hints* on what I think the most valuable of the accomplishments.

1. The first and greatest accomplishment for a lady is the *art of elegant conversation.* I call this an *art,* although most women have a natural tendency to converse with ease. But elegant and pleasant conversation must have for its basis a well-informed mind; and not only that, but one well instructed in the usages and requisitions of polite society. Much of this is to be learned from being in good society, much from the instruction of an experienced teacher, and much from the exercise of conversational talent and observation upon others.

2. The next most useful accomplishment (if not the first) is, to have a perfect acquaintance with what is called the *proprieties* of life. These are what usage, what politeness, what good feeling, and good

neighborhood require in the intercourse of society. There are a thousand nameless acts which are expected in society, and specially of women, which cannot be neglected, and which make up a part of a woman's circle of social duties. Not to be *proper*, in a woman is almost equivalent to not being moral. Society, by its usages, require many things for *propriety sake*, which may be almost called a minor code of morals.

3. *Music and drawing* seem the chief ornamental acquirements which society has assigned to the ladies. They are branches of the fine arts, and therefore, if cultivated at all except by artists, seem fairly to come within the circle of female attainments. Vocal music seems to be almost natural to the female sex. They hear the "lullaby" at the cradle, and seem to imitate and adopt the melody of the voice from their mothers. For this reason, and for the sake of sacred music, singing may be admitted as an almost indispensable accomplishment among women, and one which may safely be cultivated with much care. But when we come to instrumental music, it does not seem to be so essential. The almost universal use (among educated young women) of the piano seems to raise a doubt, whether all women can be really born with such taste and talent for the piano that one-third of two or three years should be consumed upon it. *To learn the use of the piano* has become a fashion, and, like other fashions, is carried to an extreme. The time, money, and labor of one half of those who learn

is entirely thrown away. What would you substitute? some one may say. If an instrument *must* be played upon, the simple guitar is sufficient to accompany a lady's voice, which is the principal object in learning to play on the piano. Again, the harp is a more graceful and a more melodious instrument than the piano. But one half who learn instrumental music would find themselves better paid and better satisfied by learning the *art of drawing*, which is both useful and ornamental. First, there is *linear* drawing, in which may be embraced the principles of architecture ; secondly, there is landscape drawing, in which is included perspective; thirdly, there is drawing of the human figure, which is very attractive and amusing, inasmuch as a ready hand may, with this art, sketch many subjects from living society; fourthly, there is topographical drawing, which belongs more especially to the province of engineers.

4. I need say nothing about a variety of minor accomplishments, such as fancy needle-work, &c., which are suggested naturally in the intercourse of society. I shall only add, that one or two acquirements, which may be classed under the head of *accomplishments*, is enough for most young women, and more than the mass can have. Perhaps the highest and most useful accomplishment (after the *proprieties*) is *graceful manners.* But this is a grace which cannot be defined. Its power is often wonderful, and its attractions pleasing to all classes of people. A refined taste, an acute sense of propriety, natural dignity, kind feelings, and

a wish to please, are its sources. After all, however, this pleasant talent cannot be always acquired without certain previous graces, which are the gift of Providence. All persons, however, can endeavor to please; all can show kindness, and all can be civil in their address.

RELIGIOUS TEACHINGS.

It is almost superfluous to say, that upon *mothers* devolves the earliest part of religious training, and by far the most important. The instances are rare in which a child has been instructed by its mother in certain religious principles and duties, and departs from them in after life. This instruction may not make a religious character; but it does fix certain ideas of faith and duty with a strength of memory which no time wholly eradicates. It was somewhere remarked by John Quincy Adams, that no equal number of words in English literature had been so often repeated and so long remembered as that little child's prayer:

> "Now I lay me down to sleep,
> I pray the Lord my soul to keep.
> If I should die before I wake,
> I pray the Lord my soul to take."

Strong men, who seem insensible to weakness, and whose eyes seldom see the pages of the Bible, repeat it in the watches of the night; great men, whose names are brilliant in the world's eyes, repeat this child-like orison when, for a moment, the world's glare is forgotten, and the soul takes a single glance upon the world eternal. Strength and weakness, greatness and humility, wealth and poverty, turn for a moment from the cares of life to repeat this long-remembered prayer—so simple, so powerful, so full of a mother's memory and a mother's teachings.

With such high power, and such profound responsibility, it is not to be supposed that any young women will be educated without some attention to their religious duties. The common spring of all knowledge on this head—the purest, richest, and best—is the Bible; and on the study of the Bible I have said, in another place (Chapter XIII.), all that I have to suggest.

DOMESTIC ECONOMY.

The only idea which remains to suggest is, that some knowledge of domestic economy seems essential to any proper course of female education. Generally, this has been left to home-teaching. But common sense seems to teach, that there are a great many elementary ideas of home economy which might well be taught in a female seminary; and, as the very best ideas on that subject would be given, it is very certain that many of the pupils would get information which they could not obtain at home. Upon this subject, however, as I know little, I shall say little. I believe some attention is paid to this subject in most of our female schools. At any rate, it may safely be left to the sagacity of the ladies. They are well enough aware, that while we endeavor to send the spirit forth over the widest horizon, and strengthen its pinions for the noblest flights, yet the body must be cared for, and much of happiness depends upon its little comforts. This is peculiarly the province, in our American society, of the wife, mother, and sister.

In the following programme, I have arranged a general formula of the suggestions made in the previous pages. It will serve to give a *bird's-eye* view of the *principles* I wish to bring out. Some one may say, why have you not inserted this or that particular study, which is frequently taught. For example, why have you said nothing about Latin and Greek? Because under the general term *language* in the table, is included any language which may be thought by teachers the best adapted to the end in view. Again: the study of the dead languages may safely be left *discretionary*, to be pursued or not, as may seem wisest in the particular circumstances in which a pupil is placed. They may be very proper and useful in some cases and not in others.

Again: it may be asked why I did not enumerate botany and other minor subjects. Because my object was to suggest the elements and principles of education, and what course of study is necessary to bring out and strengthen the several faculties of mind, and not to determine an order of study, which is more properly the business of an actual teacher.

PROGRAMME OF FEMALE EDUCATION.

Classification.	Subjects.	Operations of Mind.	Philosophical Ideas.
PHYSICAL SCIENCE.	*Mathematics.*	PERCEPTION, CONSCIOUSNESS, REASONING.	Logic of Demonstration.
	Chemistry.	OBSERVATION, EXPERIMENT, JUDGMENT.	Logic of Experiment.
	Natural Philosophy.	REFLECTION, CAUSATION, MEMORY.	The Relations of Cause and Effect.
	Mechanical Philosophy.	APPLICATION OF PRINCIPLES, REALIZATION OF POWER, COMPOSITION OF FORCES.	The Relations of Force and Motion.
	Astronomy.	OBSERVATION, GENERALIZATION, SYSTEMATIZING.	The Generalization of Causes.
LANGUAGE.	*The Vocabulary.*	PERCEPTION, MEMORY.	Exercise of Retentive Powers.
	Grammar.	ANALYSIS, CONSTRUCTION.	Principle of Order.
	Composition.	THOUGHT, COMBINATION, TASTE, JUDGMENT.	Principles of Attention and Discrimination.
	Reading.	THOUGHT, REFLECTION, CRITICISM.	Principles of Curiosity, Ideas of the Mind.
ACCOMPLISHMENTS.	*Art of Conversation, The Proprieties,*	SOCIAL FEELINGS, SOCIAL IDEAS.	Society.
	Manners, Drawing, Music.	LOVE OF APPEARANCE. IDEAS OF PROPORTION. IDEAS OF HARMONY.	Beauty.
DUTIES.	*Study of the Bible, Religious Instruction,*	IDEAS OF RELIGION, DEVOTION.	Relations of Man to God and Man to Man.
	Domestic Economy.	IDEAS OF THE FAMILY, IDEAS OF FAMILY DUTY.	
MISCELLANEOUS STUDIES.	*Natural History, Physiology,*	IDEAS OF NATURE.	Nature.
	Political Constitutions,	IDEAS OF POLITICAL SOCIETY.	Government.
	Intellectual Philosophy.	IDEAS OF THE MIND.	Mind.

I do not pretend to have arranged the development of the faculties of the mind with precise philosophical accuracy ; but I have given a general formula of what I think is the proper order of study, and of those branches which are necessary to exercise in succession all the talents, and make a well-balanced mind. Of course, two or three branches may be studied at the same time ; science and language may be pursued very well together : some one of the accomplishments may be taken as an accompaniment. This is the usual course; but I may remark, that mixing too many studies together is one of the prevailing faults of modern education. Two studies and one accomplishment are as much as ever ought to be pursued at one time. The mind does not act clearly or strongly when it is diverted into many channels ; nor does it proceed so fast. Let it pursue each subject distinctly and accurately, and both more progress will be made, and the faculties developed will be more strengthened.

ELEMENTARY IDEAS.

In what has here been presented on the subject of American education, I am conscious there are no discoveries. I have simply attempted to bring out the leading ideas of what is necessary for the education of a free people. The fundamental ideas are these:—

1st. A free people govern themselves.

2d. A free people must have free minds.

3d. Free minds must be enlightened; ignorance makes slavery.

4th. To *enlighten* mind, the soul itself must be strengthened and developed, intellectually and spiritually.

5th. That to strengthen the soul, it is first necessary to *think.*

6th. That to think rightly, on all subjects, it is necessary to bring out and strengthen *all the faculties* of the mind.

7th. That to bring out all the faculties in succession, education should instruct and discipline the mind in the laws of nature (science), the laws of expression (language and literature), the laws of social nature (conversation, manners, and government), and the laws of spiritual nature (the Bible and intellectual philosophy); and in addition to these instructions, such teachings as may be deemed peculiarly necessary to women.

8th. The ultimate idea in the whole scheme I have laid down is, that the great object is to give POWER AND DEVELOPMENT TO THE MIND. A strong and clear mind can turn its talents to any object or any business, and succeed better than those who have been educated to that particular business by a routine instruction. In our country, all the conditions of society, the nature of the government, and the tastes of the people, require the development of general principles in education, rather than the acquisition of special details of knowledge.

THE FUTURE.

When I read the prophetic delineations of a happy future, and behold the beautiful pictures drawn by inspired writers; when I look upon the visible universe, and see every law perfect—every animate or inanimate thing fulfilling its functions—every orb rolling with unvarying accuracy through its appointed circuit; and when I feel and know that man has every faculty of soul, and every taste adapted to perform, bring out, and enjoy the same perfect round of beautiful harmonies—nothing wanting but his own will—I also feel that the prophetic picture is not a delusion; that the time will come when humanity will exhibit the same beautiful order and harmony! when the perverted mind will be restored to its rectitude, and this earth exhibit the scene of a happy and a rejoicing people!

But *when?* It cannot be doubted that this period may be hastened or retarded by the action of the people themselves. If they prefer darkness rather than light, they may be suffered long to dwell in darkness. If they would hasten the time, they must take the light and diffuse it; the light which the *few* have must be made common to the *many:* the lump must be leavened. It is the mind—the soul—which must be enlightened. The heart of the fathers must be turned to the children, and the heart of the children to their fathers—when, in the words of the last prophet, the now risen Sun of Righteousness shall spread the healing of his wings over the earth to make it a delightsome land.

THE END.

Gillespie's Manual of Road-Making.

GILLESPIE ON ROADS AND RAILROADS.

A MANUAL OF ROAD-MAKING.

Comprising the principles and practice of the Location, Construction, and Improvement of ROADS, (common, macadam, paved, plank, &c.,) and RAILROADS. By W. M. GILLESPIE, A. M., Professor of Civil Engineering in Union College. Price $1.50.

"I have very carefully looked over Professor Gillespie's Manual of Road-Making. It is, in all respects, the best work on this subject with which I am acquainted; being, from its arrangement, comprehensiveness, and clearness, equally adapted to the wants of Students of Civil Engineering, and the purposes of persons in any way engaged in the construction or supervision of roads. The appearance of such a work, twenty years earlier, would have been a truly national benefit, and it is to be hoped that its introduction into our seminaries may be so general as to make a knowledge of the principles and practice of this branch of engineering, as popular as is its importance to all classes of the community."—*Professor Mahan, of the Military Academy.*

"This work contains in a condensed form, all the principles, both ancient and modern, of this most important art; and almost every thing useful in the great mass of writers on this subject...... Such a work as this performs a great service for those who are destined to construct roads—by showing not only what ought to be done, but what ought not to be done; thus saving immense outlay of money, and loss of time in experiments...... The committee, therefore, recommend it to the public."—*Report of a Committee of the American Institute.*

"The views of the author are sound and practical, and should be read by the people throughout the entire length and breadth of the land...... We recommend this Manual to the perusal of every tax-payer for road-making, and to the young men of the country, as they will find useful information in relation to each department of road-making, which will surely be useful to them in after-life."—*American Railroad Journal.*

"If the well-established principles of Road-Making, which are so plainly set forth in Prof. Gillespie's valuable work, and so well illustrated, could be once put into general use in this country, every traveller would bear testimony to the fact that the author is a great public benefactor."—*Silliman's American Journal of Science.*

"This small volume contains much valuable matter, derived from the best authorities, and set forth in a clear and simple style. For the want of information which is contained in this Manual, serious mistakes are frequently made, and roads are badly located and badly constructed by persons ignorant of the true principles which ought to govern in such cases."—*Journal of the Franklin Institute.*

"It would astonish many 'path-masters' to see how much they don't know with regard to the very business they have considered themselves such adepts in. Yet all is so simple, so lucid, so straightforward, so manifestly true, that the most ordinary and least instructed mind cannot fail to profit by it. We trust this useful and excellent volume may find its way into every village library if not into every school library, as well as into the hands of every man interested in road-making."—*New York Tribune*

"This elaborate and admirable work combines in a systematic and symmetrical form the results of an engineering experience in all parts of the Union, and of an examination of the great roads of Europe, with a careful digestion of all accessible authorities. The six chapters into which it is divided comprehend a methodical treatise upon every part of the whole subject; showing what roads ought to be in the vital points of direction, slope, shape, surface, and cost, and giving methods of performing all the necessary measurements of distances, directions, and heights, without the use of any instruments but such as any mechanic can make, and any farmer can use."—*Newark Daily Advertiser*

Science of the English Language

CLARK'S NEW ENGLISH GRAMMAR.

A Practical Grammar, in which WORDS, PHRASES, and SENTENCES are classified, according to their offices, and their relation to each other: illustrated by a complete system of Diagrams. By S. W. CLARK, A. M. Price 50 cts.

"It is a most capital work, and well calculated, if we mistake not, to supersede, even in our best schools, works of much loftier pretension. The peculiarity of its method grew out of the best practice of its author (as he himself assures us in its preface) while engaged in communicating the science to an *adult* class; and his success was fully commensurate with the happy and philosophic design he has unfolded."—*Rahway Register.*

"This new work strikes us very favorably. Its deviations from older books of the kind are generally judicious and often important. We wish teachers would examine it."—*New York Tribune.*

"It is prepared upon a new plan, to meet difficulties which the author has encountered in practical instruction. Grammar and the structure of language are taught throughout by analysis, and in a way which renders their acquisition easy and satisfactory. From the slight examination, which is all we have been able to give it, we are convinced it has points of very decided superiority over any of the elementary works in common use. We commend it to the attention of all who are engaged in instruction."—*New York Courier and Enquirer.*

"From a thorough examination of your method of teaching the English language, I am prepared to give it my unqualified approbation. It is a plan original and beautiful—well adapted to the capacities of learners of every age and stage of advancement."—*A. R. Simmons, Ex-Superintendent of Bristol.*

"I have, under my immediate instruction in English Grammar, a class of more than fifty ladies and gentlemen from the Teachers' Department, who, having studied the grammars in common use, concur with me in expressing a decided preference for 'Clark's New Grammar,' which we have used as a text-book since its publication, and which will be retained as such in this school hereafter."—*Professor Brittan, Principal of Lyons Union School.*

"Clark's Grammar I have never seen equalled for *practicability*, which is of the utmost importance in all school-books."—*S. B. Clark, Principal of Scarborough Academy, Maine.*

"The Grammar is just such a book as I wanted, and I shall make it *the* text-book in my school."—*William Brickley, Teacher at Canastota, N. Y.*

"This original production will, doubtless, become an indispensable auxiliary to restore the English language to its appropriate rank in our systems of education. After a cursory perusal of its contents, we are tempted to assert that it foretells the dawn of a brighter age to our mother tongue."—*Southern Literary Gazette.*

"I have examined your work on Grammar, and do not hesitate to pronounce it superior to any work with which I am acquainted. I shall introduce it into the Mount Morris Union School at the first proper opportunity."—*H. G. Winslow, A. M., Principal of Mount Morris Union School.*

"Professor Clark's new work on Grammar, containing Diagrams illustrative of his system, is, in my opinion, a most excellent treatise on 'the Science of the English Language.' The author has studiously and properly excluded from his book the technicalities, jargon, and ambiguity which so often render attempts to teach grammar unpleasant, if not impracticable. The inductive plan which he has adopted, and of which he is, in teaching grammar, the originator, is admirably adapted to the great purposes of both teaching and learning the important science of our language."—*S. N. Sweet, Author of "Sweet's Elocution."*

Parker's Rhetorical Reader.

PARKER'S RHETORICAL READER. 12mo.

Exercises in Rhetorical Reading, designed to familiarize readers with the pauses and other marks in general use, and lead them to the practice of modulation and inflection of the voice. By R. G. PARKER, author of "Exercises in English Composition," "Compendium of Natural Philosophy," &c., &c.

This work possesses many advantages which commend it to favor, among which are the following:—It is adapted to all classes and schools, from the highest to the lowest. It contains a practical illustration of all the marks employed in written language; also lessons for the cultivation, improvement, and strengthening of the voice, and instructions as well as exercises in a great variety of the principles of Rhetorical Reading, which cannot fail to render it a valuable auxiliary in the hands of any teacher. Many of the exercises are of sufficient length to afford an opportunity for each member of any class, however numerous, to participate in the same exercise—a feature which renders it convenient to examining committees. The selections for exercises in reading are from the most approved sources, possessing a salutary moral and religious tone, without the slightest tincture of sectarianism.

"I have to acknowledge the reception through your kindness of several volumes. I have not as yet found time to examine minutely all the books. Of Mr. Parker's Rhetorical Reader, however, I am prepared to speak in the highest terms. I think it so well adapted to the wants of pupils, that I shall introduce it immediately in the Academy of which I am about to take charge at Madison, in this state. It is the best thing of the kind I have yet found. I cannot say too much in its favor."—*John G. Clark, Rector of the Madison Male Academy, Athens, Ga.*

"Mr. Parker has made the public his debtor by some of his former publications—especially the 'Aids to English Composition'—and by this he has greatly increased the obligation. There are reading books almost without number, but very few of them pretend to give instructions how to read, and, unluckily, few of our teachers are competent to supply the defect. If young persons are to be taught to read well, it must generally be done in the primary schools, as the collegiate term affords too little time to begin and accomplish that work. We have seen no other 'Reader' with which we have been so well pleased; and as an evidence of our appreciation of its worth, we shall lay it aside for the use of a certain juvenile specimen of humanity in whose affairs we are specially interested."—*Christian Advocate.*

"We cannot too often urge upon teachers the importance of reading, as a part of education, and we regard it as among the auspicious signs of the times, that so much more attention is given, by the best of teachers, to the cultivation of a power which is at once a most delightful accomplishment, and of the first importance as a means of discipline and progress. In this work, Mr. Parker's volume, we are sure, will be found a valuable aid."—*Vermont Chronicle.*

"The title of this work explains its character and design, which are well carried out by the manner in which it is executed. As a class-book for students in elocution, or as an ordinary reading book, we do not think we have seen any thing superior. The distinguishing characteristic of its plan is to assume some simple and familiar example, which will be readily understood by the pupil, and which Nature will tell him how to deliver properly, and refer more difficult passages to this, as a model. There is, however, another excellence in the work, which we take pleasure in commending; it is the progressiveness with which the introductory lessons are arranged. In teaching every art and science this is indispensable, and in none more so than in that of elocution. The pieces for exercise in reading are selected with much taste and judgment We have no doubt that those who use this book will be satisfied with its success."—*Teacher's Advocate.*

SCHOOL ARCHITECTURE

OR.

CONTRIBUTIONS TO THE IMPROVEMENT OF SCHOOL-HOUSES IN THE UNITED STATES.

BY HENRY BARNARD,

COMMISSIONER OF PUBLIC SCHOOLS IN RHODE ISLAND.

CONTENTS.

From the Vermont Chronicle.

Mr. Barnard, when Secretary of the Board of Commissioners of Common Schools in Connecticut, devoted much time to School-houses, lectured upon the subject, and published his views in the School Journal, which he then edited. Since that date, (1841,) his Essay has been repeatedly published, each time with additional plans and descriptions. Parts of it have been extensively copied, and its influence has been felt in all parts of the country. He has now enlarged it to a handsome volume, which is published in a style becoming its importance and excellence. No other writer on the subject is to be compared with Mr. Barnard for the fulness and variety of his materials, and the completeness of his work in regard to all the points that are to be considered in the building and furnishing of school-houses.

Mr. Barnard does not confine himself to any one plan, but exhibits fully a great variety of excellent models for buildings, seats, desks, warming, ventilating, &c., &c., for Primary Schools, High Schools, Normal Schools; with numerous cuts and descriptions of buildings and parts of buildings in use in places where most attention has been given to the subject. At the close we have nearly a hundred pages on school apparatus and library, care of school-houses, school-regulations, books on education, suggestions for improvement, &c. The whole book is replete with information, and we heartily recommend it as one that ought to be accessible in every school-district. No school-house should be built or altered without consulting it.

Fulton & Eastman's Book-keeping.

A PRACTICAL SYSTEM OF BOOK-KEEPING.

BY LEVI S. FULTON & G. W. EASTMAN.

By Single and Double Entry.

Containing three distinct forms of Books, adapted for the Farmer, Mechanic and Merchant—to which is added a variety of useful forms for practical use viz.: Notes, Bills, Drafts, Receipts, &c., &c. Also a Compendium of Rules of Evidence applicable to Books of Account, and of Law in reference to the Collection of Promissory Notes, &c.

BOOK-KEEPING BLANKS. (Two Nos. in a set.)

Adapted to Fulton & Eastman's Book-keeping.

The use of these Blank Books will be found very important in familiarizing the scholar with the forms requisite to the keeping of accounts according to Fulton & Eastman's system.

"I have examined with much satisfaction Fulton & Eastman's System of *Book-Keeping*, and take pleasure in recommending its adoption to my immediate friends and others. It is simple and easily reduced to practice, and possesses a peculiar adaptation to the wants of the community for which it is designed. The plan for Merchants' Books, which I examined more critically than other portions of the work, is very neat, compact, and economical, and must ensure a great degree of accuracy in keeping accounts."—*Elijah Bottom, Book-keeper for John M. French & Co., Rochester, N. Y.*

"I have examined Messrs. Fulton & Eastman's 'Practical System of Book-Keeping,' and am pleased with the work. As a branch of Education, Book-Keeping is well deserving a high estimation; and, I will add, there is none of equal importance and utility more generally neglected, particularly in our public schools. The work is plain, simple, and comprehensive, and well adapted to meet the wants of the business community. In many respects I deem it superior to any other work of the kind with which I am acquainted. I shall recommend it to the schools under my charge."—*John T. Mackenzie, Town Superintendent.*

"FULTON & EASTMAN'S BOOK-KEEPING.—We had supposed that, in the multiplicity of works on Book-Keeping, hardly any thing valuable remained to be suggested by later authors, should any such present themselves. But we have been convinced of our short-sightedness in examining the work with the above title, now before us. The work is principally designed for schools—for common schools—but should be in the hands of every Farmer, Mechanic, and Merchant in the land. It opens with a system of account-keeping for farmers, followed by one for mechanics, and this, in turn, by an admirable and comprehensive system of mercantile Book-keeping, which, for its simplicity, and time and labor saving properties, possesses advantages over all other systems with which we are acquainted."—*Wayne Co. Whig.*

"We are very much pleased with the design and execution of this work. It is exceedingly practical; being by single entry, containing three different forms of books, for the Farmer, the Merchant, and Mechanic. To these are added notes, bills, drafts, receipts, and a compendium of rules of evidence applicable to books of account, and of law in reference to the collection of promissory notes. A work of such a character, and of so much practical value, speaks for itself, and stands in need of no commendation from us to ensure it a large sale among all classes."—*Albany Spectator.*

"I should think it admirably adapted as a Text-Book for schools, and the study of it of much greater importance than it has hitherto been considered. I hardly know whether the Book is of more importance to scholars in school, or to Farmers, Mechanics, or business men. The system, to which is added a variety of useful 'Forms,' which most business men have occasion to use more or less, is certainly well worth the price of the Book, to any man transacting business to the amount of twenty-five dollars a year."—*E. L. Jones, Book-keeper, Michigan.*

Davies' Grammar of Arithmetic.

DAVIES' GRAMMAR OF ARITHMETIC:

OR,

AN ANALYLIS OF THE

LANGUAGE OF FIGURES AND SCIENCE OF NUMBERS.

This work gives the results of a very full and careful analysis, both of the Science and Art of Arithmetic, and offers some suggestions on the best methods of imparting Arithmetical instruction. Perhaps a more correct description of the work cannot be given, than to copy the following notice from the *New-York Tribune.*

"GRAMMAR OF ARITHMETIC, by CHAS. DAVIES, L. L. D., (18mo. pp. 144.) In this work the language of figures and the construction of numbers are carefully analyzed. The alphabet, composed of the ten figures—the words derived from the alphabet, and the laws by which the figures are connected with each other, are all clearly explained.

"The analysis shows that there are but four hundred and eighty-eight elementary combinations in Arithmetic, each corresponding to a word of our common language; and that these combinations are so connected together as to be all expressed by only sixty-three different words. The system proposes to commit these words to memory, and then read the results instead of spelling them, as now practised.

"In another respect, the system proposes an important change—namely: to consider and treat all fractions as entire things, having a given relation to the unit ONE from which they were derived.

"We scarcely need say that the little work evinces the ingenuity and skilful mathematical analysis for which Prof. Davies' writings on this subject are justly celebrated. We commend it to the attention of practical teachers, believing that they will find it crowded with new and valuable suggestions."

MILITARY ACADEMY, Jan. 17, 1850.

"THE GRAMMAR OF ARITHMETIC, by PROF. DAVIES, presents the subject in a new light. It so analyzes Arithmetic, as to impress the mind of the learner with the first principles of mathematical science, in their right order and connection; and the new rules for the reading of figures are of great practical value."

(Signed,) W. H. C. BARTLETT,
Prof. of Natural and Ex. Philosophy.
A. E. CHURCH,
Prof. of Mathematics.
D. H. MAHAN.
Prof. of Civil Engineering.

Extract of a Letter from CHARLES A. COBURN, *President of the Teachers' Institute of the State of New-York.*

"I do not know when I have before seen so small and unpretending a mathematical work, from which I have received so much valuable information and so many practical suggestions. If teachers would follow out your plan of spelling and reading with the Arithmetical Alphabet, it would save a world of talk. I think that most teachers would receive much benefit by a careful examination of the book, and would also be able to teach arithmetic more successfully and with less labor, by taking advantage of your suggestions."

"This work supplies the want which we felt as a scholar, and did our best to supply as a teacher of the 'Science of Numbers' though little to our own satisfaction."—*Windham County Democrat.*

"This is a curious, suggestive little book. Its author is a thinker beyond the ordinary surface, or the common pavements in the subject of Numbers. Long years of study and application have given him a long sight, and his book will interest teachers generally."—*Bangor Whig.*

A. S. BARNES & COMPANY'S PUBLICATIONS.

CHAMBERS' EDUCATIONAL COURSE.

THE NATURAL SCIENCES.

The Messrs. Chambers have employed the first professors in Scotland in the preparation of these works. They are now offered to the schools of the United States, under the American revision of D. M. Reese, M. D., LL.D., *late Superintendent of Public Schools in the city and county of New York.*

I. CHAMBERS' TREASURY OF KNOWLEDGE.
II. CLARK'S ELEMENTS OF DRAWING & PERSPECTIVE.
III. CHAMBERS' ELEMENTS OF NATURAL PHILOSOPHY.
IV. REID & BAINS' CHEMISTRY AND ELECTRICITY.
V. HAMILTON'S VEGETABLE AND ANIMAL PHYSIOLOGY.
VI. CHAMBERS' ELEMENTS OF ZOOLOGY.
VII. PAGE'S ELEMENTS OF GEOLOGY.

"It is well known that the original publishers of these works (the Messrs. Chambers of Edinburgh) are able to command the best talent in the preparation of their books, and that it is their practice to deal faithfully with the public. This series will not disappoint the reasonable expectations thus excited. They are elementary works prepared by authors in every way capable of doing justice to their respective undertakings, and who have evidently bestowed upon them the necessary time and labor to adapt them to their purpose. We recommend them to teachers and parents with confidence. If not introduced as class-books in the school, they may be used to excellent advantage in general exercises, and occasional class exercise, for which every teacher ought to provide himself with an ample store of materials. The volumes may be had separately; and the one first named, in the hands of a teacher of the younger classes, might furnish an inexhaustible fund of amusement and instruction. Together, they would constitute a rich treasure to a family of intelligent children, and impart a thirst for knowledge."—*Vermont Chron.*

"Of all the numerous works of this class that have been published, there are none that have acquired a more thoroughly deserved and high reputation than this series. The Chambers of Edinburgh, well known as the careful and intelligent publishers of a vast number of works of much importance in the educational world, are the fathers of this series of books, and the American editor has exercised an unusual degree of judgment in their preparation for the use of schools as well as private families in this country."—*Philadelphia Bulletin.*

"The titles furnish a key to the contents, and it is only necessary for us to say, that the material of each volume is admirably worked up, presenting with sufficient fulness and with much clearness of method the several subjects which are treated." —*Cincinnati Gazette.*

www.ingramcontent.com/pod-product-compliance
Lightning Source LLC
LaVergne TN
LVHW010201110826
845151LV00002B/577
9781425535339